The Creation of the U.S. Constitution

Other books in the Turning Points series:

Turning|Points
IN WORLD HISTORY

The Creation of the U.S. Constitution

Loreta M. Medina, *Book Editor*

Daniel Leone, *President*
Bonnie Szumski, *Publisher*
Scott Barbour, *Managing Editor*

**GREENHAVEN
PRESS ®**

THOMSON
™
GALE

San Diego • Detroit • New York • San Francisco • Cleveland
New Haven, Conn. • Waterville, Maine • London • Munich

© 2003 by Greenhaven Press. Greenhaven Press is an imprint of The Gale Group, Inc., a division of Thomson Learning, Inc.

Greenhaven® and Thomson Learning™ are trademarks used herein under license.

For more information, contact
Greenhaven Press
27500 Drake Rd.
Farmington Hills, MI 48331-3535
Or you can visit our Internet site at http://www.gale.com

Cover credits: © Hulton/Archive by Getty Images

Dover Publications, 67
Library of Congress, 31
National Archives, 83
North Wind Picture Archives, 135

LIBRARY OF CONGRESS CATALOGING-IN-PUBLICATION DATA

The creation of the U.S. constitution / Loreta M. Medina, book editor.
    p. cm. — (Turning points in world history)
  Includes bibliographical references and index.
  ISBN 0-7377-1262-7 (lib. : alk. paper) — ISBN 0-7377-1261-9 (pbk. : alk. paper)
    1. Constitutional history—United States. 2. United States—Politics and govern-
ment—1783–1789. 3. United States—Social conditions. 4. United States—Eco-
nomic conditions. I. Medina, Loreta M. II. Turning points in world history
(Greenhaven Press)
KF4541 .C68 2003
342.73'02—dc21   2002034722

Printed in the United States of America

Contents

the states should be separated from those of the federal legislature.

Chapter 3: The Constitution Lays the Foundation of a Nation

southern states reached a compromise on commercial policy and the status of slaves. Little did they know that the issue of slavery, however, would hound them and rend the nation many years later in a civil war.

Chapter 4: The Legacy of the Constitution

Chapter 5: Critiques of the Constitution

existing problems of society at that time—all of which related to the acquisition of property. The main functions of government were to regulate property, prevent the dominance of one economic interest over others, and prevent disorder arising from economic conflicts.

Foreword

Certain past events stand out as pivotal, as having effects and outcomes that change the course of history. These events are often referred to as turning points. Historian Louis L. Snyder provides this useful definition:

> A turning point in history is an event, happening, or stage which thrusts the course of historical development into a different direction. By definition a turning point is a great event, but it is even more—a great event with the explosive impact of altering the trend of man's life on the planet.

History's turning points have taken many forms. Some were single, brief, and shattering events with immediate and obvious impact. The invasion of Britain by William the Conqueror in 1066, for example, swiftly transformed that land's political and social institutions and paved the way for the rise of the modern English nation. By contrast, other single events were deemed of minor significance when they occurred, only later recognized as turning points. The assassination of a little-known European nobleman, Archduke Franz Ferdinand, on June 28, 1914, in the Bosnian town of Sarajevo was such an event; only after it touched off a chain reaction of political-military crises that escalated into the global conflict known as World War I did the murder's true significance become evident.

Other crucial turning points occurred not in terms of a few hours, days, months, or even years, but instead as evolutionary developments spanning decades or even centuries. One of the most pivotal turning points in human history, for instance—the development of agriculture, which replaced nomadic hunter-gatherer societies with more permanent settlements—occurred over the course of many generations. Still other great turning points were neither events nor developments, but rather revolutionary new inventions and innovations that significantly altered social customs and ideas, military tactics, home life, the spread of knowledge, and the human condition in general. The developments of writing, gunpowder, the printing press, antibiotics, the electric light, atomic energy, television, and the computer, the last two of which have recently ushered in the world-altering information age, represent only some of these innovative turning points.

Each anthology in the Greenhaven Turning Points in World History series presents a group of essays chosen for their accessibility. The anthology's structure also enhances this accessibility. First, an introductory essay provides a general overview of the principal events and figures involved, placing the topic in its historical context. The essays that follow explore various aspects in more detail, some targeting political trends and consequences, others social, literary, cultural, and/or technological ramifications, and still others pivotal leaders and other influential figures. To aid the reader in choosing the material of immediate interest or need, each essay is introduced by a concise summary of the contributing writer's main themes and insights.

In addition, each volume contains extensive research tools, including a collection of excerpts from primary source documents pertaining to the historical events and figures under discussion. In the anthology on the French Revolution, for example, readers can examine the works of Rousseau, Voltaire, and other writers and thinkers whose championing of human rights helped fuel the French people's growing desire for liberty; the French *Declaration of the Rights of Man and Citizen*, presented to King Louis XVI by the French National Assembly on October 2, 1789; and eyewitness accounts of the attack on the royal palace and the horrors of the Reign of Terror. To guide students interested in pursuing further research on the subject, each volume features an extensive bibliography, which for easy access has been divided into separate sections by topic. Finally, a comprehensive index allows readers to scan and locate content efficiently. Each of the anthologies in the Greenhaven Turning Points in World History series provides students with a complete, detailed, and enlightening examination of a crucial historical watershed.

Introduction: Consensus and Conflict in the Framing of the Constitution

In 1787, a combination of social, political, and economic forces led to the gathering in Philadelphia of concerned political and business leaders who saw the need to design a new government for the thirteen sovereign states. These men had come to realize that the government they had devised under the Articles of Confederation in 1777 was not strong enough to deal with the concerns of the Union.

The government drawn up under the articles had worked to the advantage of the states during the war against Britain. Constitutional historian Clinton Rossiter cites the confederation's achievements, saying it "fought a successful war, made a viable peace, laid the foundations for a new order of diplomacy, established enough credit at home and abroad . . . created a functioning bureaucracy, and . . . maintained itself as a symbol of American unity."[1] However, when the war ended, the concerns of the individual states shifted. With the removal of an external threat, the states redirected their attention and energy to tackling domestic problems that had troubled many of them even before relations with Britain frayed. The Articles of Confederation could no longer respond to the issues that the states faced—issues that put the Union at risk. These issues included border disputes, overlapping claims over unsettled territories, unstable economies, the growing rift between the rich merchants and the indebted poor, and secessionist movements that advocated complete independence for each state.

Territorial Disputes

As land was the most important measure of wealth and power in eighteenth-century America, state rivalries over territory occurred frequently. Writing in *Are We to Be a Nation? The Making of the Constitution*, Richard B. Bernstein and Kym S. Rice note the importance of land to the states' economic growth: "A state's territory was a potentially valuable source of revenue that kept taxes down, and after sale to farmers and settlers, contributed still further to the state's economic growth. Thus, border disputes and efforts to establish claims to unsettled territories or to subdue secessionist movements became as important as modern controversies among the arid western states over water rights."[2]

An example of the territorial disputes that upset the relations of the states was the case of the land that comprises modern Vermont. Formerly under the jurisdiction of New York and New Hampshire, the Vermont territories wanted to break off from the two states' authority and form their own state. Vermont settlers brought their case to the confederation Congress, but New York and New Hampshire, which had given the original grants to the Vermont settlers, argued that they were the heirs of British authority and that this authority legitimized their claim to said territories. Vermont, uncertain of favorable action from Congress, took such aggressive steps as annexing New Hampshire towns, fighting a brief border war with New York (in 1781), and asking the British in Quebec to make the territories a British colony. The confederation Congress seemed powerless to take action, and the problem of Vermont persisted for many years while the legislature's attention focused on a multitude of other issues and concerns. Only after the U.S. Constitution was passed did Congress finally resolve the case. It recognized Vermont's independence and admitted it into the Union in 1791 as a new state, joining the original thirteen that then comprised the Union.

Economic Difficulties

Exacerbating these disputes and rivalries was the deterioration of state economies. Most of the former colonies were battered by deflation, waning profits from war-related businesses, and the inability of locally manufactured goods to compete with cheaper imports. Economic depression finally descended in 1785 and 1786, hitting indebted farmers the hardest. Saddled by high prices and debt repayment, farmers demanded laws that would bail them out of indebtedness.

To stabilize public and private finances, conservative local governments in Massachusetts and New Hampshire imposed higher property taxes to pay off Revolutionary War–era debt, put a tighter rein on paper money in circulation, and forced the settlement of debts and mortgages—all of which further fueled the agrarian unrest. Farmers initially pressed for their goals peacefully, but as their demands remained unheard, they resorted to violence. In September 1786, farmers in New Hampshire seized the state building and held state officials prisoners. Similar incidents broke out in western Massachusetts, Vermont, and Connecticut.

Things came to a head in central Massachusetts in 1786 when a group of rebels, led by Captain Daniel Shays, a former officer of the Continental army and veteran of the Revolutionary War, denounced merchants and commercial speculators as the new "aristocracy" that subjugated the people as harshly as any European monarchy. Government officials, backed up by money from the merchants, launched a military campaign to subdue the insurrection. In February 1787, during a clash between the two forces, Shays's followers were neutralized. The incident, however, sent shock waves through the rest of America.

The Need for a Stronger Union

In the midst of worries about disorder and destabilization, the confederation was on the verge of collapse. The weak central government did not have real power to regulate interstate commerce and thus improve interstate relations and reduce rivalries. Nor did it have the power to finance itself by levying taxes on interstate and foreign trade. To fund the confederation, Congress had to requisition the states; but, often the states did not send their dues. The failed financial system reduced the effectivity of Congress and, by extension, the Union.

It was clear, too, that the articles could not steer an effective foreign policy. Other nations saw the United States as a threat to their interests in their own colonized territories in North America. The British continued their hold of the

Northwest Territories along the Great Lakes. Spain blocked American attempts to gain access into the Mississippi region, a sprawling source of land. And France limited American access to its interests in the Caribbean and supported the position of Spain on its sovereignty over the Mississippi region. None of these powers in North America wished to see the union of American states present a strong front and possibly dispute the land claims of the Europeans.

As for the Americans, the fear of continued divisions, upheaval, and repudiation by other countries prodded many political and business leaders to take immediate action. These concerned men—composed of merchants, bankers, planters, physicians, and soldiers—agreed to meet in Virginia in May 1787 to revise the Articles of Confederation to make it more responsive to the young republic's pressing problems. The common vision was to fashion a political system that would ensure stability, protect property, and establish the nation's credentials in the eyes of the Europeans. In the minds of many, this meant creating a powerful central government.

In September 1786, Virginia sent out a call to the thirteen states to send commissioners to a meeting in Annapolis, Maryland, to consider trade matters. Nothing concrete came out of the poorly attended meeting. However, a report written by one of the commissioners, Alexander Hamilton, was circulated calling on the states to consider revising the articles to "render the constitution of the Foederal Government adequate to the exigencies of the Union."[3] Hamilton's call for another convention was echoed by no less than George Washington, the commander in chief of the Continental army during the Revolution and the most revered American at the time. In a letter he wrote in March 1787 to James Madison, a fellow Virginian, Washington said, "a thorough reform of the present system is indispensable" and urged that the convention must "probe the defects of the Constitution to the bottom, and provide radical cures, whether they are agreed or not."[4] Initially refraining from taking part in the convention, Washington eventually joined the Virginia delegation and became one of convention's most illustrious members.

The Imperative of a New Form of Government

Months before the second convention James Madison, considered the most learned and best prepared among the delegates, outlined several proposals which he believed should underpin discussions of a new governmental system. His proposals focused on six ideas: (1) a system of representation for the states recognizing unequal importance, (2) investing the national government with complete authority, (3) federal power to veto state legislative decisions, (4) the addition of a judiciary branch and an executive branch to the central government, (5) checks and balances among the branches and separation of powers at the national level, and (6) ratification of the new law by the people, not only by the state legislatures.

Madison's proposals reflected his belief that revising the Articles of Confederation was no longer sufficient; what was needed was a new system of government. That system was republicanism. Madison's vision was to transform the confederation of thirteen into one republic. He and his fellow Virginians—George Washington, George Mason, George Wythe, John Blair, Edmund Randolph, and James McClurg—resolved to introduce these proposals at the Philadelphia Convention.

The Men in the Convention

In February 1787, Congress requested the states to send delegates to Philadelphia for the purpose of overhauling the Articles of Confederation to make it more responsive to the needs of the Union. In all, seventy-five delegates were named, but only fifty-five actually gathered at Philadelphia in May when the convention officially started.

Historian and scholar Charles Warren notes that of the fifty-five who went to Philadelphia "thirty-nine had served in the Congress of the Confederation; eight of them had signed the Declaration of Independence; eight had helped to form their State Constitutions; five had been members of the Annapolis Convention in September, 1786; seven had been Chief Executives of their States; and twenty-one had fought . . . in the Revolutionary War."[5] Warren further notes that thirty-three had been lawyers, of whom ten had served as state judges; eight were engaged in business; six were planters; three had been physicians. In effect, these men were experienced professionals, most of whom had knowledge of government and law.

The most prominent delegations, according to Warren, came from Virginia (George Washington, James Madison, and Edmund Randolph); Massachusetts (Rufus King, Nathaniel Gorham, and Elbridge Gerry); Pennsylvania (Benjamin Franklin, James Wilson, Gouverneur Morris, and Robert Morris); Connecticut (Roger Sherman, Oliver Ellsworth, and William Samuel Johnson); and South Carolina (John Rutledge, Charles Pinckney, Charles Cotesworth Pinckney, and Pierce Butler). Of these founding fathers, many historians attribute the final form of the Constitution to ten men—Madison, Randolph, Franklin, Wilson, Gouverneur Morris, King, Rutledge, Charles Pinckney, Ellsworth, and Sherman.

Drawing on Recent Experience

At the opening of the deliberations, the Virginia delegation lost no time in introducing the Virginia Plan, which called for a republican form of government. According to the plan, the new government should contain a legislature with two branches as well as an executive office and a judiciary seat of authority. The powers of these governmental sectors should be separate and distinct, but each should impose a check on any abuse of power in the other branches.

While most delegates seemed intellectually prepared to only revise the Articles of Confederation, the idea of a new, stronger central government was not foreign to them. When the Virginians set out the Virginia Plan, the aim of the convention was radically altered. The idea of creating a new form of government was set into motion with no strong opposition. What remained to be debated were the details of the new arrangement, and it was the details that the delegates would wrangle over in subsequent discussions.

To guide them in the monumental task of drafting a new constitution to frame the new government, the delegates drew on lessons from the recent past, particularly their experience of British rule.

Constitutional historian Merrill Jensen maintains that to

most of the states representation through the legislature was not new. In his book, *The Making of the American Constitution*, Jensen notes that Virginia first established the outlines of a representative legislature in 1619, when the Virginia Company authorized the governor to call representatives of plantations to make laws for their own government. The grouping was finally recognized by Charles I in 1624, signaling the formal integration of representative legislature in the state government.

The states had also gathered experience in government as royal colonies administered directly by the British Crown; as self-governing corporations like Connecticut and Rhode Island; or as semi-independent proprietary colonies like Pennsylvania, Delaware, and Maryland.

By the end of seventeenth century through the eighteenth century, Jensen further asserts, the structures of government in the colonies were similar. Heading each government was a governor, appointed by the Crown in the colonies, by the proprietors in the proprietary colonies, and elected in Connecticut and Rhode Island. Except in the last two colonies, the governors exercised great legal powers commissioned to them by the Crown and the proprietors. While the colonies assumed various degrees of self-government, they were very much part of the British Empire, which meant they had to contend with a central authority.

The states' varied experiences in self-government and working with a central authority had earlier helped them in writing their first state constitutions after 1775. When the delegates gathered in Philadelphia in May 1787, they brought with them the added advantage of many years of direct self-governing experience. Jensen declares, "The government of the empire was in fact a vast 'federal' structure. It was awkward, unwieldy, and often unworkable, but many of its devices for achieving centralized control were to be written into the Constitution of 1787."[6]

Inspired by the Enlightenment

Apart from their understanding of self-government, the delegates were influenced by the intellectual atmosphere of the time. The Enlightenment, which held sway in Europe in the 1600s up to the 1700s, bequeathed to the framers of the Constitution the idea that human reason—not divine will—was the source of knowledge and wisdom. From Thomas Hobbes, a preeminent Enlightenment thinker, they learned the doctrine of the sovereignty of the people that made a government dependent on the consent of the governed. From John Locke the Americans culled the belief that people have inalienable rights to life, liberty, and property, and that if government violates these rights, people have the right to withdraw their allegiance to the government. Other famous thinkers who influenced the founding fathers were Charles de Montesquieu, Jean-Jacques Rousseau, and Thomas Paine; they all elucidated on the rights of man and the primacy of the will of the people.

The Constitution, in its adoption of a republican form of government that assured the participation of the governed held government leaders accountable to the people, reflected this will of the people. In deciding on a republican form of government—which Madison had labored on earlier—the delegates of 1787 were united. However, other issues would divide them as they tackled the devices and details of republicanism.

Contentious Issues Divided the Delegates

Soon after the opening of the convention in May 1787, contentious issues started to divide the delegates and threatened to dissolve the convention. First of these was the question of state representation in the legislature. Since the First Continental Congress of 1774, the states had adhered to the one-state-one-vote rule. Under that arrangement, large states like Virginia, Pennsylvania, Massachusetts, and New York had the same vote as small states like Delaware, Rhode Island, and Georgia.

The Virginia Plan, introduced at the start of the convention, recommended a bicameral legislature, a departure from the unicameral confederation Congress but a continuation of the legislatures already in place in ten of the thirteen states. Most Americans at the time, as George Mason put it, were settled on two things: "an attachment to republican government and . . . to more than one branch in the Legislature."[7] The Virginia Plan also recommended that both houses of the national legislature—the Senate and the House of Representatives—be constituted on the basis of population. States with larger populations would have more representatives than states with smaller populations. The plan naturally upset the small states, which saw the unequal representation as detrimental to their interests. After several weeks of bitter debate and threats of disunion, the delegates hammered out a compromise.

The new proposal, mediated by the delegates of Connecticut, provided that in the Senate members would be elected by the state legislatures, with each state having one vote. In the House, seats would be apportioned on the basis of the number of free inhabitants in each state plus three-fifths of the number of slaves. Mason envisioned the House, with its members directly elected by the people, to be the "grand depository of the democratic principles of the government."[8] The compromise also provided for a census every ten years to adjust the representation in the lower house according to population growth.

Another explosive issue that racked the convention was how much power the individual states would give up to the central government. One of the principal features of the Virginia Plan was the national legislature's power to veto state laws. Many delegates saw this as an assault on the sovereignty of the states. Again, a variation of the original proposal managed to stave off extended opposition from the delegates. The variation, the supremacy clause of the Constitution (Article 6, Section 1), makes the Constitution, federal laws, and treaties the supreme law of the land, elevating them above state constitutions and laws. The clause effectively sanctions the federal courts' power to declare state laws unconstitutional.

The Issue of Slavery Almost Dissolved the Union

The threat created by the clash between small and big states over representation was later overshadowed by the wrenching split between the northern and southern states. This time, the dispute was over slavery. The southern states, dependent on the slave trade for their plantations and, thus, their economy, wanted it continued; the northern states wanted it stopped on moral grounds.

In late August, as the convention progressed, the delegates from the South pressed for limits on the power of the central government to regulate the slave trade. Delegates from the northern states resisted these efforts. The heated and bitter debates that followed made it clear that if the southern states did not get what they wanted, they would withdraw from the convention, taking all hopes of a united nation with them. The northerners and the rest of the delegates realized the implications of the South's demands; they scampered to work out yet another compromise. The southerners were allowed to continue the slave trade without interference until 1880, at which time no more slaves could be imported into the nation. In return for this favor, the southerners allowed the federal Congress to regulate commerce (referred to in the deliberations as "navigation") and pass laws pertaining to trade through a simple majority (instead of the two-thirds majority required for most other laws). The provision made passing trade laws that the industrializing New England states wanted less of a hurdle.

This compromise on the slave trade spurred much debate, during as well as after the convention. On the convention floor, Luther Martin, a delegate from Maryland, denounced the compromise as a "corrupt bargain." He came out against the Constitution during the ratification process on account of its defense and protection of slavery which would, in his words, "render us contemptible to every true friend of liberty in the world."[9] Many historians have charged the founding fathers of hypocrisy and duplicity in declaring the "equality of all men," but, at the same time, disenfranchising the slaves.

Joseph J. Ellis, writing in *Founding Brothers: The Revolutionary Generation*, outlines the legacy of the founding fathers' failure to resolve this issue in their time:

> Hindsight permits us to listen to the debate of 1790 [on the abolition of slavery] with the knowledge that none of the par-

ticipants possessed. For we know full well what they could perceive dimly, if at all—namely, that slavery would become the central and defining problem for the next seventy years of American history; that the inability to take decisive action against slavery in the decades immediately following the Revolution permitted the size of the enslaved population to grow exponentially and the legal and political institutions of the developing U.S. government to become entwined in compromises with slavery's persistence; and that eventually over 600,000 Americans would die in the nation's bloodiest war to resolve the crisis, a trauma generating social shock waves that would reverberate for at least another century.[10]

Without reference to the coming civil war, other historians have defended the action of the delegates, maintaining that given a choice between obliterating slavery and holding the Union together, the delegates chose the latter. Bernstein and Rice give voice to this position:

> The delegates knew that a charter that denounced slavery, no matter how mildly, would be rejected by the southern states. . . . Similarly, they knew that a charter explicitly recognizing and sanctioning slavery would be defeated in the northern states. . . . In accommodating the interests of northern and southern states, the delegates kept before them at all times the goal of framing a Constitution that would work on a practical level, and tiptoed around issues of political and moral principle that would blow apart their fragile consensus if faced directly.[11]

It would not be until 1865, almost a century after the writing of the Constitution, that slavery would officially end with the ratification of the the Thirteenth Amendment. By then, the sectional differences, already apparent at the Constitutional Convention, had erupted into the American Civil War.

Ratification by the States

In September 1787, after four months of deliberations, when the delegates were refining the final draft of the Constitution, George Mason of Virginia argued for the inclusion of

New Hampshire
June 21, 1788

New York
July 26, 1788

Massachusetts
Feb. 6, 1788

Rhode Island
May 29, 1790

Pennsylvania
Dec. 12, 1787

Connecticut
Jan. 9, 1788

New Jersey
Dec. 19, 1787

Delaware
Dec. 7, 1787

Virginia
June 25, 1788

Maryland
April 28, 1788

North Carolina
Nov. 21, 1789

South
Carolina
May 23,
1788

Georgia
Jan. 2, 1788

**Ratification of the
Constitution**

a bill of rights that he believed was imperative in a system that valued individual rights. The body rejected Mason's proposal for several reasons. First, some delegates believed the states' respective bills of rights were enough; second, they feared a national bill of rights might challenge state rights; and third, the southern states (home to many slave owners) feared the implications of a declaration of freedom for all men. Mason, however, did not rest his case. He asserted he would not sign the draft-Constitution as long as it did not include a bill of rights, and he campaigned vigorously for such an amendment to the Constitution.

At the conclusion of the convention on September 17, 1787, marking the completion of the Constitution, only thirty-nine of the fifty-five delegates signed the document. Mason had lost his bid. The Constitution without a bill of rights was offered to the states for ratification.

The process of ratifying the draft-Constitution started soon after the dissolution of the convention. Nine of the thirteen states were required to ratify the Constitution before it would become the new law of the nation. The absence of a bill of rights would haunt the ratification debates, but more significantly it was the power of the central government and its supremacy over the state governments that would divide the state legislatures. The debates that emerged eventually crystallized into two positions—the position of the Federalists, who endorsed a strong national government and urged the ratification of the draft-Constitution, and that of the anti-Federalists, who were wary of a strong government and wanted to preserve state sovereignty and thus campaigned for nonratification. The debate, which was carried out mainly in the state legislatures, spilled over into the public arena through newspapers, pamphlets, and other publications, as well as public gatherings on the streets.

Before the end of 1787, three states had ratified the Constitution—Delaware, Pennsylvania, and New Jersey. Nine states followed suit in the following year—Georgia, Connecticut, Massachusetts, Maryland, South Carolina, New Hampshire, Virginia, New York, and North Carolina. With ratification, the Constitution became effective in March 1789. Rhode Island was the last state to ratify in May 1789.

In April 1789, the First Congress convened and declared the results of the first presidential election. The House of Representatives and Senate, in a joint session, declared George Washington the first president of the United States. In May, the legislature discussed the inclusion of a bill of rights as an amendment to the Constitution. James Madison, stirred by public demand for a bill of rights during the ratification campaign, proposed the amendment. Though Madison had earlier opposed the idea of a bill of rights, he took a turn after further reflection on the subject as well as after discussions with both Washington and Thomas Jefferson (who was at the time serving in the foreign ministry in France). In 1792, the Bill of Rights was passed by Congress. The Bill of Rights constituted the first ten amendments to the Constitution.

The Constitution Prevails

In 1887, during the centennial anniversary of the Constitution, the former prime minister of England William Ewart Gladstone, wrote that he considered the famous document "the most remarkable work . . . in modern times to have been produced by the human intellect at a single stroke."[12] Indeed, the Constitution has survived the test of time. For more than two centuries it has stood as a symbol of the American nation and its people. To most Americans—and the rest of the world—it is regarded as a nearly perfect design for government. In 1787, the Constitution established the foundation for a national government that ruled just fewer than 4 million people. Today, with twenty-seven amendments, the Constitution governs a nation of more than 280 million people.

Summing up the achievement of the Constitution in producing a strong, prosperous nation, authors Christopher Collier and James Lincoln Collier observe:

> When we measure the United States against reality—the other nations of the world—we are amazed at how well it has worked, for it is certainly the most prosperous nation in the world, and a case can be made that it is the freest. . . . Without overlooking the suppurating wounds, especially poverty and racism, that continue to stain the American fabric, it is fair to say that the United States has gone a long way toward becoming what the men at Philadelphia wanted it to be: a prosperous, orderly nation in which no man need fear the arbitrary hand of a capricious government.[13]

Notes

1. Clinton Rossiter, *1787: The Grand Convention*. New York: Macmillan, 1966, pp. 50–51.

2. Richard B. Bernstein and Kym S. Rice, *Are We to Be a Nation? The Making of the Constitution*. Cambridge, MA: Harvard University Press, 1987, p. 87.

3. Quoted in Bernstein and Rice, *Are We to Be a Nation?* p. 105.

4. Quoted in Bernstein and Rice, *Are We to Be a Nation?* p. 106.

5. Charles Warren, *The Making of the Constitution*. Boston: Little, Brown, 1929, p. 55.

6. Merrill Jensen, *The Making of the American Constitution*. New York: Van Nostrand Reinhold, 1964, pp. 14–15.

7. Quoted in Robert A. Diamond, ed., *Origins and Development of Congress*. Washington, DC: Congressional Quarterly, 1976, p. 36.

8. Quoted in Diamond, *Origins and Development of Congress*, p. 37.

9. Quoted in Joseph J. Ellis, *Founding Brothers: The Revolutionary Generation*. New York: Alfred A. Knopf, 2000, p. 94.

10. Ellis, *Founding Brothers*, p. 88.

11. Bernstein and Rice, *Are We to Be a Nation?* p. 178.

12. Quoted in Christopher Collier and James Lincoln Collier, *Decision in Philadelphia: The Constitutional Convention of 1787*. New York: Random House, 1986, acknowledgements.

13. Collier and Collier, *Decision in Philadelphia*, p. 352.

Chapter 1

A Society Divided: The Colonies at the Framing of the Constitution

Internal Struggle Between the Elite and the Underclass

Merrill Jensen

Merrill Jensen, author, educator, and scholar, challenges assumptions that are commonly made about colonial society. He points out that behind the unity that the colonies achieved in their quest to end British rule were destructive internal divisions. Jensen maintains that the Revolution was predominantly an internal struggle waged by the masses against local aristocracy. He also points out inconsistencies in the social division: Among the radicals or revolutionists who fought the British were local aristocrats, and among the groups that wanted British rule to continue (loyalists) were members of the working class. These groups forged uneasy, temporary alliances to end British rule, but when independence was finally secured, the divisions resurfaced. Jensen, a major historian of the American Revolution, has written several books on the war and the U.S. Constitution. He taught at the University of Washington, University of Wisconsin, and Oxford University. The following essay is an excerpt from his book *The Articles of Confederation*, a classic among the histories of the revolutionary era.

The American Revolution was far more than a war between the colonies and Great Britain; it was also a struggle between those who enjoyed political privileges and those who did not. Yet the conclusions which may be drawn from the history of social conflict within the colonies and applied to such matters of mutual concern as the writing of a common constitution are seldom drawn and applied. Ordinarily the Revolution is treated as the end of one age and the beginning of another; a new country was born; political parties sprang into being; political leaders, full of wisdom learned during the Revolution, sought to save the new nation from the results of ignorance and inexperience. So runs the story.

But the story is true only in an external sense. The basic social forces in colonial life were not eliminated by the Declaration of Independence. There was no break in the underlying conflict between party and party representing fundamental divisions in American society. Those divisions had their roots in the very foundation of the colonies, and by the middle of the eighteenth century there had arisen broad social groupings based on economic and political conditions. More and more, wealth and political power were concentrated along the coast, in the hands of planters in the South and of merchants in the North. There were exceptions, of course, but by and large the colonial governments were in the hands of the economic upper classes. Exceedingly conscious of its local rights, the ruling aristocracy was willing to use democratic arguments to defeat the centralizing policies of Great Britain, but it had no intention of widening the base of political power within the colonies to accord with the conclusions which could be, and were, drawn from those arguments. On the contrary, it had kept itself in power through the use of a number of political weapons. As wealth accumulated and concentrated along the coast, as the frontier moved westward and became debtor and alien in character, and as the propertyless element in the colonial towns grew larger, the owners of property demanded "a political interpretation of their favored position"—that is, political supremacy—as a protection against the economic programs of debtor agrarians and the town poor. Encouraged by the British government, they gradually secured the political safeguards they demanded—property qualifications for participation in government and representation disproportionate to their numbers. The imposition of property qualifications for the suffrage and of even higher qualifications for office effectively quelled the political ambitions of the greater part of the town population, and the denial of proportional representation to the newly settled areas prevented the growing West from capturing control of colonial governments. Laws of entail and primogeniture insured the economic basis of colonial society, so much so that Thomas Jefferson believed that their abolition in Virginia would annul the privileges of an "aristocracy of wealth."

Property Qualification for Suffrage

But the economic-political aristocracy which Jefferson hoped to abolish had not always been characteristic of the American colonies. In early Virginia and Maryland every free man, whether holding property or not, could vote. The first serious attempt to impose a property qualification for the suffrage came with the Restoration and it met with bitter opposition. One of the significant acts of Bacon's Assembly in 1676 was the abolition of the property qualification imposed by the Berkeley regime. But the victory of the poorer elements was short-lived at best, and in Virginia, as elsewhere in the colonies by the end of the seventeenth century, the property qualification was an integral part of the political system. During the eighteenth century the tendency was in the direction of ever higher qualifications, and colonial assemblies continued to refuse adequate representation to the expanding West. By the middle of the century a small minority of the colonial population wielded economic and political powers which could not be taken from them by any legal means. This political oligarchy was able to ignore most of the popular demands, and when smoldering discontent did occasionally flare up in a violent outburst, it was forcibly suppressed. Thus democracy was decreasingly a characteristic of constitutional development in the American colonies.

Opposition to the oligarchical rule of the planters and merchants came from the agrarian and proletarian elements which formed the vast majority of the colonial population. Probably most of them were politically inert, but from their ranks nevertheless came some of the effective leadership and much of the support for revolutionary activity after 1763. In the towns the poorer people, although a small part of the colonial population, far outnumbered the large property-owners. Most of them—laborers, artisans, and small trades-men—were dependent on the wealthy merchants, who ruled them economically and socially. Agrarian discontent, too, was the product of local developments: of exploitation by land speculators, "taxation without representation," and the denial of political privileges, economic benefits, and military assistance. The farmer's desire for internal revolution had al-ready been violently expressed in Bacon's Rebellion and in the Regulator Movement, events widely separated in time but similar in cause and consequence.

Colonial Radicalism

To a large extent, then, the party of colonial radicalism was composed of the masses in the towns and on the frontier. In Charleston, Philadelphia, New York, and Boston the radical parties were the foundation of the revolutionary movement in their towns and colonies. It was they who provided the or-ganization for uniting the dispersed farming population, which had not the means of organizing, but which was more than ready to act and which became the bulwark of the Rev-olution once it had started. Located at the center of things, the town radicals were able to seize upon issues as they arose and to spread propaganda by means of circular letters, com-mittees of correspondence, and provincial congresses. They brought to a focus forces that would otherwise have spent themselves in sporadic outbursts easily suppressed by the es-tablished order.

Colonial radicalism did not become effective until after the French and Indian War. Then, fostered by economic de-pression and aided by the bungling policy of Great Britain and the desire of the local governing classes for indepen-dence within the empire, it became united in an effort to throw off its local and international bonds. The discon-tented were given an opportunity to express their discontent when the British government began to enforce restrictions upon the colonies after 1763. The colonial merchants used popular demonstrations to give point to their more orderly protests against such measures as the Stamp Act, and it was only a step from such riots, incited and controlled by the merchants, to the organization of radical parties bent on the redress of local grievances which were of far more concern to the masses than the more remote and less obvious effects of British policy. Furthermore, there arose, in each of the colonies, leaders of more than ordinary ability, men who were able to create issues when none were furnished by Great Britain, and who seized on British acts as heaven-sent opportunities to attack the local aristocracy—too strongly entrenched to be overthrown on purely local issues—under the guise of a patriotic defense of American liberties. Thus, used as tools at first, the masses were soon united under capable leadership in what became as much a war against the colonial aristocracy as a war for independence.

The American Revolution thus marks the ascendancy of the radicals of the colonies, for the first time effectively united. True, this radical ascendancy was of brief duration, but while it lasted an attempt was made to write democratic ideals and theories of government into the laws and constitutions of the American states. Fulfillment was not complete, for the past was strong and in some states the conservatives retained their power and even strengthened it. And

"Give me liberty, or give me death!" from Patrick Henry's 1775 speech, became the war cry of the American Revolution.

once independence was won, the conservatives soon united in undoing, so far as they could, such political and economic democracy as had resulted from the war. Nevertheless it is significant that the attempt at democratization was made and that it was born of colonial conditions. The participation of the radicals in the creation of a common government is all-important, for they as well as the conservatives believed that a centralized government was essential to the maintenance of conservative rule. Naturally the radicals who exercised so much power in 1776 refused to set up in the Articles of Confederation a government which would guarantee the position of the conservative interests they sought to remove from power.

Conservative Interests

The conservatives gradually became aware that internal revolution might be the result of continued disputes between themselves and Great Britain, but they were not agreed on the measures necessary to retain both "home rule" and the power to "rule at home." Some of them, like Joseph Galloway, sought to tighten the bonds between the colonies and the mother country and thus to consolidate the power and bulwark the position of the colonial aristocracy. Other conservatives, like John Dickinson, denied that Parliament had any authority over the colonies and cared little for a close tie with the mother country; what they demanded was a status that was in effect home rule within the British Empire. Complete independence was to be avoided if possible, for it was fraught with the danger of social revolution within the colonies. As these men became aware that conservative rule had as much or more to fear from the people of the colonies as from British restrictions, they sought more and more for reconciliation with the mother country, in spite of her obvious intention to enforce her laws by means of arms. But they made the fatal yet unavoidable error of uniting with the radicals in meeting force with force. They made themselves believe that it was neither traitorous nor illegal to resist with arms the British measures they disliked.

When independence could no longer be delayed, the conservatives were forced to choose between England and the United States. Some became "Tories," or "Loyalists." Others, the victims of circumstances partly of their own creation, fearfully and reluctantly became revolutionists. But in so doing they did not throw away their ideals of government. They were too cool, too well versed in checkmating radicalism and in administering governments in their own interest, to be misled by the democratic propaganda of the radicals. Not even John Adams, one of the few conservatives who worked for independence, was willing to stomach the ideas of Tom Paine when it came to the task of forming governments within the American colonies.

The continued presence of groups of conservatives in all the states, weakened though they were by the Revolution, is of profound importance in the constitutional history of the United States. They appeared in strength in the first Continental Congress. In it their ideas and desires were expressed. They were still powerful at the beginning of the second Continental Congress, but gradually their hold was weakened by the growing revolutionary movement in the various states. They were strong enough, however, to obstruct the radical program during 1775 and to delay a declaration of independence in 1776 until long after the radicals believed that independence was an accomplished fact. In the bitter controversies which occurred the conservatives stated their ideas of government. In its simplest form their objection to independence was that it involved internal revolution. When forced to accept independence, they demanded the creation of a central government which would be a bulwark against internal revolution, which would aid the merchant classes, which would control Western lands, which would, in short, be a "national" government. In this they were opposed by the radicals, who created a "federal" government in the Articles of Confederation and who resisted the efforts of the conservatives to shape the character of those Articles while they were in process of writing and ratification.

Economic Instability Plagues the Union

Clinton Rossiter

Author Clinton Rossiter claims that the economic and social problems that dominated the post–Revolutionary War
era had their origins in politics. He says these problems
had persisted because of the absence of a central authority
that would impose controls on the thirteen states. He cites
the concerns of James Madison over the states' repudiation of the authority of the confederation and their numerous squabbles over interstate trade and land claims. In
1785, union leaders began to realize that the Articles of
Confederation was a failure, Congress was not viable, and
that they needed to organize a new government that
would respond to their needs and problems. Rossiter, a
distinguished constitutional historian, was professor of
American institutions at the Department of Government
at Cornell University. He also taught American history at
Cambridge University. He is the author of several books,
including *The American Presidency* and *Seedtime of the Republic*, which received numerous awards.

The first complaint of the troubled men of 1787 has a familiar ring: although the economy of the country was basically
sound, it was depressed enough in many ports and rural areas
to justify sober talk of "stagnation" and "dislocation." Eight
years of whimsical war had shut off many of the old channels
of trade, dealt a severe blow to such enterprises as fishing and
shipbuilding, disrupted the structure of prices and wages, and
destroyed an untold amount of productive property. Four
years of restless peace had first been marked by an extrava-

Clinton Rossiter, *1787: The Grand Convention*. New York: The MacMillan Company, 1966. Copyright © 1966 by Clinton Rossiter. Reproduced by permission of
the publisher.

gant importation of British and European goods, then had been marred by a rolling series of failures of firms unable either to sell or pay for these goods. Whereas inflation had been the curse of the whole economy during the war, deflation was the bane of critical parts of it in the aftermath. "In every point of view," [James] Madison wrote of Virginia in 1785, "the trade of this country is in a deplorable condition. A comparison of current prices here with those in the Northern States . . . will show that the loss direct on our produce, and indirect on our imports, is not less than fifty per cent."

In some sections of the country, to be sure, the post-war cycle of boom and bust had leveled off on a high plateau of prosperity, and many merchants and farmers were enjoying profits they had never known before. They were enjoying their profits, however, because of lucky circumstances that might not last—and at the expense of other merchants and farmers who might grow weary of being left out in the cold. The health of the American economy in 1787 was too spotty to please men who thought of the Republic, whether sentimentally or cold-bloodedly, as an interdependent array of sections and interests.

Political and Social Tensions

Their second complaint, which tied in with the first, was directed toward the state of private and public finance. Whatever gains might be made in productivity, whatever new markets might be opened up, however many banks might be founded by enterprising men, deep uneasiness was bound to prevail all through a country in which hard money was scarce and growing scarcer, paper money was a threat and growing more threatening, private debts were an invitation to political meddling, and public debts, contracted with the best of wills for the highest of purposes, were a burden that would not be lightened in a hundred years under existing modes of taxation. The critical problem was the alarming dearth of specie with which to pay for everything from taxes levied on the land to goods imported and still wanted from abroad. The drain of specie kept the back country in a state of political and social tension, while the balance of trade seemed to tip so drastically against the United States that even the most solid merchants wondered how long their credit would hold up in London and Amsterdam. At the same time, the absence of a uniform currency in the thirteen states made every dealing across a state line a small exercise in financial wizardry.

Paper money, which was issued in varying amounts and guises during the 1780's in seven states (Rhode Island, New York, New Jersey, Pennsylvania, the Carolinas, and Georgia) and was a subject of bitter controversy in three others (New Hampshire, Massachusetts, and Maryland), was the tie that joined financial dislocation to social discontent. What John Jay derided as "the doctrine of the political transubstantiation of paper into gold and silver" had a powerful appeal to men with crushing debts and unpopular taxes to pay, and with no coin in which to pay them. Although there were exceptions to the rule, as in devastated but hopeful (and therefore slave-hungry) South Carolina, most battles over paper money were fought between men of status and property and men well below them on the economic and social scale. Some of these battles were extremely nasty; a Marxist historian, if he looked hard and narrowly enough at states like Pennsylvania, New Hampshire, Maryland, and Rhode Island, could find many signs of "class struggle" in the new Republic.

The non-Marxist historian, although he may acclaim the republican consensus that kept these battles from getting entirely out of hand, is bound to admit that such incidents as the descent of an armed mob on the New Hampshire legislature in Exeter in September, 1786, and the famous "rebellion" symbolized (if not exactly led) by Captain Daniel Shays in Massachusetts were full of the animosity of distressed men toward their "betters." Beneath the veneer of deference there had always been malice and envy in the attitude of the "lower orders" toward the gentry in America, and the pressures of the 1780's brought such feelings frothing to the surface. They also set some sober members of the gentry to complaining aloud about the "heats and excesses of a mad democracy." The class structure in America has rarely been more visible, nor more visibly scarred by mistrust, than in the paper-money turmoils of the 1780's. The restoration of many loyalists to high standing in the community was another spur to social resentment. Yet another was the founding of the Society of the Cincinnati by some of Washington's officers, and even the repeal of the principle of hereditary membership in 1784 did not allay the fears of dedicated republicans (many of them in high places and themselves eligible for membership) that the Cincinnati were the forerunners of an American peerage.

For men who looked beyond the boundaries of the Republic, its weak position in the squabbling family of nations was a greater cause for worry than was a sluggish commerce or a deranged currency or even an agitated society. Of all the impulses that drove men like [George] Washington and [Alexander] Hamilton to Philadelphia in 1787, none was stronger than the uncomplicated, patriotic sense of shame at the contempt in which the United States seemed to be held—from Britain at one end of the scale of power to the Barbary states at the other. As Hamilton wrote to the editor of the *New-York Packet* as early as July 4, 1782:

> There is something . . . diminutive and contemptible in the prospect of a number of petty states, with the appearance only of union, jarring, jealous and perverse, without any determined direction, fluctuating and unhappy at home, weak and insignificant by their dissensions in the eyes of other nations.

Internal Intrigues

Although the British were the chief offenders against American interests and sensibilities—because of their discriminations against trade, their retention of seven northwest posts in defiance of the terms of the Treaty of Paris, and their refusal to send an envoy to a Republic that might or might not turn out to be a sovereign nation—France and Spain, each in its own arrogant way, pursued policies based on the cheerful suspicion that the United States would probably not survive. Few Americans, oddly enough, feared a military attack by one or more of the great powers; the immediate threat of war was not one of the impulses that drove men to Philadelphia in 1787. What concerned the Framers was not force but intrigue. They were quite certain that America could not be conquered in the foreseeable future; they were quite worried that parts of it could be bought. Enough Spanish gold flowed maliciously through the specie-starved future states of Kentucky and Tennessee to give substance to this worry. Men in this area had their own reasons to be distressed about the direction of American diplomacy, for only an angry surge of southern and western opinion in 1786 had prevented the Secretary of Foreign Affairs in the Confederation, John Jay, from bargaining away American rights to navigate the lower Mississippi for thirty years to come.

By 1787 men like Washington and Madison had come to see the commercial, financial, social, and diplomatic disorders of the new Republic as primarily political in character. The trouble with almost every state was that it was governed weakly or erratically; the trouble with the United States was that it was governed hardly at all. Since they also saw these disorders as primarily national in scope, as afflictions that no state could hope to cure on its own, the most unbearable ill was a palsied common government.

Except for Rhode Island and Connecticut, for each of which the transition from self-governing colony to statehood was a simple affair, the states had adopted new constitutions between 1776 and 1784. Most of these constitutions were commendable experiments in republicanism, and several were admirable, but none was a guarantee—no constitution ever is—against impetuosity, error, or indecision. By the middle of the 1780's the unrest in every state had impelled all but the steadiest men in power to act impetuously, all but the luckiest to make mistakes, all but the bravest to turn their backs on hard problems that clamored for attention. Despite official protestations of enduring devotion to the doctrine of the separation of powers, the governments of most states were in the hands of self-willed legislatures. Despite the energetic efforts of the gentry and its political allies, the control of most legislatures fell at one time or another into the hands of a small-farmer class that was chiefly interested in paying off old scores and new debts as speedily as possible.

Blaming the State Legislatures

The record of the more headstrong or simply shortsighted state legislatures was a major source of the discontent that finally welled up into resolute action. In compiling a list in early 1787 of some eleven "vices of the political system of the United States," Madison laid a full seven, with the hearty concurrence of every friend to whom he showed the list, at the doors of the legislatures. Whether the laws of the derelict states were guilty of "mutability" or "multiplicity" or "injustice" was then, as it is today, a point of some controversy, but no man could gainsay, although he might explain away, Madison's indictment of these states for "failure . . . to comply with the constitutional requisitions" of Congress, for "encroachments" on the "authority" of the United States, for "violations" of some of the key articles of the Treaty of Paris, and for "trespasses . . . on the rights of each other" in the form of commercial discriminations. The states had played fast and loose with the liberty and property of many of their citizens; they had failed in their elementary duty to support the common government of the United States; the "pride of independence," as even the forgiving Jefferson wrote in 1783, had taken "deep and dangerous hold on the hearts" of too many of their politicians. Although few members of the Convention would have gone so far as General Knox and pronounced the state governments to be "sources of pollution," none whose views or interests transcended state boundaries could manage more than a wry smile over the antics of turbulent Rhode Island or parochial New York in this unsettled period.

A Failed System

They could not even manage a smirk over what James Madison, a loyal and industrious member of Congress, described tartly as "the existing embarrassments and mortal diseases of the Confederacy." The government under the Articles of Confederation was on its last legs in 1786 and 1787. When the Articles had been anticipated in 1774, mulled over in 1776, proposed in 1777, and finally ratified in 1781, a confederate, congressional form of government was clearly what most Americans wanted to handle their common affairs. It had to be confederate because they were in no mood to give a faraway, central regime in the United States what they were busy denying to a faraway, central regime in Britain, and because small states like Delaware and Rhode Island believed honestly that they were, in ways that mattered, equal partners of large states like Pennsylvania and Virginia. It had to be congressional because they were in no mood to give an independent executive in the United States what they were busy denying to an independent executive in Britain. In the light of the embryonic state of American nationalism, the fear of political power that pervaded Revolutionary thinking, and the lack of experience in lawmaking and administration on a continental scale, the Articles of Confederation—in effect, a codification of the methods and experiences of the first three years of the Continental Congress—seem to have been just about as viable a form of common government as could have been offered to the American people in the second year of independence. Only a few persons were moved to think uncomfortable thoughts at the sight of a charter that gave an equal vote to each of the thirteen states, required nine votes to do anything significant in the areas of war, diplomacy, and finance (this was in fact a concession to the larger states), and required the approval of the legislatures of every state to any "alteration" in its wording. The "authors" of the Confederation, Edmund Randolph stated in behalf of the whole Convention of 1787, had "done all that patriots could do, in the then infancy of the science of constitutions and of confederacies."

By the second year of peace, however, government under the Articles had lost most of its viability, and arrangements that had made sense in 1777 were beginning to look more and more like "mortal diseases." As a result, some men had begun to wonder out loud whether a government without power to tax, to regulate trade, and to pass laws that individuals were bound to obey was a government at all. A charter of "perpetual" Union that gave equal votes to Delaware and Virginia was headed from the beginning toward trouble; a charter that relied for the replenishment of the "common treasury" on a system of requisitioning funds from the legis-latures of Delaware, Virginia, and their eleven sisters—each of which retained its "sovereignty, freedom and indepen-dence" and thus could defy any requisition—was headed to-ward atrophy or even oblivion. Although commanded by the Articles to look to the "common defense," "security," and "mutual and general welfare" of the United States, Congress lacked the power, both in fact and theory, to raise the funds necessary for the discharge of these high duties. The dele-gates in Congress were reluctant to vote substantial requisi-tions; the states were delinquent in meeting the most mod-est ones. And one state legislature—whether that of Rhode Island, New York, or Virginia—could always be counted on to block unanimous approval of any proposal to give Con-gress even a conditional power to levy tariffs. By 1785 the government of the United States was a wheedling beggar. It could not raise enough money at home or abroad to meet the modest expenses of peace; it could not even raise enough to pay interest on the debts it had contracted during the war. A convincing measure of its financial plight is the fact that the total income of this government in 1786 was less than one-third of the charges for annual interest on the national debt. So cautious a delegate as William Paterson of New Jer-sey could speak in the Convention of 1787 of the "deranged state of our finances," and so flatly anti-nationalist a delegate as Luther Martin of Maryland had to admit that Congress had been "weak, contemptibly weak."

States Refuse to Comply

The weakness of the confederate features of the Articles of Confederation was compounded by the arrangement under which the total authority of the government was centered in one institution: "the Delegates of the United States in Con-gress assembled." The first constitution of the United States—if constitution it was—set up a one-chambered as-sembly as the organ of governing and made no provision whatever for a permanent, independent executive or judi-ciary. The pressure of events, indeed the simple demands of effective government, gave rise in time to at least rudimentary executive and judicial branches. Having lumbered along ever since the extralegal days of 1774 with a system of calling upon any agency within reach to execute its decisions (including committees of its own members, state conventions or councils, the commander in chief, and other citizens with or without official status), Congress underwent a limited constitutional revolution in 1781 that put single officers in charge of each of the three areas of principal concern: diplomacy, war, and finance. While Congress itself flitted from one abode to another, and often simply vegetated because the necessary quorum of two delegates from each of seven states was not on hand, men like Benjamin Lincoln (Secretary of War, 1781–1783), Henry Knox (Secretary of War, 1785–1789), Robert R. Livingston (Secretary for Foreign Affairs, 1781–1783), John Jay (Secretary for Foreign Affairs, 1784–1789), and above all Robert Morris (the first and last Superintendent of Finance, 1781–1784) labored to give the United States the appearance of a government of permanence and promise. The three-man Court of Appeals in Cases of Capture, which operated under the authority of Congress between 1780 and 1786, did its restricted but useful judicial tasks in a manner reasonably worthy of the only plausible candidate for the title of "direct ancestor" to the Supreme Court of the United States.

It is conceivable that a stable, effective pattern of government for the Union could have emerged prescriptively out of the Confederation Congress, and that scholars today might be arguing among themselves whether Superintendent Morris, Secretary Jay, or General Washington was "really the first prime minister of the United States." But the Articles betrayed a fatal flaw, and the flaw was in the foundation, not the superstructure. The first constitution of the United States went from crisis to crisis and finally into a long slide toward death, not because it defied the commonly accepted American principle of the separation of powers by giving total authority to a single organ, but because it made the exercise of the limited authority it granted almost exclusively dependent on the good will of each of thirteen states, not one of which had any overpowering reason, even in the worst days of 1777 and 1778, to trust any or all of the other states. . . . The states failed Congress—by refusing to honor resolutions, to fill requisitions, to approve new powers, and often even to maintain a delegation at the seat of government—far more grievously than Congress failed the states. The troubles of the Republic's confederate form of government were starkly revealed in the weeks between November 26, 1783, and January 14, 1784, when the Treaty of Paris, almost a "steal" for the United States, lay unratified before a Congress that could not muster the nine state delegations necessary for approval. . . .

Congress was not a viable government for a self-respecting, self-directing, expanding, and maturing nation, which was the kind of nation most leading men wanted America to be.

A Strong National Identity Bridges Class and Social Divisions

Richard B. Bernstein with Kym S. Rice

American society in the 1780s consisted of two groups: property owners and non-property owners. The propertied class, which comprised the elite, earned voting rights and monopolized the holding of public office. They dominated the political system and shaped much of public policy. Authors Richard B. Bernstein and Kym S. Rice observe that the non-propertied class, referred to as the "common sort," deferred mostly to the elite and did not have much opportunity to participate in political life. Completely excluded from society were Native Americans (referred to as Indians), African Americans (who were mostly slaves and referred to as blacks), women, and the impoverished. At the time of writing, Richard B. Bernstein was research curator of the Bicentennial Project of the New York Public Library. Kym S. Rice was a consultant in the Exhibitions Department of the New York Public Library.

Most Americans did not take an active part in the political life of the new republic, contenting themselves with voting if they met the requirements established by state constitutions and laws. All the states maintained some form of property test for voting and still higher property qualifications for holding elective office. These requirements grew out of a few basic assumptions about political life that dominated the thinking of the eighteenth century: first, one ought to have a stake in society and be able to prove it before one could have a voice in directing that society's affairs; second,

Richard B. Bernstein with Kym S. Rice, *Are We to Be a Nation?: The Making of the Constitution.* Cambridge, MA: Harvard University Press, 1987. Copyright © 1987 by The New York Public Library. Reproduced by permission.

only truly independent voters, whose independence could be proved by their ability to satisfy the property test, were desirable participants in political life. Just how many Americans did meet these property tests for voting in this period is a matter of vigorous historical dispute, though it now seems that the property tests were far easier to satisfy than was previously believed. Of the fraction of the total population who could play a role in the political process, however, few aspired to hold office. The society that had evolved since the first British settlements at Jamestown in 1607 was governed by unspoken assumptions and principles bound up in the shorthand term *deference*. There were basically two kinds of Americans: gentlemen, who did not need to worry about earning a livelihood and thus were well suited to hold office and shape policy; and everyone else, usually grouped as "the common sort." For the most part, the common sort did not challenge the assumption that the elite were entitled to dominate the political system, but the deferential society of colonial America was buffeted and weakened by the doctrines let loose by the Revolution, and as a result the distinction between gentlemen and the common sort began to erode in the 1770s and 1780s.

This distinction was not a rigidly defined class barrier of the type found in Europe; in Denmark, for example, there existed a nine-class system in which it was a crime for members of the upper three classes to interact with members of the lower six. It was possible for the tenth son of a Boston tallow chandler, a runaway apprentice, to come to Philadelphia virtually penniless and eventually become wealthy, respected, and powerful—this was the achievement of the great Dr. [Benjamin] Franklin, who became a symbol of the possibilities of America to his admiring compatriots. Similarly, a brilliant illegitimate child could find backing to be educated at King's College (now Columbia University) and become a pillar of the New York legal profession as well as one of the ablest and most respected proponents of a stronger national government—such was the climb of Alexander Hamilton, who nonetheless strove to obscure the circumstances of his early life. The idea of the self-made man was thus an early development in American thought, though it was still the exception rather than the rule.

In addition, the elite of American society were themselves heterogeneous, divided by occupation, education, religion, and geography. New England divines, merchants, and lawyers found it difficult to establish common ground with southern planters, and vice versa. The cleavages and divergences between the various states and regions that made up the United States were among the most daunting obstacles to forging a union of the American states.

Outsiders: Indians, Blacks, and Women

Whatever the structure of American politics and the fluid and evanescent quality of the distinctions between the elite and the common sort, several key groups were excluded by common consent even from the common sort and thus had no direct role in shaping American politics—Indians, blacks, women, and the desperately poor or debtor class.

Of these groups, the Indians loomed largest in the minds of most Americans. From the outset, native Americans had viewed the Europeans' colonization of North America with puzzlement and suspicion. They had at first sought to help the struggling settlements but soon realized that their differing views on the concept of land ownership and exploitation of natural resources made such cooperation impossible. Some tribes maintained friendly or "arm's-length" relations with the colonial governments and later with the states and the Confederation; others withdrew from contact or sought to drive the new settlers out of North America by waging war. During the colonial wars of the seventeenth and eighteenth centuries, the British and French forged alliances with various Indian tribes, and the outcomes of those conflicts spelled extinction for tribes unfortunate enough to be allies of the losing imperial power; similar alliances were made during the Revolution, with similar consequences. By the mid-1780s, most Americans had at least heard rumors of the "savagery" or "barbarism" of the Indians' methods of warfare, if they had not actually witnessed it; consequently, in frontier settlements in the West and South, fear of Indian attacks prompted settlers to support a strong general government that could field and support an army to repel such attacks and preserve their security.

In Virginia, in the same year that witnessed the founding of the Virginia House of Burgesses, a ship bearing twenty "Nigars" docked in Jamestown harbor. These first black residents of British North America were indentured servants, who had committed themselves to work for a term of years as deferred payment for their passage to Virginia. Within a generation, however, the white settlers had laid the foundations for the system of chattel slavery. By 1787, the black population of the United States numbered some 650,000, most of whom were slaves. Slavery existed in nearly every state, though many northern states were either contemplating or moving toward abolition of the institution. Most slaveholders lived in the southern states, where the cultivation of labor-intensive crops such as tobacco, rice, and indigo made dependence on slave labor necessary. Large slaveholding estates, however, were the exception rather than the rule. Most slaveholders owned fewer than five slaves; few operated on the scale of Virginia's George Mason, who owned as many as ninety slaves to till his seventy-five-thousand-acre plantation, Gunston Hall. These slaves were deemed to be property, pure and simple, though their lives were not as harsh as those of their descendants in the next century, the age of King Cotton.

Nonetheless, the institution of chattel slavery was a blight on the new republic, distorting and crippling opportunities for the comparatively few free blacks in the North and condemning hundreds of thousands of men, women, and children to lives of unremitting toil and degradation. Furthermore, the issue of slavery threatened the political stability of the United States. In the 1770s and 1780s, distinguished northerners such as Benjamin Franklin, Benjamin Rush, and John Jay founded or joined manumission societies and campaigned for the abolition of slavery. Enlightened southerners such as Washington, Jefferson, Mason, and Madison hoped that slavery somehow would eventually wither away, though they took few steps themselves to help bring this

about. Other southerners, such as the Rutledges and Pinck-
neys of South Carolina, defended the institution as a necessary part of the plantation economy and the southern way of
life, and even as a positive good for the slaves themselves.
Slavery thus had the potential to cause irreparable cleavage
in the American political community, and most politicians of
the period regarded it as a problem to be handled with extreme care—if indeed at all.

Consigned to Home

The role of women in American society in the Revolutionary era is one of the major new fields of historical inquiry.
Recent scholarship has illuminated not only this specific
subject but also the general character of the Revolution.
Most women in this period found themselves consigned
largely to the private realm of home, family, and childbear-
ing and -rearing. Some women, such as the Baltimore
printer Mary K. Goddard or the historian, poet, dramatist,
and polemicist Mercy Otis Warren of Boston, were able to
lead their own lives and take at least some part in the public
controversies of the day. Nonetheless, the prevailing legal
and political assumptions of colonial America persisted into
the Revolutionary period. Although academies for young
women brought literacy and learning to some, it was a matter of controversy whether women should be educated at all,
on the rationale that education would only tend to make
them dissatisfied with their place in society. Married women
were still subject to the common-law doctrine of coverture,
under which a married couple was considered as one person—the husband; married women thus had no claim to
property during the existence of their marriage. As [histo-
rian] Linda K. Kerber has pointed out, thanks to the old political assumptions linking property with political rights and
participation, the conventional wisdom concluded that married women had no capacity to play a role in political affairs.
Nonetheless, the Revolution had profound consequences for
the role of women in politics and society. The various economic boycotts of British goods in the pre-Revolutionary
period depended for their effectiveness on the cooperation

of women . . . and gradually, painfully, a theory of patriotism applicable to women began to coalesce. Women also came to play critical roles in the fighting of the Revolution itself—not as combatants, but in the equally crucial role of providing logistical support for the Continental Army, such as food, cleaning, nursing, clothing, and even intelligence work. The doctrine of coverture also raised issues of loyalty and patriotism when the new states and the Revolutionary government came to consider the plight of wives of Loyalists: were they bound to their husbands' choices of allegiance under law, unable legally to make political choices on their own, or did they have independent political capacity?

Choices such as these required women in the Revolutionary era to rethink the old view that they were exclusively creatures of the private sphere and must leave the public sphere of politics, diplomacy, and war to men. Indeed, the wives of a few key Revolutionary leaders showed themselves equal to many of their husbands and male kinsmen in their grasp of political realities and ideas, shrewd sense for valid and erroneous political news, and daringness and originality of political thought. And yet the Revolution did not lead to a comparable transformation of women's political rights and responsibilities in the new republic. Although the symbolism of America and of liberty was primarily female—we need only look at the many political cartoons of the period depicting America as a halfclad Indian maiden or as the reincarnation of the Greek goddess Athene—the women of the new nation were not permitted to enter fully into the political life of the new republic. Rather, the dominant ideology of the period, with its roots in republican political theory and classical history, recognized women as embodiments of the ideal of "republican motherhood," namely, that women could best serve the republic by acting as good wives and mothers and transmitting the values of republicanism and the American polity to their children, who, depending on their sex, would either continue this tradition by passing these values to the next generation or would grow up to become good citizens.

The least obvious group of Americans excluded from political decision-making in this period was not the women of the new nation, nor the free and slave blacks, nor the Indians, but those who were too poor to have a legitimate voice in politics—in a popular phrase of the time, the "desperate debtors." Many people, male and female, came to the British

The Exclusion of the Indians

In colonial times, the Indian tribes were not part of American society. They often forged alliances with the European powers to protect their independence and fend off the march of the colonies for western lands. During the Revolution, the greater number of them fought with the British as an act of war against the colonies, whom they perceived as a threat to their land. In the following letter, Washakie, a Shoshone Indian, writes to Governor John W. Hoyt of the Wyoming territory, expressing his disgust and sorrow over the exploitation and brutality his people have suffered from the American settlers who have come to occupy their lands.

Governor:

We are right glad, sir, that you have so bravely and kindly come among us. I shall, indeed, speak to you freely of the many wrongs we have suffered at the hands of the white man. They are things to be noted and remembered. But I cannot hope to express to you the half that is in our hearts. They are too full for words.

Disappointment; then a deep sadness; then a grief inexpressible; then, at times, a bitterness that makes us think of the rifle, the knife and the tomahawk, and kindles in our hearts the fires of desperation—that, sir, is the story of our experience, of our wretched lives.

The white man, who possesses this whole vast country from sea to sea, who roams over it at pleasure, and lives where he likes, cannot know the cramp we feel in this little spot, with the undying remembrance of the fact, which you know as well as we, that every foot of what you proudly call America, not very long ago belonged to the red man. The Great Spirit gave it to us. There was room enough for all his many tribes, and all were happy in their freedom. But the white man had, in ways we know not of, colonies and later to the United States as indentured servants, to pay for their passage from Europe. Indentured servants were not treated as property in theory or in practice, and they also knew that they were bound only for a finite period; in all other respects, however, they were virtually in-

learned some things we had not learned; among them, how to make superior tools and terrible weapons, better for war than bows and arrows; and there seemed no end to the hordes of men that followed them from other lands beyond the sea.

And so, at last, our fathers were steadily driven out, or killed, and we, their sons, but sorry remnants of tribes once mighty, are cornered in little spots of the earth all ours of right—cornered like guilty prisoners, and watched by men with guns, who are more than anxious to kill us off.

Nor is that all. The white man's government promised that if we, the Shoshones, would be content with the little patch allowed us, it would keep us well supplied with everything necessary to comfortable living, and would see that no white man should cross our borders for our game, or for anything that is ours. *But is has not kept its word!* The white man kills our game, captures our furs, and sometimes feeds his herds upon our meadows. And your great and mighty government—Oh sir, I hesitate, for I cannot tell the half! It does not protect us in our rights. It leaves us without the promised seed, without tools for cultivating the land, without implements for harvesting our crops, without breeding animals better than ours, without the food we still lack, after all we can do, without the many comforts we cannot produce, without the schools we so much need for our children.

I say again, the government does not keep its word! And so, after all we can get cultivating the land, and by hunting and fishing, we are sometimes nearly starved, and go half naked, as you see us!

Knowing all this, do you wonder, sir, that we have fits of desperation and think to be avenged?

Andrew Carroll, ed., *Letters of a Nation.* New York: Broadway Books, 1997, pp. 23–25.

distinguishable from chattel slaves.

Those who were not bound for service were not immune from economic collapse. Because there was very little specie, or hard cash, in the United States in this period, the dominant medium of exchange was the note. The person making the note would promise to pay a specified sum at a specified date in exchange for goods or services to be provided by the person to whom he gave the note. The recipients of these notes then endorsed them over to other persons in payment for other goods and services; thus the economic life of the period ran on these written statements of credit and debt. The hope of the maker of a note was that, by the time the note became due or was presented to him for payment, he would have accumulated enough hard currency or other notes to be able to satisfy the obligation. Unfortunately, thanks to the uncertainties of agriculture and of commerce, many Americans' notes came back to them at times when they could not satisfy the demands.

The problem of debt affected Americans at every level of society. . . . Many wealthy planters actually had to carry mountainous loads of debt, which on occasion brought them crashing down to ruin; so Thomas Jefferson discovered in the last years of his life, when the creditors of Wilson Cary Nicholas, for whom he had cosigned a note, came to Jefferson to satisfy the note when Nicholas defaulted. Associate Justice James Wilson of the Supreme Court died, senselessly raving, in a small inn in North Carolina, pursued by creditors after his huge and impracticable financial speculations disintegrated, leaving him and his family destitute. But the problem of debt struck most often and most cruelly at the small farmers and tradesmen; for every failure of a Jefferson or a Wilson, there were hundreds if not thousands of failures of much smaller scale, though equally catastrophic for the debtors involved. In some states, those who owed debts sought to induce the state governments to cause inflation by printing new issues of paper money; by flooding the money supply with depreciated currency, they reasoned, they could pay off their debts more quickly and exorcise the twin specters of litigation and debtor's prison. This pattern of inflationary politics appeared most frequently in Rhode Island, giving the tiny state an almost unshakable reputation for turbulence, faithlessness, and radicalism. This fear of Rhode Island's and other states' actions to cause inflation, to impede out-of-state and British creditors from collecting debts, and otherwise to vitiate or destroy the value of debts owed by their citizens was a major stimulus to the efforts to strengthen the general government of the United States.

Common Interest

American Society in the 1770s and 1780s was thus a rich mosaic of groups, interests, and social strata, and it seems almost incredible that such a crazy-quilt collection of people could coalesce into a nation. Nonetheless, the American people were able to forge a national identity and sense of purpose that strengthened as the century drew to a close. This emergent nationalism was the product of several factors. For one thing, the Americans all spoke a common language, though there were regional variations in dialect and an occasional pocket of people like the Dutch-speaking patroons of the upper Hudson River valley in New York. For another, despite the sectarian differences between Congregationalists and Baptists, between Anglicans and Presbyterians, most Americans in this period shared the common religious heritage of Protestant Christianity—although, again, there were scattered pockets of Catholics in Maryland and other middle Atlantic states and a handful of Jews in New York, Rhode Island, and Philadelphia. Despite local loyalties, many Americans who pursued a college education crossed state lines to do so; southerners occasionally attended Harvard, Yale, or Princeton, and northerners enrolled in the new university in Philadelphia. Similarly, learned societies sprang up in the new republic and attracted members from all over America; the American Philosophical Society of Philadelphia and the American Academy of Boston are but two examples.

Ultimately, however, what united the Americans, whether members of the elite or the common sort or even those ordinarily excluded from politics, was the experience of the

Revolution itself. The Revolution compelled citizens of different states to consider the possibility that they were more than New Yorkers or Pennsylvanians or Georgians. The idea gradually emerged that there might be a national interest and common good transcending state and local loyalties and interests. Especially for those who served in the Confederation Congress or the Continental Army, the idea of an American nation took on a reality and an immediacy that eventually translated themselves into political action. Because the Revolution essentially focused on issues of political theory and questions of governmental structure and powers, the idea of national identity was intimately bound up with conceptions of politics. And the reverse was true, as well: once they were willing to conceive of the United States of America as a nation rather than as a collection of autonomous states, the Americans were ready to risk new political experiments to construct a national government.

Chapter 2

The Roots of the Constitution

Turning Points

IN WORLD HISTORY

Defining Principles of a New, Federal Government

Bernard Bailyn

In the following essay, history professor Bernard Bailyn notes that certain radical principles, which had stirred the colonies during the revolutionary period, became the foundation of a new system of government for America. The first of these principles was the notion that government depends on the consent of the people, and therefore the people must be represented in all governing bodies. Second was the idea of a permanent constitution that defines and sets limits on the government, as well as safeguards people's inalienable human rights. The third principle was the concept of sovereignty that establishes a division of power between the colonial governments and the federal government. Professor Bailyn, who has been called the "dean of American colonial history," has written and edited major works on the subject. Two of his widely acclaimed books, *The Ideological Origins of the American Revolution* (the source of this essay) and *Voyages to the West: A Passage in the Peopling of America on the Eve of the Revolution*, won the Pulitzer Prize in 1967 and 1986, respectively.

What had taken place in the earlier years of colonial history was the partial re-creation, as a matter of fact and not of theory, of a kind of representation that had flourished in medieval England but that had faded and been superseded by another during the fifteenth and sixteenth centuries. In its original, medieval, form elective representation to Parliament had been a device by which "local men, locally minded, whose business began and ended with the interests of the

Bernard Bailyn, *The Ideological Origins of the American Revolution*. Cambridge, MA: The Belknap Press of Harvard University Press, 1967. Copyright © 1967 by the President and Fellows of Harvard College. Reproduced by permission.

constituency," were enabled, as attorneys for their electors, to seek redress from the royal court of Parliament, in return for which they were expected to commit their constituents to grants of financial aid. Attendance at Parliament of representatives of the commons was for the most part an obligation unwillingly performed, and local communities bound their representatives to local interests in every way possible: by requiring local residency or the ownership of local property as a qualification for election, by closely controlling the payment of wages for official services performed, by instructing representatives minutely as to their powers and the limits of permissible concessions, and by making them strictly accountable for all actions taken in the name of the constituents. As a result, representatives of the commons in the medieval Parliaments did not speak for that estate in general or for any other body or group larger than the specific one that had elected them.

Changing circumstances, however, had drastically altered this form and practice of representation. By the time the institutions of government were taking firm shape in the American colonies, Parliament in England had been transformed. The restrictions that had been placed upon representatives of the commons to make them attorneys of their constituencies fell away; members came to sit "not merely as parochial representatives, but as delegates of all the commons of the land." Symbolically incorporating the state, Parliament in effect had become the nation for purposes of government, and its members virtually if not actually, symbolically if not by sealed orders, spoke for all as well as for the group that had chosen them. They stood for the interest of the realm. . . .

The colonists, reproducing English institutions in miniature, had been led by force of circumstance to move in the opposite direction. Starting with seventeenth-century assumptions, out of necessity they drifted backward, as it were, toward the medieval forms of attorneyship in representation. Their surroundings had recreated to a significant extent the conditions that had shaped the earlier experiences of the English people. The colonial towns and counties, like their medieval counterparts, were largely autonomous, and they stood to lose more than they were likely to gain from a loose acquiescence in the action of central government. More often than not they felt themselves to be the benefactors rather than the beneficiaries of central government, provincial or imperial; and when they sought favors from higher authorities they sought local and particular—in effect private—favors. Having little reason to identify their interests with those of the central government, they sought to keep the voices of local interests clear and distinct; and where it seemed necessary, they moved—though with little sense of innovating or taking actions of broad significance, and nowhere comprehensively or systematically—to bind representatives to local interests. . . .

Representation and Consent

The view of representation developing in America [years before the 1787 Constitutional Convention] implied if it did not state that direct consent of the people in government was not restricted, as [English philosopher John] Locke would have had it, to those climactic moments when government was overthrown by the people in a last final effort to defend their rights, nor even to those repeated, benign moments when a government was peaceably dissolved and another chosen in its place. Where government was such an accurate mirror of the people, sensitively reflecting their desires and feelings, consent was a continuous, everyday process. In effect the people were present through their representatives, and were themselves, step by step and point by point, acting in the conduct of public affairs. No longer merely an ultimate check on government, they *were* in some sense the government. Government had no separate existence apart from them; it was *by* the people as well as *for* the people; it gained its authority from their continuous consent. The very nature and meaning of law was involved. The traditional sense, proclaimed by [English advocate of common law William] Blackstone no less than by [English philosopher Thomas] Hobbes, that law was a command "prescribed by source superior and which the inferior is bound to obey"—such a sense of law as the declaration of a person or body existing independently above the subjects of law and imposing its will upon them, was brought into question by the developing notion of representation. Already in these years there were adumbrations of the sweeping repudiation James Wilson and others would make of Blackstone's definition of law, and of the view they would put in its place: the view that the binding power of law flowed from the continuous assent of the subjects of law; the view "that the only reason why a free and independent man was bound by human laws was this—that he bound himself."

These were deep-lying implications of making representation—systematically, in principle as well as in fact—"a substitute for legislation by direct action of the people." They were radical possibilities, glimpsed but not wholly grasped, thrown up in the creative clash of ideas that preceded the Revolution, and drawn into the discussion of the first state constitutions even before Independence was declared. They were perhaps, in these early years, understood most clearly by the more perceptive of the Tories, who stood outside and viewed with apprehension the tendency of events and the drift of theory. "The position," the Anglican minister Samuel Seabury wrote in 1774, "that we are bound by no laws to which we have not consented either by ourselves or our representatives is a novel position unsupported by any authoritative record of the British constitution, ancient or modern. It is republican in its very nature, and tends to the utter subversion of the English monarchy.". . .

A Constitution Marks Out Boundaries

In 1776 there came conclusive pronouncements [about the definition of a constitution]. Two pamphlets of that year, brilliant sparks thrown off by the clash of Revolutionary politics in Pennsylvania, lit up the final steps of the path that led directly to the first constitutions of the American states. "A constitution and a form of government," the author of *Four Letters on Important Subjects* wrote, "are frequently confounded together and spoken of as synonymous things, whereas are not only different but are established for different purposes." All nations have governments, "but few, or perhaps none, have truly a constitution." The primary function of a constitution was to mark out the boundaries of governmental powers—hence in England, where there was no constitution, there were no limits (save for the effect of trial by jury) to what the legislature might do. In order to confine the ordinary actions of government, the constitution must be grounded in some fundamental source of authority, some "higher authority than the giving out [of] temporary laws." This special authority could be gained if the constitution were created by "an act of *all*," and it would acquire permanence if it were embodied "in some written charter." Defects, of course, might be discovered and would have to be repaired: there would have to be some procedure by which to alter the constitution without disturbing its controlling power as fundamental law. . . . Thus created and thus secured, the constitution could effectively designate what "part of their liberty" the people are to sacrifice to the necessity of having government, by furnishing answers to "the two following questions: first, what shall the form of government be? And secondly, what shall be its power?" In addition, "it is the part of a constitution to fix the manner in which the officers of government shall be chosen, and determine the principal outlines of their power, their time of duration, manner of commissioning them, etc." Finally, "all the great rights which man never mean, nor ever ought, to lose should be *guaranteed*, not *granted*, by the constitution, for at the forming a constitution, we ought to have in mind that whatever is left to be secured by law only may be altered by another law."

The same ideas, in some ways even more clearly worked out, appear in the second Pennsylvania pamphlet of 1776, *The Genuine Principles of the Ancient Saxon or English Constitution*, which was largely composed of excerpts from Obadiah Hulme's *An Historical Essay on the English Constitution*, published in London in 1771, a book both determinative and representative of the historical understanding that lay behind the emerging American constitutionalism. Here too was stated the idea of a constitution as a "*set of fundamental rules* by which even the supreme power of the state shall be governed" and which the legislature is absolutely forbidden to alter. But in this pamphlet there are more explicit explanations of how such documents come into being and of their permanence and importance. They are to be formed "by a convention of the delegates of the people appointed for that express purpose," the pamphlet states, and they are never to be "added to, diminished from, nor altered in any respect by any power besides the power which first framed [them]." They are to remain permanent, and so to have the most profound effect on the lives of people. . . .

Inalienable Rights

Accompanying this shift in the understanding of constitutionalism, and part of it, was another change, which also began as a relocation of emphasis and ended as a contribution to the transforming radicalism of the Revolution. The *rights* that constitutions existed to protect were understood in the early years of the period . . . to be at once the inalienable, indefeasible rights inherent in all people by virtue of their humanity, and the concrete provisions of English law as expressed in statutes, charters, and court decisions; it was assumed that the "constitution" in its normal workings would specify and protect the inalienable rights of man. . . .

Alexander Hamilton . . . wrote in bold, arresting words that "the sacred rights of mankind are not to be rummaged for among old parchments or musty records. They are written, as with a sunbeam, in the whole *volume* of human nature, by the hand of divinity itself, and can never be erased or obscured by mortal power." But if some found this statement too enthusiastic, few by 1774—few even of the Tories—disagreed with the calmer formulation of the same idea, by Philip Livingston. . . . Livingston declared . . . legal rights are "those rights which we are entitled to by the eternal laws of right reason"; they exist independent of positive law, and stand as the measure of its legitimacy.

Neither Hamilton nor Livingston, nor any of the other writers who touched on the subject, meant to repudiate the heritage of English common and statutory law. Their claim was only that the source of rights be recognized, in Jefferson's words, as "the laws of nature, and not as the gift of their chief magistrate," and that as a consequence the ideal must be understood to exist before the real and to remain superior to it, controlling it and limiting it. But what was the ideal? What precisely were the ideal rights of man? They were, everyone knew, in some sense Life, Liberty, and Property. . . .

A Concept of Sovereignty

Of all the intellectual problems the colonists faced, one was absolutely crucial: in the last analysis it was over this issue that the Revolution was fought. On the pivotal question of sovereignty, which is the question of the nature and location of the ultimate power in the state, American thinkers attempted to depart sharply from one of the most firmly fixed points in eighteenth-century political thought; and though they failed to gain acceptance for their strange and awkward views, they succeeded nevertheless in opening this fundamental issue to critical discussion, preparing the way for a new departure in the organization of power.

The idea of sovereignty current in the English-speaking world of the 1760's was scarcely more than a century old. It had first emerged during the English Civil War, in the early 1640's, and had been established as a canon of Whig political thought in the Revolution of 1688. It was composed essentially of two elements. The first was the notion that there must reside somewhere in every political unit a single, undivided, final power, higher in legal authority than any other power, subject to no law, a law unto itself. Derived in part from the political theory of classical antiquity, in part from Roman law, and in part from medieval thought, this idea came to England most directly in . . . sixteenth-century writings. . . .

A Different View in the Colonies

If in England the concept of sovereignty was not only logical but realistic, it was far from that in the colonies. From the beginning of settlement, circumstances in America had run directly counter to the exercise of unlimited and undivided sovereignty. Despite the efforts that had been made by the English government in the late seventeenth century to reduce the areas of local jurisdiction in the colonies, local provincial autonomy continued to characterize American life. Never had Parliament or the crown, or both together, operated in actuality as theory indicated sovereign powers should. They had exercised authority, of course. The crown had retained the final power of legalizing or annulling actions of the colonial legislatures and of the colonial courts; it had made appointments to high office; it had laid down rules and policies for its colonial officials to follow; it had held in its own hand major decisions, civil and military, affecting relations with other nations; and it had continued to claim control of, if not actually to control, vast areas of wild land in the west as well as certain settled territories in the east. Similarly, Parliament had created the colonial postal system, regulated naturalization, and laid down rules for certain economic activities in the colonies, of which the laws of trade and navigation were the most important. But these were far from total powers; together they did not constitute governance in depth, nor did they exclude the exercise of real power by lesser bodies or organs of government. . . . All other powers were enjoyed, in fact if not in constitutional theory, by local, colonial organs of government. This area of residual authority, constituting the "internal police" of the community, included most of the substance of everyday life.

It had in fact been local American agencies that effectively created and maintained law and order, for there had been no imperial constabulary, and such elements of England's military power as had appeared in America from time to time had acted for purposes that only incidentally involved the daily lives of the colonists. It had in fact been local, common law courts that administered justice in the colonies; the courts associated with the home government had been condemned as "prerogative," their jurisdiction repeatedly challenged and closely restricted. And it had in fact been local bodies—towns and counties in the first instance, ultimately the provincial Assemblies—that laid down the rules for daily life. . . .

The condition of British America by the end of the Seven Years' War was therefore anomalous: extreme decentralization of authority within an empire presumably ruled by a single, absolute, undivided sovereign. And anomalous it had been known to be at the time. For decades before 1763 the situation had been remarked on, and reforms proposed by officers of the crown in the colonies as well as by administrators and theorists in England. But since, in the age of Walpole and Newcastle, no sustained effort had been made to alter the situation, the colonists found themselves in 1763 faced not merely with new policies but with a challenge to their settled way of life—a way of life that had been familiar in some places for a century or more. The arguments the colonists put forward against Parliament's claims to the right

A Shared Belief in Government

The delegates to the convention, though all shepherded by the American Revolution, were first and foremost planters, merchants, and professionals. They considered the convention a political necessity but perhaps not a historic undertaking. Still, as author Merrill Jensen acknowledges, these men shared common ideas on history, especially lessons from the ancient world on the goals and functions of government, that they wanted to be incorporated into the new American agenda.

The members of the Convention shared a common education that was centered around the history and political philosophy of the ancient world and of England. As a result, some of them believed that they could draw upon the history of the past, in fact must draw upon it, if they were to achieve a workable constitution. Thus James Madison spent a part of the winter before the Convention studying the constitutions of ancient and modern confederacies, while in Europe John Adams outlined the history of a host of past states to set forth their defects and the causes of their fall.

The lesson of history was clear and the outcome inevitable. History taught, such men believed, that there were only three kinds of government—monarchy, aristocracy, and democracy— and that each had fatal defects. They believed too that if any one class in society got control of government, it would exploit all the others. The solution, so political theorists ever since to exercise sovereign power in America were efforts to express in logical form, to state in the language of constitutional theory, the truth of the world they knew. They were at first, necessarily, fumbling and unsure efforts, for there were no arguments—there was no vocabulary—to resort to: the ideas, the terminology, had to be invented.

How was this to be done? What arguments, what words, could be used to elevate to the status of constitutional principle the division of authority that had for so long existed and which the colonists associated with the freedom they had enjoyed? . . .

Aristotle had taught, was a "balanced government" in which each class in society was represented and given a check upon the others to protect its interests. The history they read and believed showed that every democracy in the past had ended in class warfare between the poor and the rich. As John Adams put it: "There never was a democracy that did not commit suicide."

The delegates recognized that the United States in 1787 did not suffer from the maldistribution of property which had characterized ancient states and which was true of contemporary Europe. But they believed it inevitable that in the future the United States would become like every other state in history, and that the majority of the American people would, in time, be without property. Experience since 1776 demonstrated, so more than one delegate said, that the American state governments were too democratic. The task before the delegates was, therefore, a double one: to check the "levelling spirit" which, they believed, had arisen since 1776, and to provide protection for property in that future time when property owners would be a minority in the United States. It was in such specific terms that James Madison explained what the Convention should do, and no delegate disagreed with him.

Merrill Jensen, *The Making of the American Constitution*. New York: Van Nostrand Reinhold, 1964, pp. 8–9.

In 1764 Richard Bland, searching for a principle by which to assign exclusive powers to colonial governments and yet retain the colonies' dependency on England, found the distinction between things internal and things external to be essential to his purpose. If Virginians are freemen, he argued, they must have a representative assembly capable of enacting "laws for the INTERNAL government of the colony"—"internal" being defined so as to exclude "all power derogatory to their dependence upon the mother kingdom . . . In every instance, therefore, of our EXTERNAL government we are and must be subject to the authority of the British Parliament, but in no others; for if the Parliament should impose laws upon us merely relative to our INTERNAL government, it deprives us, as far as those laws extend, of the most valuable part of our birthright as Englishmen . . ." And if Parliament is limited in its legislative power over the colonies to external matters, "then any tax respecting our INTERNAL polity which may hereafter be imposed on us by act of Parliament is arbitrary, as depriving us of our rights, and may be opposed."

When the Stamp Act controversy exploded, the distinction naturally became part of the discussion of the rights involved. Stephen Hopkins, writing for the colony of Rhode Island, began by defining stamp duties as internal taxes and hence properly within the jurisdiction of the separate colonial legislatures, which had responsibility for the "internal government" of the colonies. The colonial jurisdiction of Parliament, he wrote, was quite different. Its proper power was over

> things of a more general nature, quite out of the reach of these particular legislatures . . . One of this kind is the commerce of the whole British empire, taken collectively, and that of each kingdom and colony in it as it makes a part of that whole. Indeed, everything that concerns the proper interest and fit government of the whole commonwealth, of keeping the peace, and subordination of all the parts towards the whole and one among another, must be considered in this light.

For all such "matters of general nature" there must be some "supreme and overruling authority" to make laws and "compel their execution," and such a supreme power, everyone knows, Hopkins wrote, lies in "that grand and august legislative body," Parliament. He did not at this point develop the idea that if "internal" taxes were denied Parliament, "external" taxes might not be; he was not attempting to distinguish among types of taxes but to deal with the broader issue of spheres of authority within which taxation fell. . . .

John Dickinson

No one could have been better informed on the state of American thinking and on the armory of weapons the colonists had devised to attack Parliamentary taxation than [Benjamin] Franklin. . . . The colonists were not, he said, denying Parliament's right to collect moneys from them. They had long acknowledged Parliament's right "of laying duties to regulate commerce." What they were objecting to as "unconstitutional and unjust" was Parliament's effort "to lay internal taxes," for such a right "was never supposed to be in Parliament, as we are not represented there." His interrogators pressed him: Did he really believe that such a distinction was valid? Yes, Franklin assured them, he did; the difference between "external" and "internal" taxing was "very great.". . .

John Dickinson, in his *Farmer's Letters* (1767–68), . . . examining the problem of Parliament's power with greater acuity than any writer had shown before, went on to a new stage in the exploration of the idea of sovereignty.

All taxation, Dickinson wrote in his famous pamphlet, being an "imposition to raise money," is essentially the same, and so there is no difference between "external" and "internal" taxation. Parliament has no right to levy taxes on Americans for any purpose whatsoever: that much was clear. What was not so clear, what needed discussion, and what he followed out in his thought boldly and imaginatively, was the

proper role of a central government in a truly imperial constitution. The legislature of an empire, he said, was different
from the legislature of a nation. Though the two might exist
in the same body, they bad different functions and powers as
organs of government. Over the American colonies Parliament must have all the power, but only the power, necessary
to maintain the essential connections of empire, and this
meant the power to regulate commerce and other aspects of
the economy "in such a manner as [England] thought most
conducive to their mutual advantage and her own welfare."
The duties imposed in the course of such regulation, he
made clear, would be legitimate, for such "external impositions" do not grant property away but only prevent its acquisition. England's other imperial powers were quite specific, and inhered not in Parliament but in the crown: the
power to repeal colonial legislation, to exercise "the *executive*
authority of government," and to sit in appeal "from all
judgments in the administration of justice."

In admitting that Parliament had such regulatory authority but yet no taxing powers whatever over America, Dickinson was approaching a conception of sovereignty different in
essence from what had been accepted hitherto. For in as-
suming an empire to be basically different from a unitary nation, he was saying now explicitly that its sovereign body
need not be supreme everywhere and in all matters in the
territory it controlled, but only on some issues and in some
ways, and that other, lesser bodies might exercise absolute
and arbitrary powers—sovereign powers in effect—within
spheres specifically allotted to them. . . .

This argument, radical for the mid-1760's, had by 1775
become a conservative bastion; it was defended not only in
point of theory by authentic leaders of the American cause
who, like John Dickinson, hesitated to proceed to the more
extreme position, but also by outspoken Tories who, continuing to ridicule the theory of divided sovereignty, accepted
it in practice as they sought to establish some measure of
rapport with the new forces of American life. To "disavow
the authority of Parliament" and still claim allegiance to the
King, the New York Tory leader Samuel Seabury wrote in

1774, "is another piece of Whiggish nonsense"; and he cited [William] Pitt's speeches in Parliament and Dickinson's *Farmer's Letters* to defend the argument, now comfortably old-fashioned, that the line to be drawn—in fact if not in theory—between "the supremacy of Great Britain and the dependency of the colonies" should leave "all internal taxation . . . in our own legislatures, and the right of regulating trade . . . [and] enacting all general laws for the good of the colonies" in Parliament. So also, with minor variations, wrote the English traveler John Lind; so too wrote Daniel Leonard in Massachusetts; so too Joseph Galloway in Pennsylvania; so too Thomas Bradbury Chandler in New York; and so too, in the end—though still ambiguously and much too late—did the government of George III. . . .

Only in 1778—after Independence had invoked the ultimate sovereignty of the people; after most of the states had organized their own governments, and the Articles of Confederation of the new nation had been drawn up and submitted to the states for ratification; and only under the pressure of the catastrophe at Saratoga and of France's entrance into the war—only then . . . did the North administration [England's government during the American Revolution was headed by Lord North] relent sufficiently to endorse, though still not in theory, the position that Dickinson had advanced so long ago in the *Farmer's Letters.* . . .

The course of intellectual, as well as of political and military, events had brought into question the entire concept of a unitary, concentrated, and absolute governmental sovereignty. It had been challenged, implicitly or explicitly, by all those who had sought constitutional grounds for limiting Parliament's power in America. In its place had come the sense, premised on the assumption that the ultimate sovereignty—ultimate yet still real and effective—rested with the people, that it was not only conceivable but in certain circumstances salutary to divide and distribute the attributes of governmental sovereignty among different levels of institutions. The notion had proved unacceptable as a solution of the problem of Anglo-American relations, but it was acted upon immediately and instinctively in forming the new union of sovereign states. . . . Later analysts, starting where the colonists had left off before Independence and habituated to think in terms of "qualified sovereignty," "lesser sovereignties," "the divisibility of sovereignty," would continue the effort to make federalism a logical as well as a practical system of government.

They would not entirely succeed; the task would be a continuing one, never fully completed. Generations later there would still be those, states rightists and nationalists, who would repudiate this legacy of the Revolution. . . . But the federalist tradition, born in the colonists' efforts to state in constitutional language the qualification of Parliament's authority they had known—to comprehend, systematize, and generalize the unplanned circumstance of colonial life—nevertheless survived, and remains, to justify the distribution of absolute power among governments no one of which can claim to be total, and so to keep the central government from amassing "a degree of energy, in order to sustain itself, dangerous to the liberties of the people."

Early Experiments with Mixed Government

Gordon S. Wood

In the following essay, author Gordon S. Wood discusses how the newly liberated colonies, using the British system as their model, were bent on adopting a mixed government in their new constitutions. The system would combine aspects of monarchy, or the rule of a single person; aristocracy, or the rule of a few wise men; and democracy, or the rule of the many. The colonists debated variations of the balance of power that they would institute in their new state republics, a balance that would ensure both stability and liberty. Wood's book *The Creation of the American Republic* won the 1970 National Book Award, while another work, *The Radicalism of the American Revolution*, won the Pulitzer Prize in 1993. Wood, a professor of history at Brown University at the time of writing, also wrote *The Confederation and the Constitution: The Crucial Issues.*

The theory of mixed government was as old as the Greeks and had dominated Western political thinking for centuries. It was based on the ancient categorization of forms of government into three ideal types, monarchy, aristocracy, and democracy—a classical scheme derived from the number and character of the ruling power. "There are only Three simple Forms of Government," said John Adams in an oration delivered at Braintree [Massachusetts] in 1772. When the entire ruling power was entrusted to the discretion of a single person, the government was called a monarchy, or the rule of one. When it was placed in the hands of a "few great, rich, wise Men," the government was an aristocracy, or the rule of the few. And when the whole power of the society was lodged with all the people, the government was termed a democracy, or the rule of the many. Each of these simple forms possessed a certain quality of excellence: for monarchy, it was order or energy; for aristocracy, it was wisdom; and for democracy, it was honesty or goodness. But the maintenance of these peculiar qualities depended on the forms of government standing fast on the imagined spectrum of power. Yet men being what they were, experience had tragically taught that none of these simple forms of government by itself could remain stable. Left alone each ran headlong into perversion in the eager search by the rulers, whether one, few, or many, for more power. Monarchy lunged toward its extremity and ended in a cruel despotism. Aristocracy, located midway on the band of power, pulled in both directions and created "faction and multiplied usurpation." Democracy, seeking more power in the hands of the people, degenerated into anarchy and tumult. The mixed or balanced polity was designed to prevent these perversions. By including each of the classic simple forms of government in the same constitution, political fluctuations would cease. The forces pulling in one direction would be counterbalanced by opposing forces. Monarchy and democracy would each prevent the other from sliding off toward an extremity on the power spectrum; and to keep the government from oscillating like a pendulum the aristocracy would act as a centering stabilizer. Only through this reciprocal sharing of political power by the one, the few, and the many, could the desirable qualities of each be preserved. As John Adams told his Braintree audience, "Liberty depends upon an exact Balance, a nice Counterpoise of all the Powers of the state. . . . The best Governments of the World have been mixed.". . .

Although by the nineteenth century the theory had lost its relevance for Western political thought because the state and government had become detached from what was seen as an increasingly complicated social structure, in the previous century through its expression in the English constitution it attained a vitality and prominence it had not had since antiquity. "The British constitution . . . ," said Joseph War-

ren in Boston in 1772, "is a happy compound of the three
forms . . . , monarchy, aristocracy, and democracy; of these
three the British legislature is composed.". . .

The States and Mixed Government

Most Americans set about the building of their new states in
1776 within the confines of [the] theory of mixed government, for independence and the abolition of monarchy had
not altered the basic postulates of the science of politics.
"The Constitution of Britain had for its object the union of
the three grand qualities of virtue, wisdom, and power as the
characteristicks of perfect Government," William Hooper
informed the North Carolina Congress framing a constitution in the fall of 1776. "Might not this or something like
this serve as a Model for us." Since the English had obviously not been able to sustain a proper balance, "altho' it was
the professed aim of that System," it remained for the Americans in their new republics to "correct those errors and defects which are to be found in the most perfect constitution
of government which ever the world has yet been blessed
with." In fact, in most of the states the theory of mixed government was so axiomatic, so much a part of the Whig science of politics, that it went largely unquestioned, particularly since the colonists' debate with England had not
compelled them to explore it comprehensively. . . .

There can be no doubt that [John] Adams's *Thoughts on
Government*, published in 1776 and widely circulated among
the leading Revolutionaries in several states, was the most influential pamphlet in the early constitution-making period.

Adams immediately raised the central problem the
constitution-makers faced in devising a balanced government in their new republics. In Adams's mind, as in the
minds of most of the framers in 1776, it was not a question
of whether there would be a mixture or not, but rather a
question of what sort of mixture. "Of republics," he wrote,
"there is an inexhaustible variety, because the possible combinations of the powers of society are capable of innumerable variations." Whatever their general agreement on the
theory of mixed government, Americans in 1776 at once

found themselves arguing over these "innumerable variations," in the search for "that particular arrangement of the
powers of society" which would guarantee both stability and
liberty in their new republics. . . .

The issue separating a conservative Whig, like Carter
Braxton, from a Revolutionary Whig, like Richard Henry
Lee, was not the theory of mixed government itself, but the
proportion of power to be allotted to each of the elements in
the constitution. Braxton in his plan of government for Virginia suggested that the governor hold office during good
behavior in order to give him "the dignity to command necessary respect and authority," and "to enable him to execute
the laws without being deterred by the fear of giving offence." He also proposed that twenty-four persons be chosen by the Assembly "to constitute a Council of State, who
should form a distinct or intermediate Branch of the Legislature, and hold their places for life, in order that they might
possess all the weight, stability, and dignity, due to the importance of their office." Richard Henry Lee dismissed
Braxton's pamphlet as a "Contemptible little Tract"; yet in
the very same breath he defined the problem facing the
constitution-makers in 1776 as consisting "certainly in a
blending of the three simple forms of Government in such a
manner as to prevent the inordinate views of either from unduly affecting the others." What angered Lee and other radical Whigs about Braxton's governmental proposals was not
the idea of balance, but the emphasis Braxton had put on the
monarchical and aristocratical element in his suggested
mixed constitution—an expression, said Lee, of Braxton's
"aristocratic pride," betraying "the little Knot or Junto from
whence it proceeded." Indeed, most of the numerous drafts
for the constitutions of the new governments proposed in
debates, pamphlets, and newspapers in 1776, like Lee's and
Braxton's, were only variations, although decidedly important variations, on Adams's theme of "a balance between . . .
contending powers." For the mixed governments of the
American states did not have to be, indeed should not be,
replicas of the eighteenth-century English constitution in
order to be considered mixed. There could in fact be nearly

as many possible blends and balances of the social powers as there were differences in social outlook.

Variations of Balance

"Some talk of having two councils, one legislative, and the other executive: some of a small executive council only; which should have nothing to do with framing the laws. Some would have the Governor, an integral part of the legislature: others, only president of the council with a casting voice." All were reflections of the gradations of radicalism among the Whigs, differences that were ultimately measured by each man's confidence in the people and thus by the degrees of power to be allotted the several elements—monarchical, aristocratic and democratic—in the new republics. In many states apprehensions over too much power in the hands of the people, in the hands of "Men without Character and without Fortune," fed into the Americans' plans for the new constitutions, creating a division, as Gouverneur Morris remarked of New York, over the character of the mixture in the new republics, "whether it should be founded upon Aristocratic or Democratic principles." The ideal, said one New Jerseyite, was to avoid the two extremes implicit in republicanism: "the one is, that noble birth, or wealth and riches, should be considered as an hereditary title to the government of the republic . . . the other extreme is, that the government be managed by the *promiscuous multitude of the community*," who "though honest, yet from many natural defects, are generally in the execution of government, violent, changeable and liable to many fatal errors." In establishing "the internal Police" of their states, as even Samuel Adams admitted, the Americans had "Scilla and Charybdis to avoid."

While some like John Dickinson despaired of independence and the establishment of any republic, fearing that if the counterpoise of monarchy were taken away the democratic power would carry all before it and destroy all possibility of balanced government, most Whigs in 1776 remained confident that even without a king they could still maintain the right equilibrium and mixture of the powers of the society. Republicanism itself was no obstacle to the institution of the mixed polity. The American states, observed Thomas Pownall in his *Memorial Addressed to the Sovereigns of America*, had preserved the traditional balanced structure of their former colonial governments; "Nor are they less Commonwealths or Republics for taking this mixed form." After all, said John Adams in 1772, "the Republics of Greece, Rome, Carthage were all mixed Governments." And, as James Burgh had remarked, this mixture had never been an objection against their being republican. Had not the English classical republicans . . . demonstrated that a republic was superior to a monarchy in realizing the ideal of a mixed state? Having the governors elected frequently by the people—making them, as William Hooper said, "the creatures of the people"—was entirely compatible with the theory of mixed government. In other words, it was possible, as Milton had argued, that the monarchical element might be present in a constitution without there being any king. It was this Commonwealth understanding of the mixed polity, perceived through "Aristotle, Livy and Harrington," that enabled John Adams in 1775 to argue that the uncorrupted "British constitution is nothing more nor less than a republic, in which the king is first magistrate." Even though the upper houses and the governors were now to be periodically selected by the people, no one clearly foresaw in 1776 that their essential nature was to be thereby changed. The upper houses, elective or not, were still the embodiment of "the few," or the aristocratic element; and the governors, elective or not, were still the embodiment of "the one," or the monarchical element in the mixed republics.

Chapter 3

The Constitution Lays the Foundation of a Nation

Turning Points
IN WORLD HISTORY

Ensuring the Independence of the Three Branches of Government

George W. Carey

Author George W. Carey observes that in adopting the idea of separation of powers, the delegates' primary concern was how to achieve a republican legislature that was not susceptible to mob rule. Because of this fear, they put restraints on the legislature and entrusted more powers to the executive and judiciary branches of government. The following essay, culled from the book *Founding Principles of American Government: Two Hundred Years of Democracy on Trial*, notes that the concern for the separation and independence of the three branches defined important choices—the composition and election of the Senate, the veto power of a single executive, and the selection of the judiciary. George W. Carey, professor of government, taught at Georgetown University in Washington, D.C. He is the author of several books, including *In Defense of the Constitution* and *The Federalist*. He has edited books on politics, history, and government.

Two major difficulties confronted the framers of our Constitution. The first of these emerged out of the fact that European theories relative to a separation of powers were not entirely applicable to the American situation. Montesquieu's theory, for example, was based on the existence of monarchy and aristocracy. The United States, however, lacked a nobility. This fact was well noted during the debates at the Constitutional Convention. . . . For this reason, significant modifications in implementing the doctrine were called for, and certain questions naturally arose; for instance, since the for-

George W. Carey, "The Separation of Powers," *Founding Principles of American Government: Two Hundred Years of Democracy on Trial*, edited by George J. Graham Jr. and Scarlett G. Graham. Bloomington: Indiana University Press, 1977. Copyright © 1977 by George W. Carey. Reproduced by permission.

mer colonies lacked the social and economic classes to be found in European systems, what interests should be checked against each other? How would the representation of these interests be provided for? To these and related concerns we must add other complicating factors like the desire to establish a republican form of government, wherein sovereignty resided in the people; along with the conviction on the part of some that the federal or confederate principle, in accordance with which each state would retain a share of sovereignty, ought to be incorporated into the new constitution.

The second difficulty lay in the fact that, while a separation of powers was an almost universally accepted objective at the time of founding, for the most part this acceptance was merely verbal. As the late and noted constitutional authority, Edward Corwin, wrote:

> That the majority of the Revolutionary constitutions recorded recognition of the principle of the separation of powers is, of course, well known. What is not so generally understood is that the recognition was verbal merely, for the reason that the material terms in which it was couched still remained undefined; and that this was true in particular of "legislative power" in relation to "judicial power."

The task of the framers, then, certainly was not a simple one, for, as the proceedings will indicate, various notions were entertained concerning what the doctrine entailed in practice....

The Virginia Plan

Two major and relatively detailed plans for a new government were set before the Philadelphia Convention: the Virginia ("the large state" or Randolph) plan, and the New Jersey ("the small state" or Paterson) plan. The most important was the Virginia plan. It formed the basis for most of the discussion and debate. While it provided for a separation of powers by suggesting three branches of government, it is more notable for its wide departure in fundamental respects from the pure or model doctrine. Article 7 provided that the national executive "be chosen by the national legislature." Article 4, which dealt with the lower house of the legislature, stipulated that its "members ought to be elected by the people of the several states;" but Article 5, which dealt with the upper house, provided that "the members of the second branch ought to be elected, by those of the first, out of a proper number of persons nominated by the individual legislatures."

Perhaps the most interesting provision was Article 8, which called for a *council of revision*. It read in its entirety:

> Resolved, that the executive, and a convenient number of the national judiciary, ought to compose a council of revision, with authority to examine every act of the national legislature, before it shall operate, and every act of a particular legislature before a negative thereon shall be final; and that the dissent of the said council shall amount to a rejection, unless the act of the national legislature be again passed, or that of a particular legislature be again negatived by [the number to be agreed upon] of the members of each branch.

This *council of revision* should not be confused with the judiciary. While it is true that members of the latter would compose the bulk of its membership, the judiciary and its functions were elaborated in section 9, which called for independent tribunals whose members were to be selected by the national legislature, and would serve during "good behavior."

The New Jersey Plan

The New Jersey plan was more in keeping with the Articles of Confederation, both in terms of its structure and the powers granted to the national government. Under its provisions, the Congress of the Articles was to be retained, with certain added powers, principally that of requisitioning funds needed for the operation of the government. This meant, of course, that the legislature would be unicameral, with each state possessing one vote in all decisions.

Other features of the plan are noteworthy from the viewpoint of a separation of powers. With respect to the executive, the plan provided: "That the United States in Congress be authorized to elect a federal executive, to consist of—persons. . . ." This article apparently was written with the supposition that executive powers could be exercised more effectively and safely by a few rather than by just one. Article 5, the judiciary article, read in part: "That a federal judiciary be established, to consist of a supreme tribunal, the judges of which to be appointed by the executive, and to hold their offices during good behavior. . . ."

Each of the two plans, while adhering to the doctrine of a separation of powers in creating three branches of government, provided a degree of *interdependency* between the branches which was lacking in previous formulations of the doctrine. In the Virginia plan, for instance, the composition of the upper house was entirely dependent on that of the lower. Likewise, in each plan the national executive was to be elected by the legislative branch. Moreover, both plans, because of this interdependency, can be viewed as legislative-supremacy documents, for, in both, the legislature (only the lower house in the Virginia plan) was to be the "mainspring" upon which, in one degree or another, all other branches were dependent.

While it can be said that the New Jersey plan corresponded rather closely to the pure doctrine, the Virginia plan deviated rather markedly in its provision calling for a *council of revision*. Not only did the composition of this council represent a blending of personnel (the executive with selected members of the judiciary), it also involved a sharing of powers (legislative and executive). In effect, by suggesting that the judiciary and the executive be united, a "fourth" branch, unparalleled in the history of the doctrine, had been proposed.

Grappling with Three Issues

In these two plans various ideas were expressed concerning the proper relationship, the powers, and the structure of the branches. The resultant compromises are to be found in our present Constitution. What is vitally important to remember when viewing the final product is the fact that the members of the Philadelphia Convention were, so to speak, "juggling three balls": *federalism*, or state participation in the constitutional order; *republicanism*, or popular participation in and control over the national government, which would be direct in the sense that the states would not act as intermediaries between the people and the national government; and a *separation of powers*, which required a division of functions between the independent branches, without which no viable and non-tyrannical government was thought to be possible.

As far as a separation of powers is concerned, the proposed plans—as we have just seen—did call for a high degree of interdependence, with the legislative body acting as a "kingpin" or "centerstone." A good deal of the deliberations, therefore, centered on securing the independence of the other branches from the legislature. . . .

Why, we can ask, was there this fear of the legislative branch? The answer is to be found in the fact that the framers of the Constitution almost to a man had reservations about unlimited popular control which, because of the republican character of the legislature, was bound to come from that quarter. In other words, the legislature—particularly the lower house—was most likely to respond to the passions of the multitude, thereby doing harm to the society. Some were quite outspoken in their fear of, and contempt for, popular rule. Elbridge Gerry's comments are of this order:

> The evils we experience flow from the excess of democracy. The people do not want virtue, but are the dupes of the pretended patriots. In Massachusetts, it had been fully confirmed by experience, that they are daily misled into the most baneful measures and opinions, by the false reports circulated by designing men, and which no one on the spot can refute.

Others, speaking to the need for a second legislative chamber and for restraints on the legislative branch in general, expressed more moderate views; but they still saw a need for restraint because of the nature of the people. Gouverneur Morris, inquiring into the purpose of a second branch, put the matter in these terms:

> To check the precipitation, changeableness, and excesses, of the first branch. Every man of observation had seen in the democratic branches of the state legislatures, precipitation—in Congress, changeableness—in every department,

excesses against personal liberty, private property, and personal safety. . . .

The greatest single controversy in the Convention took place over the composition and mode of selection of the second chamber. Should the upper chamber be selected by the lower? Should the people participate directly in the selection or election of senators? What role should the state legislature play? As we know, these matters, after long and heated debate, were resolved by the Connecticut (or "Great") compromise, which provided for election by the state legislatures and equality of representation in the upper chamber. While the doctrine of a separation of powers in no way dictated any such compromise or solution, we cannot help but note that its historical development had provided for, albeit for totally different reasons, a second chamber. This in itself is important, for, we can say that the doctrine as it was understood at that time also provided an institution which gave room for the issues involved in the Connecticut compromise to be worked out and resolved. Specifically, a second chamber allowed room for the incorporation of the confederate principle of equal representation of the states. One is left to wonder what kind of a compromise could have been achieved if the doctrine had been mute in the matter of a second chamber.

Of more importance from the standpoint of guaranteeing

The framers of the Constitution grappled with many difficult issues, including the power and structure of the three branches of government.

the independence of the other branches, a bicameral legislature, with different modes of selection, was an important step toward insuring that the legislature not act in a hasty and ill-considered fashion to gather all governmental functions into its own hands. The compliance of both houses would be necessary to execute any such scheme.

In this connection, we must note another matter often overlooked today but which, at the time of founding, was felt to be important, namely, that no member of the legislative branch hold any other office under the United States. Section 6 of Article I fixes this principle in our Constitution with the following provisions:

> No senator or representative shall, during the time for which he was elected, be appointed to any civil office under the authority of the United States, which shall have been created, or the emoluments whereof shall have been increased, during such time; and no person, holding any office under the United States, shall be a member of either House during his continuance in office.

Not only does this provide for a separation of personnel in keeping with the general tenor of the doctrine, it also reduces the chances that the executive might be able to hold out lucrative positions, in order to sway the deliberations of legislators.

Quite obviously, independence of the branches also required that the executive be isolated as far as possible from the legislature. Both plans before the convention called for the legislature to select the executive; but, not unexpectedly, strong objections of varying character were presented against any such means of selection. One objection rested naturally on the grounds that election by the legislature would make the executive unduly dependent on it. . . . James Madison, in supporting election by the people, reiterated his strongly held belief in the separation and independence of the branches:

> If it be a fundamental principle of free government, that the legislative, executive, and judiciary powers should be *sepa-*

rately exercised, it is equally so that they be *independently* exercised. There is the same, and perhaps greater, reason why the executive should be independent of the legislature, than why the judiciary should. A coalition of the two former powers would be more immediately and certainly dangerous to public liberty. It is essential, then, that the appointment of the executive should either be drawn from some source, or held by some tenure, that will give him a free agency with regard to the legislature. This could not be, if he was to be appointable from time to time, by the legislature.

We have seen that fear of the legislature impelled a majority of the framers of the Constitution to divide that branch into two distinct and relatively independent bodies. By the same reasoning, a majority felt that unity in the executive branch, as represented in a single executive, was called for. Only with unity could the executive act firmly and with resolution to the demands of the office and the possible threats posed by the legislature.

While today we take a single executive for granted, the issue of whether the office should be filled with one man or more than one (the usual figure suggested: three) was far from settled at the beginning of the Convention. The New Jersey plan, as we have noted, appeared to call for a plural executive; and a number of the framers urged such upon the Convention. Even Randolph, who had introduced the Virginia plan, was a staunch opponent of a single executive. . . .

Elbridge Gerry introduced still another consideration which seemed to carry great weight in the Convention. He "was at a loss," he stated, "to discover the policy of three members for the executive. It would be extremely inconvenient in many instances, particularly in military matters, whether relating to the militia, an army, or a navy. It would be a general with three heads." Principally for these reasons, only three states (each acting as a unit) voted against a single executive.

Not content with the foregoing measures designed to provide for executive independence, the Convention also conferred upon the President the veto power. At an early point in the deliberations, Wilson remarked: "If the legislature, executive, and judiciary, ought to be distinct and independent, the executive ought to have an absolute negative. Without such a self-defence, the legislature can at any moment sink it into nonexistence;" but the final form which the veto power assumed was intimately connected with deliberations concerning the Council of Revision. This segment of the debates, in which the framers differentiated between executive and judicial functions, represents our most unique and significant contribution to the doctrine of the separation of powers. One may appreciate this by recalling that heretofore, with the exception of Montesquieu who did not carry the matter very far, the executive and judicial functions were theoretically blended or subsumed under the executive function. Now, in the United States the judiciary was recognized as a distinct branch, and the task fell to the framers to differentiate its functions from those of the executive. . . .

Wilson, Madison, and Mason were the foremost proponents of associating the national judiciary with the exercise of the veto power. Here again the desire to limit and check the legislature seemed to be uppermost in their minds. More than this: it seems that they did not believe a veto power vested in the executive alone would be sufficient for this purpose. Mason thought that such a provision "would give a confidence to the executive which he would not otherwise have, and without which the revisionary power would be of little avail." Wilson thought that a sharing of the "revisionary power" with the judiciary would allow the judges to counteract "by the weight of their opinions, the improper views of the legislature;" and Madison did not see any grounds for apprehension that the executive and judicial branches would possess "too much strength" vis à vis the legislature. . . .

The response of the opponents to any such union of executive and judicial powers was entirely predictable. Gerry, who throughout the debates remained a staunch opponent of any such mixture, summed up what seemed to be the feeling of the majority:

> The object, he conceived, of the revisionary power was merely to secure the executive department against legislative

encroachment. The executive, therefore, who will be known and be ready to defend his rights, ought alone to have the defence of them. The motion was liable to strong objections. It was combining and mixing together the legislative and the other departments. It was making statesmen of the judges, and setting them up as guardians of the rights of the people. He relied, for his part, on the representatives of the people, as the guardians of their rights and interests. . . .

As we know, Madison did not win the day, and the veto power was vested exclusively in a single executive. This veto power did not take the form of an absolute negative, as Wilson suggested, principally because the delegates felt this would be too great a grant of power which conceivably might bring the entire government to a standstill. The provision requiring a two-thirds vote of both houses of Congress was decided upon largely as a compromise between those who advocated a simple majority of both houses for this purpose and others who deemed a three-fourths vote necessary to preserve executive independence.

Check Through Impeachment

Having provided for executive independence and powers, the framers were keenly aware that some check was needed to guard against executive encroachment on the other branches as well as to insure that the executive perform his functions in accordance with the Constitution. Some were content with merely the electoral process by which an executive could be removed at the expiration of his term. The delegates did divide on whether the Constitution should provide for removal of the chief executive through an impeachment process. Gouverneur Morris set forth the principal arguments of those who were opposed to impeachment and removal of the President. His remarks on this score are worthy of extensive quotation:

> The executive is also to be impeachable. This is a dangerous part of the plan. It will hold him in such dependence, that he will be no check on the legislature, will not be a firm guardian of the people and of the public interest. He will be the tool of a faction, of some leading demagogue in the legislature. . . .

As to the danger from an unimpeachable magistrate, he could not regard it as formidable. There must be certain great officers of state, a minister of finance, of war, of foreign affairs, etc. These, he presumes, will exercise their functions in subordination to the executive, and will be amenable, by impeachment, to the public justice. Without these ministers, the executive can do nothing of consequence.

This position, we should note, is a return to the solution provided by Montesquieu, namely, that the chief executive be kept in line through legislative control of his subordinates. The position was not without strong support, particularly on the grounds that the branches, as Morris intimated, would not be separate and distinct as long as the legislature possessed the power to remove the chief executive. Rufus King was adamant on this point: "Under no circumstances ought he to be impeachable by the legislature. This would be destructive of his independence and of the principles of the Constitution. He relied on the vigor of the executive, as a great security for the public liberties."

Madison and others successfully countered these arguments. Madison noted that: "The limitation of the period of his service was not a sufficient security. He might lose his capacity after his appointment. He might pervert his administration into a scheme of peculation or oppression. He might betray his trust to a foreign power.". . .

The impeachment process as specified in our Constitution was again, no doubt, the result of compromise. Most importantly, the impeachment process could not be carried through too easily or the independence of the executive would be threatened; nor could it be made so difficult as to be ineffectual when circumstances required it.

Deliberations in the Convention concerning the structure of the judiciary gave rise to other difficulties with reference to a separation of powers. Appointment or nomination by the President was opposed by some, like Mason, who felt that this would constitute "a dangerous prerogative," because it would give the executive "an influence over the judiciary itself." Others felt that the executive would not be familiar enough with "fit" characters to make suitable appointments to the bench. Ellsworth contended, "As he will be stationary, it was not to be supposed he could have a better knowledge of characters" than the Senate. Moreover, Ellsworth maintained, "He will be more open to caresses and intrigues than the Senate." Those who favored presidential nomination and Senate confirmation, however, were not without answers to these and like contentions. Randolph argued that "appointments by the legislatures have generally resulted from cabal, from personal regard, or some other consideration than a title derived from the proper qualifications.". . .

Although the Convention originally rejected the provision requiring nomination by the President and confirmation by the Senate, it finally came around to this method for filling judicial positions. The process, of course, involved a blending: the executive *and* part of the legislature would select the members of the judiciary.

Establishing the Powers of the Executive Office

Jack N. Rakove

The following essay discusses how the framers debated on several critical factors that defined the presidency and ensured its independence from the legislative branch. These issues include the manner of election, length of tenure, eliminating reelection, devising a mechanism for impeachment, and crafting a system for checking legislation through the presidential power of limited veto. The author of the essay, Jack N. Rakove, contends that the president's role was new to most of the delegates, so they were uncertain about many things. At certain points, the body could not agree on whether to assign to the Senate or to the president the act of declaring war and managing foreign relations, including entering into treaties with other nations. Rakove's essay was taken from his *Original Meanings: Politics and Ideas in the Making of the Constitution*, which won the Pulitzer Prize in history in 1997. At the time of writing, Rakove was professor of history at Stanford University. He is the author of *The Beginnings of National Politics: An Interpretive History of the Continental Congress* and *James Madison and the Creation of the American Republic*. He is also the editor of *Interpreting the Constitution: The Debate over Original Intent*.

[During the Constitutional Convention in 1787] there were three distinct phases in the evolution of the presidency. The first (June 1–6) produced agreement on two major points: to vest the executive power in a single person, who would in turn wield a limited veto over legislation. During the second

Jack N. Rakove, *Original Meanings: Politics and Ideas in the Making of the Constitution*. New York: Vintage Books, 1996. Copyright © 1996 by Jack N. Rakove. Reproduced by permission of Alfred A. Knopf, Inc.

phase (July 17–26), the framers struggled to reconcile the general principle of an independent executive with different options for rules of election and tenure. Much of this discussion involved weighing the relative *dis*advantages of election by the legislature, the people, or an electoral college. These doubts persisted into the final stage of debate (September 4–8), but the decisions taken as adjournment neared also made the presidency the net beneficiary of growing reservations about the Senate.

The Virginia Plan offered only a minimalist approach to the problem of executive power. Article 7 proposed that the executive "be chosen by the National Legislature" for a single term of unspecified length, receive "a fixed compensation," and possess "general authority to execute the National laws" and "to enjoy the Executive rights vested in Congress by the Confederation." Whether those "executive rights" included matters of war and diplomacy was left unresolved; nor did the Virginia Plan make any provision for powers of appointment. Article 8 further proposed to join the executive "and a convenient number of the National Judiciary" in a council of revision armed with a limited veto over national legislation. . . .

The committee of the whole endorsed the clauses of the Virginia Plan calling for the executive to be elected by the national legislature for a single term now fixed at seven years. Two days later (June 4), the committee approved the idea of a unitary executive.

The most revealing passage in this exploratory discussion occurred when the delegates took up the council of revision. Elbridge Gerry immediately moved to give a limited veto to the executive alone, and he prefaced his motion with the striking claim that the judiciary need not be involved in the veto because "they will have a sufficient check agst. encroachments on their own department by their exposition of the laws, which involved a power of deciding on their constitutionality.". . . [James] Wilson and [Alexander] Hamilton then offered a rival amendment to give the executive an *absolute* veto. This was so offensive that only its movers and [Rufus] King voted in its favor. Gerry's proposal for a limited veto then passed nearly as decisively, eight states to two. But when [James] Madison and Wilson renewed the case for the council of revision as a more prudent and effective check on the legislature, their motion failed eight states to three.

This decision effectively completed the first round of debate on the executive. Notwithstanding the alarm that [George] Mason and [Edmund] Randolph sounded against incipient monarchy, the delegates had already revived the executive in notable ways by creating a unitary office with constitutionally prescribed duties, a check on legislation, and a tenure that would render it independent of the legislature immediately after election. This was substantial progress, but it was made only by skirting issues that later proved vexatious.

The second round of discussion brought the most perplexing passage of the entire Convention. It began deceptively when the delegates affirmed the principle of a unitary executive on July 17 and ended nine days later where it began, with an executive elected by the legislature for a single seven-year term. Between these two points, the framers cycled through a series of motions and counterproposals as they weighed the disadvantages of legislative election, rejected popular election while endorsing a plan for an electoral college, grappled with the issues of length of term and reeligibility as functions of these modes of election, reconsidered the council of revision, asked whether powers of appointment should be vested solely in the executive or jointly with the Senate, and then worked back to their starting position as qualms about both an electoral college and popular election prevailed over the desire to make reeligibility an incentive for sound administration.

A New Office

Within this matrix, the nearest thing to a first principle or independent variable was the desire to enable the executive to resist legislative "encroachments." If that is kept in mind, the logic of the positions the framers took on nearly every other aspect of the executive becomes much more explicable. But another factor repeatedly worked to make consensus elusive. In their debates over Congress, the framers were content to allow the states to decide how representatives would be elected. But the rules for electing the executive had to be fixed constitutionally, and here they labored under doubts and uncertainties that reflected the very novelty of the office they were designing. The interplay of these two crucial factors becomes evident if we examine the major questions the framers considered between July 17 and July 26.

Election. The framers considered three basic modes of election, and each proved vulnerable to serious criticism. The most obvious alternative was to give the choice to the national legislature, which had the advantage of placing the decision in the nation's most knowledgeable leaders. The countervailing concern, [Gouverneur] Morris warned, was that the result would inevitably be the "work of intrigue, of cabal, and of faction," producing a pliable official who would become the willing tool of his supporters. The first alternative to this mode was election by the people, which Morris, Wilson, and Madison boldly endorsed on principle. . . .

The third option was to establish an electoral college, an idea first raised by Wilson on June 2, revived by Rufus King, and then revised further when Gerry and [Oliver] Ellsworth proposed to have the state legislatures appoint twenty-five electors. . . . When the delegates gathered on July 26, Mason canvassed the defects in the various modes of election before concluding "that an election by the Natl Legislature as originally proposed"—for a single term of seven years—"was the best. If it was liable to objections, it was liable to fewer than any others." With the committee of detail about to begin its work, the Convention endorsed Mason's motion seven states to three (with Massachusetts unaccountably absent).

Reeligibility. Mason could take this position because he strongly believed that it was "the very palladium of Civil liberty, that the great officers of State, and particularly the executive, should at fixed periods return to that mass from which they were at first taken. . . . But other delegates regarded eligibility for reelection as valuable in itself. As [Roger] Sherman and King both argued, "he who has proved himself to be most fit for an Office, ought not to be excluded by the constitution from holding it." Two votes on this issue indicated that a majority of delegates agreed, but only so long as they were satisfied that the power of election was safely placed outside Congress. When that prospect evaporated, the Convention had to restrict the executive to a single term.

Length of term. . . . Competence in the administrative aspects of government could not be gained in a day, nor should its benefits be yielded almost as soon as they were felt. Morris made this case forthrightly. When Dr. [John] McClurg of Virginia offered a substitute motion for tenure "during good behavior" after the Convention initially voted for reeligibility, Morris exclaimed, "This was the way to get a good Government." But statements like those could only spark a nervous reaction in those who worried that a president who grew too comfortable in office would acquire monarchical ambitions. No magic number defined the optimal term an executive should serve; this calculation also depended on the mode of election and the matter of reeligibility.

Impeachment. The longer the term the executive received, the more important it was to find a mechanism "for defending the Community agst the incapacity, negligence or perfidy of the chief Magistrate." But here, too, perplexing questions awaited. Was impeachment really necessary for an executive serving a fixed term? Why not limit its reach to the "coadjutors" of the president? What independence could the executive retain if this power was given to the legislature? But what body other than the legislature could exercise this formidable power?

Council of revision. The discussion of all these questions of tenure was shaped by the framers' overriding concern with the need to curb legislative "encroachments." The debate over the joint executive-judicial council of revision, however, encouraged the framers to consider executive power and influence in broader terms. . . .

In early June, the committee of the whole had vested a limited negative in the executive. Simply reaching this point was a substantial step away from the republican orthodoxy of 1776, for it meant that the Convention already agreed that the legislature should be subject to an external "check." But

Wilson and Madison remained strongly committed to the council of revision, and on July 21 they nearly deadlocked the Convention on its merits. . . .

The opponents of the council of revision were more inclined to emphasize the principle of separation of powers, and to limit their concern to enabling the two weaker branches to protect themselves separately against legislative encroachments. Judges would exercise their own negative, Luther Martin noted, by determining "the Constitutionality of laws." But the case against the council had its own pragmatic side. Prior participation in lawmaking would in fact make it more difficult for judges to exercise their proper power and special knowledge when cases came before them. . . .

It was not evident how the Convention would pursue its general goal of securing executive independence. Nor was it yet certain that the executive would possess any powers other than administrative ones. At this point in their deliberations, the framers still expected the power to negotiate treaties and to make appointments to other major offices to reside in the Senate.

That expectation shaped the report of the committee of detail, which gave the Senate the "power to make treaties, and to appoint Ambassadors, and Judges of the supreme Court," and the quasi-judicial function of overseeing interstate disputes "respecting territory and jurisdiction." The Senate would thus possess not only legislative but aspects of executive, federative, and judicial power alike. The president could convey information and recommendations to Congress; but his essential duties were to "take care that the laws . . . be duly and faithfully executed"; to "appoint officers in all cases not otherwise provided for"; and to act as commander in chief of the armed forces. Executive power in foreign relations involved only the ceremonial function of receiving ambassadors.

Reaction Against the Senate

Over the next five weeks, however, a growing reaction against the Senate worked in favor of the presidency. . . . Morris and Wilson suggested that it would be better to give the executive an absolute negative, again implying that the Senate would not check the House when measures were afoot to promote legislative control of the executive. Their arguments were strong enough to carry an amendment raising the majority required to overturn a veto from two-thirds to three-fourths of each house.

The other two debates that enhanced presidential authority fell within the realm of federative power. Late in the session of August 17, after a cryptic but momentous debate, the Convention modified the clause authorizing Congress "to make war" to read "to declare war.". . . Though Congress could still exert great influence through its power of the purse, allowing it to *make* war (in the sense of directing operations) was another form of encroachment that would compromise the benefits of holding the president as responsible for the conduct of war as for the administration of government. . . .

But as this debate and the discussion of the treaty power six days later revealed, a number of framers now thought that the Senate alone should not control American diplomacy. Their objections did not immediately work to enlarge the federative powers of the presidency. In fact, Morris and Wilson, who might be expected to have favored a broader presidential role, preferred to require treaties to be "ratified by a law"—in effect bringing both the president and the House into this process. But while the size of the House and the presumed inexperience of its members rendered it a doubtful partner in this delicate realm, the executive now emerged as the likely beneficiary of the misgivings that the framers were increasingly voicing about the Senate.

The Convention took up the election of the executive on August 24. It first agreed, with difficulty, that Congress should ballot in joint session. Morris then roundly denounced legislative election as a formula for a supine executive who would be willing to "sacrific[e] his Executive rights." Two test votes now found the delegates evenly divided on the "abstract question" of restoring an electoral college. With this impasse, further consideration of the issue fell to the eleven-member committee. . . .

In its second report (September 4), the committee offered several proposals that bore directly on the election of the executive and its relation to the Senate. Most important was its revival of the electoral college, now modified to give each state the same number of electors as its membership in Congress. . . . The committee proposed three further changes. First, the president would serve for four years and be eligible for reelection. Second, the power "to make treaties" and to nominate and appoint "Ambassadors and other public Ministers, Judges of the supreme Court, and all other officers of the U.S. whose appointments are not otherwise herein provided for" was now given to the president, acting "by and with the advice and consent of the Senate." Third, the committee devised a removal procedure under which the House would impeach the president and the Senate try the charges brought against him.

More Ambiguities

As three ensuing days of debate revealed, the link between the president and the Senate was liable to one critical objection. The committee had responded to the reservations raised about the Senate by giving the president a major role in treaty making and appointments, but it undercut this revision by empowering the Senate to elect the president whenever the electoral college failed to produce a majority. . . . As Randolph, Mason, Wilson, [John] Rutledge, [Charles] Pinckney, and Williamson argued, the plan would give the Senate "such an influence . . . over the election of the President in addition to its other powers, [as] to convert that body into a real & dangerous Aristocracy," not least because it would then control all other executive and judicial appointments, down to the level of "tidewaiter." Add its power to try impeachments and make treaties, Wilson complained, and one would see that "the Legislative, Executive, & Judiciary powers are all blended in one branch of the Government.". . .

These objections did not outweigh the explicitly political calculations underlying the committee's proposal, which built on the "compromise" of July 16 by giving the large states the advantage in promoting candidates while the smaller states would enjoy greater influence when the final choice devolved on the Senate. If either Congress or the

House made this election, the large states would have the advantage at both stages. Unable to escape this dilemma, the Convention on September 6 approved both the electoral college and eventual election by the Senate. But almost immediately two committee members found an ingenious solution to the problem. Williamson first moved that the "eventual choice" be made by Congress "voting *by states* and not *per capita*," and Sherman then modified this idea to substitute the House of Representatives for the whole Congress. This had the twofold advantage of preserving the political compromise among the states while "lessening the aristocratic influence of the Senate." Sherman's amendment passed with hardly a word of debate and only Delaware dissenting.

As this concern with the role of the House and Senate suggests, few of the framers anticipated, much less intended, that the election of the president would soon emerge as the most important stimulus for political innovation and the creation of alliances running across state lines. Madison came closest to foreseeing this result when he urged the delegates to recall that their aim was "to render an eventual resort to any part of the Legislature improbable" by encouraging the large states "to make the appointment in the first instance conclusive." Abraham Baldwin and Wilson also voiced a prescient hope that effective government and "the increasing intercourse among the people" would "multiply" the number of "Continental Characters" from whom electors could make a decisive choice. But the prevailing expectation was that the electoral college would only limit, not eliminate, a legislative role in selecting the president.

Something of this ambiguity also marked the debates of September 7–8. By severing the electoral ties between the Senate and the president and placing the power to impeach in the House, the Convention enlarged the power of the executive at the expense of the Senate in the areas (treaties and appointments) where their authority overlapped. On the matter of diplomatic and judicial appointments, the framers reached near-consensus on the virtues of combining the "responsibility" of executive nomination with the "security" of senatorial advice and consent. But the lengthier debate over the treaty clause revealed a greater disparity of opinion. . . .

Foreign Relations Under the Executive

The framers better revealed the limits of their conception of executive power by entertaining a flurry of amendments to modify the clause requiring treaties to be approved by two-thirds of the Senate. Although none passed, all presupposed that the Senate would remain the locus of decision for the exercise of this crucial power.

Nothing in this debate suggests that the framers viewed the president as the principal and independent author of foreign policy, or that they would have reduced the advice and consent required of the Senate to the formal approval of treaties negotiated solely at the initiative and discretion of the executive. The prosaic aspects of foreign relations—routine correspondence, consular affairs, minor incidents of diplomacy—would clearly fall to the executive. Thinking of treaties as the cornerstones in the future structure of American foreign relations, and hardly foreseeing the dilemmas that a quarter century of European war soon posed for American diplomacy, few of the framers thought that the executive virtues of "energy" and "despatch" would come into play with quite the frequency or subtlety required of European rulers operating amid an ever-fluctuating balance of power. Yet by repeatedly expressing mistrust for the Senate, the framers indicated that they regarded the president as something more than a convenient conduit for negotiations. Much of the jockeying over the two-thirds clause reflected fears that particular regional interests might be "sacrificed" in a Senate that still closely resembled the Continental Congress. In 1779 and 1786, Congress had plunged into bitterly divisive debates, first over securing access to the Newfoundland fisheries, then over the free navigation of the Mississippi. Both disputes erupted while Congress was drafting instructions for treaty negotiations, and thus illustrated the problem of framing foreign policy in a quasi-legislative manner; both spilled beyond its chambers to foment public mistrust of Congress. Familiar as the framers were with these episodes, they could readily appreciate the diplomatic and political advantages of allowing the president a significant initiative in the conduct of foreign relations. Interpreted in this way, this debate suggests that the placement of the treaty power in Article II was more than a quirk of draftsmanship but less than a complete endorsement of the idea that the general conduct of foreign relations was an inherently executive function. . . .

This debate also illustrates the difficulty of converting the strong views that individual framers expressed about the executive into a coherent set of intentions for the Convention collectively. The growth of the presidency owed more to doubts about the Senate than to the enthusiasm with which Hamilton, Morris, and Wilson endorsed the virtues of an energetic administration. The electoral college similarly owed more to the perceived defects in alternative modes of election than to any great confidence that this ingenious mechanism would work in practice. Whether it would give the president the "firmness" to wield the veto not only to resist congressional encroachments but also to serve as a check against unjust legislation was far from certain. Moreover, precisely because the electoral college extended "the great compromise" over representation, with its dubious expectation that the division between small and large states would persist beyond 1787, its formal logic proved irrelevant to the actual politics of presidential election.

The problems that confounded the framers' efforts to imagine how any system of presidential selection would work anticipated the prolonged experimentation that accompanied the ebb and flow of party competition in the early Republic. No feature of the Constitution stimulated the organization of political parties more than the recognition that control of the national government depended on control of the presidency. That was hardly the result the framers intended, nor was it even an outcome that they could plausibly imagine.

The Great Compromise Determines Representation in Congress

Max Farrand

In this essay, historian Max Farrand discusses the convention's debate over how representation would be determined in the national legislature. Large states wanted representation based on population. Smaller states wanted each state to have equal representation so their opinions would not easily be outvoted. After much debate, the convention delegates reached what is known as the Great Compromise. It was agreed that the federal Congress would be composed of two houses. The House of Representatives would have a membership that reflected state populations, while the Senate would contain an equal number of members from each state. To determine state populations, the convention advocated regular census taking of taxpaying citizens. The delegates also agreed that three-fifths of the states' slave populations would be used in determining the overall population of each state. The essay is an excerpt from Farrand's *The Framing of the Constitution of the United States*. Farrand, a professor emeritus at Yale University, wrote several books, which are all considered major works, including *Fathers of the Constitution* and *The Development of the United States from Colonies to a World Power*.

For a few days [at the start of the convention in June 1787] everything went comparatively smoothly. But it was only the lull before the storm which every one could see approaching, and the suspense was hard to endure. If the storm could not

Max Farrand, "The Great Compromise," *The Framing of the Constitution of the United States*. New Haven, CT: Yale University Press, 1926.

be weathered, it was better to have the end come quickly. So on June 27, when [John] Rutledge made the motion, the convention voted unanimously to proceed at once to the resolutions involving "the most fundamental points, the rules of suffrage in the two branches [of Congress]."

With the convention impatient to meet the issue, Luther Martin chose this most inopportune time, and in a spell of hot weather, too, to deliver a lengthy harangue. For more than three hours he continued and, having exhausted his own strength, to say nothing of the patience of his audience, he announced to the dismay of all that he would resume his discourse the next day. . . .

When the convention finally got at the question of proportional representation, nearly three weeks were spent in reaching a conclusion. More than once any satisfactory solution of the difficulty seemed impossible, and the convention was on the point of breaking up. Gouverneur Morris afterwards said that "the fate of America was suspended by a hair.". . .

Initial Decisions

On July 5, the compromise committee [of the convention] presented its report, recommending two propositions "on condition that both shall be generally adopted." The substance of these proposals was: 1. That in the first branch [i.e., the House of Representatives] each state should have one representative for every 40,000 inhabitants, counting three-fifths of the slaves, and that money-bills should originate in the first branch and should not be amended by the second branch. 2. That in the second branch [i.e., the Senate] each state should have an equal vote.

Immediately the debate broke forth again and recriminations were indulged in. . . .

On July 9, the special committee recommended: that the first house of representatives should consist of fifty-six members, of which number New Hampshire was to have two, Massachusetts seven, etc.; and that the legislature should be authorized to regulate future representation upon the principles of wealth and number of inhabitants. The latter part of this report was promptly passed without debate and by a large majority, but the first part, specifying the number of members from the various states, was unsatisfactory, so that after a short discussion it was referred to a committee of a member from each state. Then the house adjourned.

Promptly the next morning this committee of eleven made its report, increasing the number of representatives in the first legislature to sixty-five. There may well have been some truth in the charge that the numbers were "artfully lessened for the large States . . . in order to prevent the undue influence which the large States will have in the government from being too apparent," but the numbers assigned to the different states had doubtless been a matter of compromise among the members of the committee, and several proposals in the convention to vary these were defeated by large majorities.

The provision for future changes had been vaguely expressed and [Edmund] Randolph now proposed that, in order to ascertain the alterations in the population and wealth of the several states, a census should be taken at regular intervals and representation arranged accordingly. [Hugh] Williamson suggested, and Randolph readily accepted the modification, that the census should be taken of the free white inhabitants and three-fifths "of those of other descriptions.". . . It was unanimously agreed that representation should be regulated according to the census. It was agreed by a vote of six states to four that a census of the "free inhabitants" should be taken, but to include "three fifths of the inhabitants of other description" was by a similar majority voted down. There was no sharp division here between slave and free states. On the first vote Delaware and Maryland joined with South Carolina and Georgia in the negative. In the second vote, to include three-fifths of the slaves, the states in favor of it were Connecticut, Virginia, North Carolina, and Georgia. . . . Almost immediately afterwards the whole resolution, in the form in which it then stood, was rejected unanimously, and the convention found itself without having advanced a single step.

The discussion of this point had occupied the sessions of one day, July 11. The first thing on the morning of July 12,

Gouverneur Morris proposed to add to the clause, empowering the legislature to vary the representation according to the principles of wealth and number of inhabitants, a proviso that taxation should be in proportion to representation. There was a brief discussion, the wording was modified to limit it to direct taxation, and it was then adopted by the convention unanimously. The main difficulty was thus solved and further details were quite easily agreed upon. It is worthy of note that Gouverneur Morris later wished to have this provision stricken out, although he himself had proposed it, because it did not accord with his own opinions and "he had only meant it as a bridge to assist us over a certain gulph." Before the day was over it had been decided that "representation ought to be proportioned according to direct Taxation and in order to ascertain the alteration . . . which may be required from time to time . . . that a Census be taken within six years . . . and once within the term of every Ten years afterwards of all the inhabitants of the United States in the manner and according to the ratio recommended by Congress in their resolution of April 18, 1783." The ratio recommended in 1783 was, of course, the three-fifths ratio. An amendment to have the blacks rated equally with the whites was voted down by eight states against two. . . .

On Monday morning, July 16, the whole compromise was adopted. . . .

Final Features of the Compromise

The important feature of the compromise was that in the upper house of the legislature each state should have an equal vote. The principle of proportional representation in the lower house was not a part of the compromise, although the details for carrying out that principle were involved. An absolute number of representatives from the several states was agreed upon in the formation of the first legislature, and the future apportionment was to be made by the legislature itself on the basis of numbers of population, counting three-fifths of the slaves, and direct taxation was to be in proportion to that representation. The proviso that money-bills should originate in the first branch and should not be amended in the second branch was regarded by some delegates as of great importance, but there were others who considered it of no importance at all.

The credit for the great compromise has been claimed by different men, and it has been ascribed to others. Of more recent years . . . the credit has been very generally attributed to the Connecticut delegation, and the compromise has been quite commonly known as the "Connecticut compromise." It is true that the delegates from Connecticut were responsible for bringing forward the formal question. Introduced by Doctor [William] Johnson, who spoke seldom but very much to the point and was therefore accorded a respectful hearing, the motion was made by [Oliver] Ellsworth "that in the second branch . . . each State shall have an equal vote." In the debate of the following day this was referred to at least once as the "Connecticut proposal" and once as the "Connecticut motion." It is undoubtedly true that the Connecticut delegates took an important part in getting the compromise adopted. But credit to the exclusion of others cannot be given to any individual, nor to any delegation, nor to any group of men other than to the small-state men in general. The combination of two methods of representation in one legislature was hinted at on May 30, the very first day that the Virginia plan was under discussion. On the day following, it was definitely and specifically suggested, and from then on it was frequently referred to until its final embodiment in the great compromise. With proportional popular representation established for one house, equal state representation for the other was inevitable, both from the ideas of representation that were current at the time and from the division of opinions in the convention.

Roots of the Three-Fifths Ratio

The counting of three-fifths of the slaves, the so-called "three-fifths rule," has very generally been referred to as a compromise and as one of the important compromises of the convention. This is certainly not the case. Attention has already been called to the fact that this ratio was embodied by the congress of the confederation in the revenue amendment of 1783, that the committee of the whole by a vote of nine states to two had added it as an amendment to the Virginia plan, that it was embodied in the New Jersey plan, and that when it was incorporated in the great compromise it was described as "the ratio recommended by Congress in their resolution of April 18, 1783." Indeed, one finds references in contemporary writings to the "Federal ratio", as if it were well understood what was meant by that term. A few months later, in the Massachusetts state convention, Rufus King very aptly said that "this rule . . . was adopted, because it was the language of all America." In reality the three-fifths rule was a mere incident in that part of the great compromise which declared that "representation ought to be proportioned according to direct Taxation."

In view of subsequent developments in this country, it is not surprising that historical writers have very generally overemphasized the differing interests of north and south in the convention. A correct understanding of the situation, however, can only be obtained if it is realized that in the first stages of the discussion of proportional representation the conflicting interests of east and west were more important than those of slave and free states. In colonial times, as population increased and settlement extended into the back country, the conservative moneyed interests of the coast insisted upon retaining the control of government in their own hands and refused to grant to the interior counties the share in government to which their numbers of population entitled them. This was seen in its most obvious form in the inequality of representation in the legislature. Notably was this the case in Pennsylvania, Virginia, and the Carolinas. And this inequality was maintained in the state governments that were formed after the outbreak of the Revolution. In the federal convention, the same interests demanded similar restrictions. Pennsylvania's method of dealing with the frontier counties was cited with approval. As it had worked well there for the older portions of the state to keep the power in their own hands, so now in the United States, it was insisted, new states ought not to be admitted on an equal footing with the old states. Gouverneur Morris was the champion of the commercial and propertied interests, and when the great compromise was under discussion he declared in favor of considering property as well as the number of inhabitants in apportioning representatives. In explanation of his position he stated that he had in mind the "range of new States which would soon be formed in the west," and "he thought the rule of representation ought to be so fixed as to secure to the Atlantic States a prevalence in the National Councils." Morris was also chairman of the first committee of five appointed to determine the numbers of representatives from the existing states in the first instance and to provide for future apportionment. As a member of the committee, [Nathaniel] Gorham frankly explained that one of the objects in their report which the committee had had in view was to give to the Atlantic States the power of "dealing out the right of Representation in safe proportions to the Western States." This portion of the report was at first adopted, but was afterwards disregarded in the readjustment by which both representation and direct taxation were to be apportioned according to numbers of population.

In 1787, slavery was not the important question, it might be said that it was not the moral question that it later became. The proceedings of the federal convention did not become known until the slavery question had grown into the paramount issue of the day. Men naturally were eager to know what the framers of the constitution had said and done upon this all-absorbing topic. This led to an overemphasis of the slavery question in the convention that has persisted to the present day. As a matter of fact, there was comparatively little said on the subject in the convention. [James] Madison was one of the very few men who seemed to appreciate the real division of interests in this country. It is significant that in the debate on proportional representation, he felt it necessary to warn the convention that it was not the size of the states but that "the great danger to our general government is the great southern and northern interests of the continent, being opposed to each other."

Election of Senators

Again the ever-recurring interest in the question of the popular election of senators has led to misinterpretation of things that were said and done in the convention. In the proceedings of the committee of the whole, a momentary interest had been aroused over the election of the members of the upper house by the state legislatures. A good many years afterward, Madison went over his notes very carefully with the idea of their posthumous publication and at that point, in view of subsequent developments, he tried to make sure that there should be no misunderstanding by inserting the following explanation: "It will throw light on this discussion, to remark that an election by the State Legislatures involved a surrender of the principle insisted on by the large States and dreaded by the small ones, namely that of a proportional representation in the Senate." To make assurance doubly sure, when the subject came up again in the debate leading to the great compromise, Madison inserted another note: "It must be kept in view that the largest States particularly Pennsylvania and Virginia always considered the choice of the second Branch by the State Legislatures as opposed to a proportional Representation to which they were attached as a fundamental principle of just Government." It cannot be too strongly insisted that whatever opinions were expressed in debate, and whatever arguments were advanced for or against the election of the members of the upper house by the state legislatures—and all sorts of proposals of other methods were made and all sorts of opinions were expressed—they should be interpreted with reference to the one question at issue, that of proportional representation. It might also be noted that from the moment of the adoption of the great compromise the method of electing the members of the upper house was never questioned in the convention.

Protecting Commercial Interest and Sealing the Fate of Slaves

Christopher Collier and James Lincoln Collier

The issue of slavery became a bargaining point during discussions on trade policy at the Constitutional Convention. The northern states pressed for limits on the slave trade, but did not press hard because they wanted concessions on trade policies. They believed the slave trade would end naturally; they did not foresee it would become a wound that would continue to fester in the nation for decades to come. In this essay, Christopher Collier and James Lincoln Collier maintain that had the northern states pressed for the abolition of slavery, the southern states would have boycotted the convention, and there would have been no constitution. On the other hand, they observe that had the northerners not compromised on the issue of slavery, the Civil War that erupted in later years might have been avoided. At the time of writing, Christopher Collier was historian for the State of Connecticut, professor of American history at the University of Connecticut, and editor of Connecticut's public records. He is the author of books and articles on early American history, including *Roger Sherman's Connecticut: Yankee Politics and the American Revolution* and *The Literature of Connecticut History*. James Lincoln Collier is the author of *The Making of Jazz* as well as other historical and biographical books. Together, the brothers have written several historical books for children.

One of the principal causes of the American Revolution had been the effort by the British to control the trade of the colonies to its own benefit. In general, the British in London

Christopher Collier and James Lincoln Collier, *Decision in Philadelphia: The Constitutional Convention of 1787*. New York: Readers' Digest Press and Random House of Canada Limited, 1986. Copyright © 1986 by Christopher Collier and James Lincoln Collier. Reproduced by permission of Alfred K. Knopf, a division of Random House, Inc., and the authors.

did not want the colonies trading independently with foreign nations. They wanted instead to force the trade to pass through England, where it could be taxed, and middleman profits could be extracted. They also required that colonial goods be shipped in British or colonial ships. In exchange, the colonies were given trading advantages with the mother country and each other over foreign competitors.

Parliament began passing the so-called navigation acts as early as 1650, and continued to pass them virtually up to the moment of the Revolution. The acts were not always seen as burdensome by Americans, because they did help to keep down foreign competition, especially in the lucrative West Indies trade. But in the years leading up to the Revolution they were increasingly resented, and were got around whenever possible. Many Americans favored the moves toward independence primarily to escape British regulation of their trade.

The term "navigation acts" thus was a loaded one, and the whole question of how foreign trade was to be regulated proved thorny right from the moment the colonies achieved their freedom. The problem, as was so frequently the case in the union, was that the different states had different commercial interests. Pennsylvania, New York, Virginia, and Massachusetts imported great quantities of goods, a substantial proportion of which were passed along to neighboring states, such as New Hampshire, Maryland, New Jersey, and Delaware. It was to the advantage of the big importing states to levy for themselves high import taxes, which could be collected from the ultimate consumers in other states.

The major importers were not averse to taxes on exports, either. Export taxes were standard among commercial nations in the eighteenth century and had been for some time. Indeed, it was more usual to tax exports than imports, because export taxes could be passed along to customers in other nations, while import taxes would be borne at home. All the big trading states, of course, exported, but the largest portion of any export taxes would be collected on the products of the southern states, whose economy was built around exporting tobacco, rice, and indigo. Such taxes would raise the prices of their exports and reduce their markets.

The big importing states also had a strong interest in gaining trading privileges from foreign nations. In order to negotiate trade treaties they needed to present a unified front. But under the Articles of Confederation, which left most commercial matters in the hands of the individual states, a coordinated policy was difficult to put together. . . .

The major trading states . . . wanted a government with substantial powers to regulate foreign trade and negotiate trade treaties. The small states, too, wanted a firm national control over trade, but for somewhat different reasons. They assumed that a government with power to regulate trade would take the power to tax imports away from the individual states, and use the duties for the benefit of all.

The interests of the southerners, however, were different. They were afraid that a national government with a free hand to regulate commerce might levy export taxes on the produce that was central to their economy. They also did not want a national government that could require them to use American bottoms, which would effectively give northerners a monopoly on shipping. And because the North would initially have a majority in both houses of Congress, southerners considered it essential to build into the Constitution some limitations on what the national government could do in respect to trade, or "navigation," as they usually termed it.

To sum up a rather complex question, then, both North and South had very strong reasons for not wanting the other section to control commerce; but for the North it was especially critical to establish a national government that could, and would, manage trade.

A Biased Committee

The North-South battle over navigation acts began on July 24 with the appointment by the Convention of what came to be known as the Committee of Detail. This committee was handed the task of going through the resolutions passed by the Convention and bringing some sort of order to them. . . .

Its membership . . . is a matter of a good deal of interest. It comprised two northerners, two southerners, and one man from the middle states. One of the northerners was

Nathaniel Gorham of Massachusetts, a nationalist who had just served a term as president of the old Congress, and a businessman who had become modestly wealthy through commerce. The other was the snuff-taking Connecticut lawyer Oliver Ellsworth, who operated under the influence of Roger Sherman. The southerners were the politically sharp John Rutledge and Edmund Randolph of Virginia, a careful politician who in the end refused to sign the Constitution because he was afraid his Virginia constituents would not like it. The man from the middle states was James Wilson, a business ally of Rutledge's, whom Rutledge lived with for the first three weeks of the Convention, and who had been [James] Madison's major supporter in putting together the Big Three–Deep South alliance.

In picking this committee, the Convention made a misstep. Congressional control over commerce, then, was of great interest to southerners, but it was vital to northerners—as vital as slavery was to southerners. According to Donald Robinson, who has studied the matter closely, "The Convention could not have produced at this critical point an intersectional committee in whose hands the interests of slave owners would have been safer." Randolph and Rutledge were totally committed to the defense of slavery, Wilson had accepted it as the price of Deep South support for proportional representation, and Ellsworth was part of the Connecticut–South Carolina axis. Only Nathaniel Gorham was likely to protest against slavery, and he could hardly prevail alone.

And in fact he did not. The Convention adjourned from July 27 to August 6 to allow the Committee of Detail to do its work. When it gave its report on Monday, August 6, it was immediately clear to at least some of the northerners that they had been sold out. Robinson says, "The report of the Committee of Detail was a monument to Southern craft and gall."

The key portions of the report read:

No tax or duty shall be laid by the legislature on articles exported from any states; nor on the migration or importation of such persons [i.e., black slaves] as the several states shall think proper to admit; nor shall such migration or importation be prohibited. . . . No capitation tax shall be laid, unless in proportion to the census. . . . No navigation act shall be passed without the assent of two thirds of the members present in each House.

The Central Issue of Slavery

The Committee of Detail had given the South everything it wanted. There would be no export taxes on their rice and indigo. The Constitution would forbid the new government from ending the hated foreign slave trade. There would be no "capitation," or head, taxes on the slaves, and the two-thirds requirement for passage of navigation acts would give the South an effective veto over them. . . .

When the report was read out, the portions dealing with slavery so dismayed at least some of the delegates that they made an effort to adjourn the Convention for a day so that they could mount a counterattack. Virginia and Maryland were particularly upset by the lack of limitations on the slave trade, which many of the delegates, including [George] Washington, [George] Mason, and Madison, intensely disliked. But the delegates by this time were tired and eager to get finished. They voted down the adjournment, and proceeded to take up the draft Constitution of the Committee of Detail, step by step. . . .

[On] August 8, the independent-minded Rufus King of Massachusetts leapt ahead to what he considered the central issues. The admission of slaves was a most grating "circumstance," he announced. He had agreed to the three-fifths formula [i.e., counting three-fifths of slave populations when determining state representation in the House of Representatives], he said, because he had assumed that in return for this concession, the South would agree to accept a strong national government, free to make decisions on other matters as it saw fit. But in this report, "In two great points the hands of the legislature were absolutely tied. The importation of slaves could not be prohibited—exports could not be taxed.". . .

"He had hoped that some accommodation would have taken place on this subject; that at least a time would have been limited for the importation of slaves. He never could agree to let them be imported without limitation and then be represented in the National Legislature. . . . Either slaves should not be represented, or exports should be taxable."

A deal, in other words, was a deal, King insisted. But it is apparent some other deal had been struck, because as soon as King sat down, Roger Sherman rose and gently pointed out that King was out of order, and the points he had raised must be debated in their proper place. Sherman would support the South on the issue.

But other northerners were not having it. Gouverneur Morris immediately rose and gave by far the strongest antislavery speech of the Convention, an angry peroration in which he said that slavery

> was a nefarious institution . . . the curse of Heaven on the states where it prevailed . . . . Upon what principle is it that the slaves shall be computed in the representation? Are they men? Then make them citizens and let them vote. . . . The admission of slaves into the representation when fairly explained comes to this: that the inhabitant of Georgia and South Carolina who goes to the Coast of Africa, and in defiance of the most sacred laws of humanity tears away his fellow creatures from their dearest connections and damns them to the most cruel bondages, shall have more votes in a government instituted for protection of the rights of mankind, than the citizen of Pennsylvania or New Jersey who views with a laudable horror so nefarious a practise.

Morris may have been taking an extreme position for bargaining purposes, or just exhibiting some of the rhetorical flamboyance for which he was noted. But he went on to say that the northern states were going to be taxed to pay for the defense of the South against slave insurrections. The legislature would be able to tax imports, and the North got a considerable part of its living by importing goods, which it sold to the South. But the national government would not be able to tax exports, by which the South made its living. . . .

The issue was forced when the Convention began to debate the clause in the committee's report that prohibited taxes on exports. Moderates in the North believed that export taxes might be necessary at some point and certainly should not be flatly prohibited. Even James Madison argued that the national government's hands should not be tied, and in one of the few instances in which Washington's vote was recorded, he agreed. But the South hated and feared the possibility of an export tax, and it voted as a solid bloc for not permitting it. Virginia, despite the influence of Madison and Washington, voted with the rest of the South. Two northern states did so, too. One was Massachusetts, where Gorham, who had been on the committee, presumably brought his fellow delegates into camp. The other, of course, was Connecticut. The prohibition on export taxes was carried.

However, the moment it was, Luther Martin got up and insisted that the resolution be amended to allow either prohibition of the importation of slaves, or at least a tax on them if importation was permitted. Slavery presented a danger to one part of the union, which the other part would have to defend, and besides, "it was inconsistent with the principles of the Revolution and dishonorable to the American character to have such a feature in the Constitution."

The only effect of this speech was to cause the southerners to become more obdurate. Rutledge said flatly that "religion and humanity had nothing to do with this question. Interest alone is the governing principle with nations. The true question at present is whether the Southern states shall or shall not be parties to the union." And Charles Pinckney said even more flatly that "South Carolina can never receive the plan if it prohibits the [foreign] slave trade.". . .

Once again it was the Connecticut men who broke ranks with their northern neighbors. At the close of debate on August 21 Oliver Ellsworth, who had been on the Committee of Detail, said, "The morality or wisdom of slavery are considerations belonging to the states themselves." And the first thing the next morning, August 22, Roger Sherman said that although he disapproved of the slave trade, the "public good" did not require its prohibition, and he "thought it best to leave the matter" as it was, in order not to drive the South out of the union. He added that slavery was dying out anyway and would by degrees disappear. Connecticut would continue to support the Deep South.

It was a Virginian, the prickly George Mason, who rose to make a strong speech against the slave trade. Mason owned scores of slaves and was not seeking the abolition of slavery; but the Virginians generally opposed the slave *trade*, in part because they felt it degraded master as well as servant, but also because the ending of slave importation would increase the value of Virginia's surplus slaves. Motives, once again, were mixed. . . .

Despite the support of Connecticut, the men from the Deep South were beginning to realize that they had better give ground somewhere. They recognized, as Randolph said, that slave importation "would revolt the Quakers, Methodists, and many others in the states having no slaves." In other words, at least Pennsylvania, and possibly others of the northern states, would refuse to ratify a Constitution that left the slave trade untouched. So the southerners backed off a little: Charles Cotesworth Pinckney suggested that a committee be put together to consider whether new slaves coming into the country should be taxed as other goods would be, "which he thought right and which would remove one difficulty that had been started." Rutledge seconded the motion; and Morris immediately said that he "wished the whole subject to be committed, including the clauses relating to taxes on exports and to a navigation act.". . .

The composition of the new committee, one of a number called the Committee of Eleven, is, as usual, of considerable interest. ([Robert] Yates and [John] Lansing of New York left on July 10; John Langdon and Nicholas Gilman of New Hampshire arrived on July 23). Its members were, in the main, conciliatory men, a number of whom had spoken little on the issue and had given no indication of strong feeling one way or another—William Livingston of New Jersey, George Clymer of Pennsylvania, Hugh Williamson of North Carolina. It also included some of the men who had already indicated that they were prepared to bargain—Charles Cotesworth Pinckney and John Langdon of New Hampshire.

On Friday, August 24, the Committee of Eleven brought in its report, which contained four provisions:

Congress could prohibit the importation of slaves after 1800.

Imported slaves could be taxed.

No exports could be taxed.

Navigation acts could be passed by simple majorities in Congress.

A Complex Bargain

A complex bargain, modifying the report of the Committee of Detail, which had been so favorable to southerners, had been struck. In essence, the southerners, in order to hang on to the prohibition against export taxes, had given in to the northerners on other kinds of navigation acts, which northern majorities in Congress would now be able to pass as they liked. The South had also accepted what at the time seemed a very minor limitation on the slave trade—the proviso that the new government could not interfere with it until 1800. Much later, as David Davis points out, when the issue of slavery began to tear at the country, Charles Pinckney called this clause a "negative pregnant." It forbade action for a time, and did not require any afterward, leaving open the possibility of the growth and expansion of the slave population. It was generally assumed, of course, that by 1800 the South might well have a majority in the House of Representatives and would be able to forestall congressional action on the slave trade.

The report was debated on August 25. Immediately Charles Cotesworth Pinckney arose and moved that the slave trade should be allowed to continue not merely until 1800 but for a full twenty years. How many of the northern delegates grasped this we do not know, but only James Madison spoke against extending the life of the slave trade. . . .

Next the Convention took up the second part of the bargain, that slaves could be taxed. A number of people spoke against it, including Roger Sherman, who said that he was against "acknowledging men to be property, by taxing them as such." But King of Massachusetts and Langdon of New Hampshire pointed out that a deal was a deal, and a tax on slaves was "the price" of permitting the slave trade to continue for so long. The South Carolinian Charles Cotesworth Pinckney "admitted that it was so." Nonetheless, southerners managed to get a limitation of ten dollars for each imported slave. In view of the fact that a healthy slave was worth several hundred dollars, the tax was only a sop. But the northerners accepted it.

The third part of the deal, the prohibition on export taxes, was not even debated, as it was understood by the northern delegates that it was the quid pro quo for the time limit on the slave trade. . . .

The Fugitive Clause

On August 28, the Convention began debating the question of the extradition of criminals from one state to another. In the course of the debate the South Carolinians [Pierce] Butler and Pinckney proposed to add to the extradition clause a clause that would "require fugitive slaves and servants to be delivered up like criminals." There was resistance to the idea—Wilson said that the cost would fall on the taxpayers, and Sherman said he "saw no more propriety in the public seizing and surrendering a slave or a servant, than a horse.". . .

The next day the Convention returned to the subject of navigation acts, which the Committee of Eleven had decided should be passed by simple majorities, as the North wished. Now the maverick Charles Pinckney offered a motion reintroducing the requirement of a two-thirds majority for passage of navigation acts, which would effectively give the South a veto. Very quickly his cousin Charles Cotesworth Pinckney rose and said:

> . . . it was the true interest of the southern states to have no regulation of commerce; but considering the loss brought on the commerce of the eastern states [i.e., New England] by the Revolution, their liberal conduct towards the views of South Carolina, and the interest the weak southern states had in being united with the strong eastern states, he thought it proper that no fetters should be imposed on the power of making commercial regulations; and that his constituents though prejudiced against the eastern states, would be reconciled to this liberality. He had himself, he said, prej-

udices against the eastern states before he came here, but would acknowledge that he had found them as liberal and candid as any men whatever.

. . . Several northerners followed, insisting on the importance of navigation acts to them, and speaking against the requirement of two-thirds majorities for them. They were supported by the South Carolinian Pierce Butler, who also wanted to keep the deal intact. He announced that he, too, despite his antipathy to navigation acts was "desirous of conciliating the affections of the east," and would vote against the two-thirds requirement. It was a signal: when the vote came, South Carolina was the only southern state to vote with the North in killing the two-thirds requirement.

And in virtually the next breath South Carolina's Butler rose and offered this motion:

> If any person bound to service or labor in any of the United States shall escape into another state he or she . . . shall be delivered up to the person justly claiming their service or labor.

This was the same as the fugitive slave clause that had been written into the Northwest Ordinance in July by the old Congress sitting in New York, as part of the price for prohibiting slavery north of the Ohio River. In Philadelphia on this August 29 it was written into the Constitution in part payment for allowing simple majorities for passage of navigation acts. It is almost as if the actors in the drama were following a script. First Charles Pinckney demands two-thirds majorities; then the other South Carolinians contradict him, saying they are "desirous of conciliating the affections of the New Englanders" for "their liberal conduct toward the views of South Carolina." Pinckney's call for two-thirds majorities is duly rejected without debate or a vote, and immediately Pierce Butler proposes the fugitive slave clause, which is duly accepted by general assent without a debate or a vote. . . .

What Would Have Happened?

And this now brings us to the question that still haunts our thinking about the Constitutional Convention: could the northern delegates have put closer limits on slavery, perhaps sparing the country the disastrous Civil War, and the racial animosities that have dogged it ever since?

To begin with, virtually no one, North or South, was advocating immediate abolition. Nor was there any possibility of even a phased abolition stretching out for decades. The white voters of the Deep South would never have ratified a constitution calling for abolition, and it would have been impossible to get such a constitution through Virginia, too. New York and Rhode Island, hostile to the whole idea of a new constitution, would have used the defection of the southern states as reason for not joining—Rhode Island failed to join the union until conditions forced it to do so, and New York ratified only by the slimmest of margins. In sum, if the North had pressed for the abolition of slavery, there would have been no Constitution, and everybody at the Convention knew it.

Nonetheless, the Deep South states were in a poor position to go it alone. Georgia was desperately underpopulated and defenseless against Spanish, Indians, and their own blacks, numbers of whom had found safe harbor with Florida Indians. North Carolina was not much more populous, and South Carolina, while richer and more peopled, had nonetheless succumbed rapidly to the British during the Revolution. It is difficult to see how the three states of the Deep South could have survived long in isolation against the array of enemies set against them—the states to the north; foreign nations with substantial fleets and greedy eyes alit at the sight of southern agricultural wealth; Indians; their own slaves. And most of these Deep South delegates knew better than anyone else just how vulnerable they were: some of them had been in British prison camps not many years before.

It is our belief that by playing on these very real fears, the northern delegates could have forced into the Constitution stricter limits on slavery. The South would probably have accepted the 1800 end to the slave trade proposed by the Committee of Eleven. This would at least have prevented the importation of tens of thousands of slaves and slowed the spread of slavery. It is also possible that the North could have secured prohibitions against slavery in *any* new states, north or south. There had not been much opposition to this idea when Thomas Jefferson and his committee had proposed it to the old Congress in 1784. It would not have been popular in the South; but the southerners might have been forced to swallow it by a determined northern coalition. Indeed, some southerners were willing to limit the spread of slavery in order to prevent competition in growing hemp, tobacco, and other staples. These two measures alone would have had the effect of confining slavery to the Southeast, and would perhaps have prevented the Civil War.

Finally, the North almost certainly could have fought off the fugitive slave clause. In fact, the effect of the act was more symbolic than real. It was always difficult for plantation owners from Georgia or Virginia to trace and recapture slaves who had run into Massachusetts or upstate New York. The fugitive slave act would have been useful mainly to slave owners on the borders of the Ohio River, who could chase slaves attempting to swim to freedom. As it worked out, the real effect of the fugitive slave act was to allow man-stealers to go into northern states and kidnap free blacks, under the pretense that they were escaped slaves. Unfortunately, black freedmen usually had only their friends and family to help them, and tens of thousands of freedmen were kidnapped into slavery under the fugitive slave act. If nothing else, defeat of this article would have saved these thousands of humans from lives of misery.

But the men of the North did not make the fight. They did not because most of them genuinely believed that blacks were inferior and, even as freedmen, could work only at menial labor. Furthermore they felt that slavery was bound to die out anyway, especially as the slave trade seemed likely to end. Even though most of the northern delegates believed that slavery was wrong in theory, they did not see it as a central issue of the time, as we tend to see racial friction today. As Madison's secretary said, it was a "distracting question," which was "retarding the labors" of the Convention. As a consequence, few northerners were prepared to risk jeopardizing the union in a battle over the happiness of blacks. What mattered to the North primarily was fear of southern dominance of a new government. And the result was that the blacks became bargaining chips in a set of complex compromises, which were meant to adjust the delicate balance of North and South in the new government.

In what they did and what they left undone, the delegates to the Convention were reflecting the opinions of most Americans. At the ratifying conventions later there would be little outcry against the delegates' decisions about slavery. That the 20 percent of the population that was black were used as pawns with no rights the white man was bound to respect only means that the Founders were living in the eighteenth century, not the twentieth. They committed one of the worst mistakes in American history, but that can be seen better under twentieth-century illumination than it could by the light of eighteenth-century ideological lamps. With hindsight, we can see that the Founding Fathers might have provided for the phasing out of slavery over a relatively long term, principally by confining it geographically. But they saw things, as we all do, according to their lights and they acted on their own vision.

And of course the irony of it all was that the South gave up power to the North because it expected it would soon be dominant anyway, and the North gave up slavery to the South because it thought it would die out anyway, and both were wrong. The final lesson, then, may be that institutions, once established, are not easily changed.

Guaranteeing Civil Liberties in the First Amendment

Richard B. Bernstein with Jerome Agel

Richard B. Bernstein and Jerome Agel observe that during the ratification campaign, the Anti-Federalists' main contention with the proposed constitution was that it did not have a bill of rights. The oppositionists contended that such a document was needed to limit the power of the government over individual liberties. Nevertheless, the Constitution was ratified by most of the states without the call for a bill of rights. When the First Congress convened on March 4, 1789, Anti-Federalist James Madison took the opportunity to introduce a bill of rights as the first amendment to the Constitution. Debates on the document continued for weeks and months in both houses of Congress until the amendment was approved in September of the same year. To the authors, the nation owes the Bill of Rights to Madison, who applied the full force of his intellect and character in bringing a very significant document into existence. At the time of writing, Richard B. Bernstein was adjunct associate professor of law at New York Law School. He has written and edited several books on American constitutional history, including *Are We to Be a Nation?: The Making of the Constitution* (with Kym S. Rice). He has served as historical consultant to the Library of Congress and research director of the New York State Commission on the Bicentennial of the Constitution. Jerome Agel has written numerous books, including collaborations with Carl Sagan, Marshall McLuhan, Stanley Kubrick, and Isaac Asimov.

Richard B. Bernstein with Jerome Agel, *Amending America*. New York: Times Books, 1993. Copyright © 1993 by Jerome Agel and Richard B. Bernstein. Reproduced by permission.

In 1787–1788, both the Anti-Federalists and those who sought to remain neutral in the ratification controversy worried that the Constitution authorized a government so powerful that it would destroy the states and the rights of the people. Such Federalists as James Wilson and Alexander Hamilton derided these fears as groundless, explaining that the general government could exercise only those powers conferred on it by the Constitution. Moreover, they contended, the people were the ultimate sovereigns; how could the people violate their own rights? They also cited such provisions as Article I, section 9, cataloging a series of limitations on federal power, to refute the Anti-Federal charge that the Constitution conferred unlimited powers on the general government. Finally, they maintained, the state governments were far from bastions of liberty themselves; throughout the 1770s and 1780s they had been responsible for the most frequent and blatant violations of individual rights.

Unconvinced, Anti-Federalists insisted that the Constitution provided few explicit limitations on governmental power, making even more glaring the document's lack of a bill of rights. They brushed aside the Federalists' attacks on state governments, pointing out that the powers of a new, untried federal government were the issue under debate. And they refused even to consider the argument (so popular with Federalist polemicists) that the people could not violate their own rights. Clinging to the traditional view that the government and the people were and could only be adversaries, Anti-Federalists could not embrace the new Federalist theories of popular sovereignty. And, they knew, many Americans who were otherwise friendly to the Constitution shared their views on the need to limit the federal government's power over rights.

As this debate moved from one state ratifying convention to the next, the Constitution's lack of a bill of rights limiting the powers of the general government over the individual became the Anti-Federalists' most compelling argument. Moreover, Anti-Federalists were able to point to state constitutions that either began with declarations of rights, as in Virginia and Massachusetts, or incorporated rights-protecting provisions, as in New York. That the Constitution created a government possessing the power to operate on individual citizens, they insisted, meant that (like the state constitutions that it resembled) it ought to include provisions defining and protecting rights. . . .

Leadership to obtain a bill of rights from the First Congress [of March 1789] came from someone who, only a year earlier, would have been a most unlikely candidate for the role. James Madison had reversed his stand from the opening stages of the struggle for ratification, having made a public commitment at the Virginia ratifying convention to work to amend the Constitution. This about-face was the most noteworthy development in the ratification controversy with respect to future amendments. Madison brought many strengths to the movement for a declaration of rights: his national political stature, his ability to secure President Washington's backing of the call for amendments securing individual rights, and his extraordinary intellectual talents and capacity for hard work. . . .

Madison's Proposed Amendments

Thus, when the First Congress convened the following spring, Madison was already hard at work, studying with great care a pamphlet published by Augustine Davis, a Virginia printer, setting forth the more than two hundred amendments to the Constitution recommended by the ratifying conventions. Madison realized that the existence of this pamphlet and its circulation far beyond its original place of publication confirmed that the question of amendments was still alive. He therefore scoured its pages, noting redundancies and sorting out those amendments designed to identify and protect rights from those that would otherwise alter the structure of government provided by the Constitution.

Madison used other political demands on his time and energies to advance the cause of amendments. At the same time that he immersed himself in the Davis pamphlet, he was deep in consultation with President-elect George Washington. . . .

When June 8 came [with Congress in session], Madison claimed recognition from the floor to fulfill his promise to his colleagues and to the nation to introduce the subject of amendments. He was confident of success, having worked hard to prepare a set of proposals that would satisfy the goals he and the President had set in Washington's inaugural address. With the people's expectations about to be gratified, and the support of the President, how could he fail?

Madison's list of proposed amendments included none that would limit the necessary powers of the general gov-

---

A Bill of Rights Is Necessary

In 1784, Thomas Jefferson, who earlier wrote the Declaration of Independence, went off to Paris as minister to France from the newly independent United States. He and James Madison, both from Virginia, had by then maintained a friendship and they regularly corresponded with each other on the ongoing deliberations in the convention. In the following letter from Paris, Jefferson writes to Madison and urges that the inclusion of a bill of rights in the Constitution is absolutely necessary.

I like much the general idea of framing a government, which should go on of itself, peaceably, without needing continual recurrence to the State legislatures. I like the organization of the government into legislative, judiciary and executive. I like the power given the legislature to levy taxes, and for that reason solely, I approve of the greater House being chosen by the people directly. . . . I am much pleased too, with the substitution of the method of voting [in Congress] by person, instead of that of voting by States; and I like the negative [veto] given to the Executive, conjointly with a third of either House; though I should have liked it better had the judiciary been associated for that purpose, or invested separately with a similar power. There are other good things of less moment.

I will now tell you what I do not like. First, the omission of a bill of rights, providing clearly, and without the aid of sophism, for freedom of religion, freedom of the press, protection against standing armies, restriction of monopolies, the eternal and unremitting force of the habeas corpus laws, and trials by jury in all

ernment. The Virginian aimed instead to state basic principles of republican government and to protect individual rights. Virtually every one of the twelve amendments ultimately proposed by Congress in 1789 has roots in Madison's list. He also included four provisions, derived from the Virginia Declaration of Rights and the American Declaration of Independence, affirming that government is derived from the people and is instituted to protect their liberty, safety,

---

matters of fact triable by the laws of the land, and not by the laws of nations. To say, as Mr. Wilson does, that a bill of rights was not necessary, because all is reserved in the case of the general government which is not given, while in the particular ones, all is given which is not reserved, might do for the audience to which it was addressed; but it is surely a *gratis dictum*, the reverse of which might just as well be said; and it is opposed by strong influences from the body of the instrument, as well as from the omission of the cause of our present Confederation, which had made the reservation in express terms. It was hard to conclude, because there has been a want of uniformity among the States as to the cases triable by jury, because some have been so incautious as to dispense with this mode of trial in certain cases, therefore, the more prudent States shall be reduced to the same level of calamity. It would have been much more just and wise to have concluded the other way, that as most of the States had preserved with jealousy this sacred palladium of liberty, those who wandered, should be brought back to it; and to have established general right rather than general wrong. For I consider all the ill as established, which may be established. I have a right to nothing, which another has a right to take away; and Congress will have a right to take away trials by jury in all civil cases. Let me add, that a bill of rights is what the people are entitled to against every government on earth, general or particular, and what no just government should refuse, or rest on inference.

Andrew Carroll, ed., *Letters of a Nation*. New York: Broadway Books, 1997, pp. 75–80.

and happiness, and that "the people have an indubitable, un-alienable, and indefeasible right to reform or change their Government, whenever it be found adverse or inadequate to the purposes of its institution." Finally, he included one other amendment not derived from any proposal, formal or informal, made during the ratification controversy: "No state shall violate the equal rights of conscience, or the free-dom of the press, or the trial by jury in criminal cases.". . .

Protection of People's Rights

Madison had originally drafted what we now know as the Bill of Rights as a set of Amendments to various provisions of the Constitution. Even in the final form as proposed to the states, these Amendments appear in the order of the pro-visions they were intended to modify.

Of the twelve Amendments proposed by Congress, the first two had nothing to do with rights. They pertained to the structure of Congress (outlined in the first sections of Article I), responding to Anti-Federal critiques of that insti-tution. The remaining ten Amendments were intended to revise sections 9 and 10 of Article I, which established limi-tations on the substantive powers of federal and state gov-ernments, respectively. . . .

Taken together, the ten amendments we know as the Bill of Rights reinforced the basic premise of a written constitu-tion: government must be limited if the rights of the people are to be protected. Even today, when we think of the prin-ciples of the American republic, we think first of the ca-dences of the Bill of Rights: freedom of religion, freedom of speech, freedom of the press, freedom of assembly, the right to keep and bear arms, the ban on unreasonable searches and seizures, due process of law, the prohibition of cruel and un-usual punishment, and so forth.

Yet the Bill of Rights differs from the original body of the Constitution in a fundamental way. Instead of spelling out the powers of the national government, it specifies proce-dures the government must follow when it exercises its au-thority over individual citizens and actions it may not take when using that authority. For this reason, the Bill of Rights is framed in a different manner from declarations of rights in the state constitutions of the 1770s and 1780s. Those declarations spelled out the principles of a free polity, expressed as admonitions (using "ought" or "should" language) rather than enforceable commands (using "shall" or "shall not" language). Because the Constitution did not begin with a declaration of rights but with a series of grants of power, the federal Bill of Rights was written in the language of command, establishing limitations on previous grants of government power.

Ironically, however, by March 1, 1792, when Secretary of State Thomas Jefferson certified that the Bill of Rights had become part of the Constitution, the first ten amendments had been transformed from the focus of national politics to a set of shared though unexamined assumptions about American public life. Within a few months after their submission to the states, they were eclipsed by other issues, less elevated but more dramatic: the contest over the location of the temporary and permanent capitals of the United States, the proposals of Secretary of the Treasury Alexander Hamilton to assume the debts of the states and consolidate them with the Confederation and federal debts, the controversy over the bill to create a Bank of the United States, and the foreign policy issues sparked by the French Revolution. Not until the twentieth century would the first ten amendments to the Constitution, and the proposition that rights are at the core of the American constitutional experiment, exert a powerful influence on constitutional law and the public mind.

The Bill of Rights has been the single largest grafting of new principles and doctrines in the history of the Constitution and its amending process. At the same time, these first ten amendments codified understandings having deep roots in Anglo-American history and law—the American people's understandings of individual rights and limits on government power.

It would be misleading to think of the Bill of Rights as "amending America," for ideas of rights always have been vital to American national identity and to the American experiment. Demands for a national bill of rights predated, accompanied, and even (because of the existence of Article V) made possible the adoption of the Constitution. Thus, the first ten amendments confirmed, rather than revised, the conception of the American nation held by the American people between 1789 and 1791. But the existence of these amendments as symbols of liberty, and their evolving function as judicially enforceable safeguards, helped to move ideas of rights to the core of American public life. We may well regard the pursuit, definition, and enforcement of rights as a central theme of the history of the United States. And, as we continue our disputes over the appropriate or necessary scope of rights, the Bill of Rights continues to amend America, over two centuries after its ratification.

Chapter 4

The Legacy of the Constitution

Turning Points
IN WORLD HISTORY

The Flourish of Free Enterprise

Nation's Business

In the early days of the republic, the individual states, which had previously united against a foreign foe, were often at odds in pursuing their narrow economic interests. James Madison and Alexander Hamilton believed that what could unite the nation was the promise of prosperity through the acquisition of property, free trade, and commerce. According to this essay from *Nation's Business*, it was this motivation for trade and commerce that saved the union from fragmentation after independence. The essay goes on to assert that the Constitution, enshrining this fundamental right to prosperity, has been instrumental in turning the United States into an industrial superpower. *Nation's Business* is published by the U.S. Chamber of Commerce.

The U.S. Constitution may seem just a fragile relic, its yellowed parchment pages sealed in a helium-filled enclosure in the National Archives . . . [but it is a vital document].

It has provided not only the mechanics of government and protections of such individual rights as freedom of speech and religion, but also has helped create an environment in which free enterprise has flourished.

The 55 delegates called to Philadelphia in 1787 to strengthen the Articles of Confederation convened at a time of serious economic difficulties in the new nation.

The confederacy's credit was exhausted, its securities selling at steep discounts. Farmers were being bankrupted by debt. Commerce was shackled by tariffs and other barriers the newly independent states had thrown up against one another. Southern agriculture and northern mercantile/financial inter-

Nation's Business, "200 and Going Strong: The Founding Fathers of the United States Drafted the Constitution That for Two Centuries Has Enabled Free Enterprise to Flourish," *Nation's Business*, vol. 75, July 1987, p. 49. Copyright © 1987 by Nation's Business. Reproduced by permission.

ests were in sharp conflict. Fears had arisen that the infant nation would fragment into regional confederations with their own governments serving narrow economic ends.

The framers—in particular James Madison and Alexander Hamilton—believed that fragmentation could be avoided if the people could be encouraged to turn to commerce. If the new government could give everyone the opportunity to earn property, to amass capital, to have a stake in the nation, then they would support it rather than conflicting local interests.

They shared the belief that owning property was a natural right and, through the Constitution, encouraged a unity based on the sanctity of property and the individual who held it. In short, the Constitution was at its root a document that promoted free enterprise.

"Both Madison and Hamilton knew that national prosperity would not just happen," says Betty Southard Murphy, a member of the law firm of Baker & Hostetler in Washington and former chairman of the National Labor Relations Board. "It had to be fostered by a constitution which encouraged it and protected it and by legislators who, deep in their souls, believed in it."

The first article of the Constitution authorized Congress to:

"Borrow money on the credit of the United States;

"Regulate commerce with foreign nations and among the several states;

"Establish . . . uniform laws on the subject of bankruptcies;

"Coin money . . . and fix the standard of weights and measures;

"Provide for the punishment of counterfeiting the securities and current coin of the United States;

"Establish post offices."

That same article prohibits states from enacting any law "impairing the obligation of contracts." Further, the Fifth Amendment, adopted in 1791 as part of the Bill of Rights, says, "No person shall be . . . deprived of life, liberty or property, without due process of law; nor shall private property be taken for public use without just compensation."

Marketplace Freedoms

The essential protection meant that those who came to America could have something unattainable for them elsewhere in the world—the freedom to work and acquire possessions. And they could keep it for themselves and their descendants. No one could take their property without paying for it.

Peter Onuf, associate professor of history at Worcester Polytechnic Institute and an authority on the founding of the nation, says the framers of the Constitution established "an arena of free enterprise" and "viewed trade and commerce—both domestic and international—as the bases of an enduring union." Over the past two centuries, legislative and judicial actions have greatly expanded government's role in regulating enterprise.

The U.S. Supreme Court has played a critical role. In 1803, in *Marbury v. Madison*, the Court, under strong-willed Chief Justice John Marshall, asserted its power to determine the constitutionality of legislation—the doctrine of judicial review.

The Marshall Court went on to lay the foundations of what became a national marketplace. In *McCulloch v. Maryland* (1819), the Court established federal supremacy in a conflict between federal and state law. The decision denied the state of Maryland's right to tax the Baltimore branch of the Bank of the United States (created by Congress) and sanctioned broad congressional actions:

"Let the end be legitimate, let it be within the scope of the Constitution, and all means which are appropriate, which are plainly adapted to that end, which are not prohibited, but consistent with the letter and spirit of the Constitution, are constitutional."

In its *Dartmouth College* decision (1819), the Court invalidated a New Hampshire law that sought to abolish the charter of Dartmouth College and bring the school under state control. The Chief Justice wrote in the decision that the charter was a contract protected by the Constitution from state impairment.

In one of the most significant of the Court's interpretations, Marshall also defined what the Constitution meant when it granted Congress the right to "regulate commerce with foreign nations and among the several states."

In *Gibbons v. Ogden*, a case involving an attempt by New York State to establish a monopoly on steamboat service in New York harbor, which includes ports on the New Jersey side, the Court held that congressional power over commerce was not confined by state lines but "acts upon its own subject matter where it is to be found."

Federal Power to Regulate Commerce

Thus, state law had to yield to Congress, and the resulting federal regulation of interstate and foreign commerce guaranteed uniformity. The doctrine stimulated an already growing national economy.

The pendulum swung, however, under Chief Justice Roger Taney, who served from 1835 to 1864. In his view, the federal government and the states possessed exclusive areas of authority in which each was supreme. Taney made it clear that he would not strip away rights reserved to the states. That position led to modification of the earlier *Dartmouth College* decision.

A procession in honor of the Constitution, a document that has helped create an environment in which free enterprise has flourished.

A state-chartered company operating a toll bridge in Boston argued that its charter (or contract, under the *Dartmouth* decision) had been impaired by passage of a state law authorizing construction of a nontoll, parallel bridge. Taney's opinion upheld the right of the state to build the second bridge, stating that a corporate charter could not imply the power to act against the public interest—a doctrine still prevalent.

The next shift in the judicial view of the Constitution as it applied to business began amid allegations of monopoly and fraud in industry and finance. The Court supported the government in a series of antitrust cases alleging predatory market practices. One famous case action in that era resulted in the breakup of Standard Oil Company, which had been founded in 1882 by John D. Rockefeller.

It was in the trustbusting atmosphere of the 1880s that Congress passed the Sherman Antitrust Act of 1890, which declared illegal any combination that restrained trade or commerce among the states or abroad. The purpose was in line with the original intent of Hamilton and Madison to give everyone a chance to have a stake in the nation's economy.

On the other hand, the Supreme Court rebuffed the government in the 1930s, when Congress, seeking to end the Depression, passed several farreaching laws affecting business. Among the most momentous decisions in the history of the U.S. Supreme Court was one involving the National Recovery Administration (NRA), which administered a system of production and price controls.

The Supreme Court struck down the NRA as unconstitutional, holding that it represented an illegal delegation of congressional authority to the executive branch of government.

As a result of Supreme Court decisions against major New Deal initiatives, President Franklin D. Roosevelt proposed to expand—critics used the term "pack"—the Court by appointing up to six new justices who would be more friendly to his legislative program. That proposal was rejected by Congress, but a new majority soon emerged on the existing Court and the Roosevelt administration began winning its cases there. Reluctance to interfere with congressional activism in regulating business set the general tone for successive Courts.

Contemporary Concerns

While the requirement for due process was once a strong barrier to regulation of business, the Supreme Court's unwillingness over the past half century to use it in that fashion has spawned the federal and state regulatory climate in which businesses operate today.

Where the Court once required strict standards to justify regulation, it is now willing to accept such reasons as "in the public interest" and "for public convenience and necessity.". . .

[Contemporary] issues being raised include employer rights, the lengths to which the government can go to protect the environment, business' free-speech rights and . . . interpretations of various provisions of the massive tax reform act passed [in 1986].

Although business is frequently unhappy with Supreme Court interpretations of the Constitution, the document remains a critical source of protection for the free enterprise system, constitutional experts say.

Drafted in an age of sail and horses for an agricultural society of 4 million people, the Constitution is proving flexible enough to serve, after just 14 changes since 1791, as the supreme law of an industrial superpower of 240 million.

An Inspiration to Other Nations

John Greenwald

The principles of rights and freedoms enshrined in the U.S. Constitution have been reflected in the constitutions of other nations. Over time, as author John Greenwald observes, U.S.-inspired constitutions have gone their own ways. In Catholic Ireland and Communist China, in Latin America and Africa, in democracies and in dictatorships, in industrialized nations and developing ones, the ideas manifest in the Constitution have been suited to the needs of others in foreign lands hungry for freedom. John Greenwald wrote the following essay for *Time* magazine.

In overwhelmingly Catholic Ireland, the constitution outlaws abortion and divorce and proclaims the Holy Trinity the source of all political power. Japan's national charter renounces war. Portugal's forbids private ownership of television stations. Peru reprints its charter in the Lima telephone directory, filling ten pages of fine print. Yet beneath such diversity, each document can trace its rights and freedoms to U.S. soil. Says Joseph Magnet, a law professor at Canada's University of Ottawa: "America has been and remains the great constitutional laboratory for the entire world."

Of the 170 countries that exist today [1987], more than 160 have written charters modeled directly or indirectly on the U.S. version. Those states range from the giant Soviet Union to the tiny Caribbean island country of Grenada. While Poland and France became the first to follow America's lead when they drafted modern constitutions in 1791, the largest impact has been recent. More than three-quarters of today's charters were adopted after World War II. Jawaharlal Nehru, India's first Prime Minister, could have been

John Greenwald, "A Gift to All Nations," *Time*, vol. 130, July 6, 1987. Copyright © 1987 by Time, Inc. Reproduced by permission.

speaking for the rest of the Third World when he told the U.S. Congress in 1949, "We have been greatly influenced by your own Constitution."

Some charters are roundly ignored. China's declaration of human rights was powerless to stop the abuses of the 1960s Cultural Revolution. In Latin America dictators often simply disregard national charters during times of unrest. Many African leaders have stymied democracy by outlawing opposing political parties and turning their countries into one-party states, often without bothering to amend their charters. Yet so strongly have constitutional ideals taken hold worldwide that few countries dare to abandon them completely.

Indeed, constitutions are living documents that are constantly being created and reshaped. Voters in the Philippines went to the polls in January [1987] to approve a new charter, the country's fifth, that prohibits human rights violations and retains Corazon Aquino as President until 1992. In Nicaragua this year, the Marxist-influenced Sandinista leadership unveiled that country's twelfth constitution in 149 years. Haitians in March [1987] approved their 23rd charter since 1804 in the country's first free election in three decades.

As such figures show, many constitutions have managed to survive only until the next upheaval or military coup. Three-quarters of the world's constitutions have been completely rewritten since they were first adopted, making America's fidelity to a single charter highly unusual. Some experts contend that frequent constitutional changes can be healthy. Says Albert Blaustein, a Rutgers University law professor who has helped draft six foreign charters: "Jefferson concluded that every 20 years the new generation should have its own constitution to meet current needs. That might not be a good idea for the U.S., but it's really not a bad idea for other countries."

Restraint in Modern Charters

Some constitutions are born of disaster. After World War II, Americans played a key role in drafting charters for the defeated nations of Japan and West Germany. The Japanese charter declares that the country will never again make war or maintain an army, navy or air force. As a result, Japan spends only about 1% of its gross national product on defense, freeing the economy for more productive purposes. Ironically, the U.S. is pressing the Japanese to boost defense outlays.

The West German constitution, written under the watchful eye of U.S. occupation leaders, sought to prevent the rise of another Hitler by limiting the executive branch. Recalls Joachim von Elbe, a Bonn legal expert: "We did not want to make the Germans just imitate the American constitutional model but rely on themselves to reform, rebuild and overcome the Nazi period." The framers decreed that the Bundestag, or parliament, could not oust a Chancellor without first choosing a successor. That has helped prevent a return of the political chaos that brought the Nazis to power in the 1930s.

Italians, with memories of Mussolini still fresh in their minds, went even further than the Germans in reining in the executive branch. While this has guarded against a new outbreak of tyranny, the inability of any one of Italy's parties to win a majority in parliament has led to frequent political turnover: Italy has had 46 governments since 1945.

The constitutions of Eastern Europe bestow supreme power on the Communist Party. While charters from Bulgaria to Poland ring with declarations of human and civil rights, they all contain loopholes that permit governments to set such rights aside should the party so require. Thus many guarantees—like the widely promised right to complain about government misdeeds without fear of retribution—are honored mainly in the breach, and supposedly independent courts almost never hand down rulings the party does not like.

The same gulf between rhetoric and reality exists in China. The country's current charter, its fifth since 1949, grants "freedom of speech, of the press, of assembly, of association, of procession and of demonstration." Peking nonetheless responded to widespread student protests [in 1986] by detaining the leaders, firing university officials and halting demonstrations. Authorities then shut down half a dozen liberal periodicals and banned scores of books, magazines and films throughout the country.

Third World Charter

Among Third World nations, India has often seemed the most faithful to its U.S.-inspired constitutional ideals. The world's largest democracy included a declaration of "fundamental rights" in its 1949 charter and backed them up by borrowing the U.S. system of judicial review. "Thank God they put in the fundamental rights," says Nani Palkhivala, a constitutional expert who was India's Ambassador to Washington in the late 1970s. He observes, "Since 1947 we have had more harsh and repressive laws than were ever imposed under British rule." Indian courts, however, overturned most of them.

Leaders in Africa, confronted by tribal rivalries and the constant threat of coups, have taken far greater pains to stay in power than to preserve democratic rights. Troublesome constitutions are usually ignored or tailored to suit. "If anyone speaks to you about a multiparty political system, catch him and hit him hard," declared Gabon President Albert-Bernard (Omar) Bongo in a widely quoted 1983 speech. At least 28 of the continent's 53 states have only one political party, and 27 African nations are under military rule. Countries ranging from Guinea in West Africa to Somalia in the east have gone so far as to declare dissent a treasonable crime that can be punished by death. Notes British Historian Lord Blake: "The political tradition in many parts of Africa is authoritarian, and that's what has taken over."

In Latin America, coups and military dictatorships have often been the rule. Chile's 1981 constitution grants dictatorial authority to President Augusto Pinochet, the general who seized power in 1973. In Argentina, the three-year effort at civilian rule under constitutionally mandated human-rights principles still sways precariously if the military glowers too hard. Mexico is politically stable and boasts a constitution that provides for separation of powers between branches of government, but the Institutional Revolutionary Party and its forerunner have controlled the presidency—and much of the other branches—since 1929.

Though many U.S.-inspired constitutions have gone their own ways over the years, the seed planted in Philadelphia in 1789 should continue to flower. "The idea that individuals have rights against government is probably the most profound influence of the U.S. Constitution," says Oscar Schachter, professor emeritus of international law and diplomacy at Columbia University. "The whole notion of human rights as a worldwide movement was grounded in part in the Constitution." Those rights may not always be honored, but they have fired the imaginations of individuals, free and otherwise, around the world. After two centuries, the U.S. Constitution remains the standard against which people of all sorts measure their governments, and some governments even measure themselves.

The Question of Slavery: Preserving the Union at the Expense of Justice

Herbert J. Storing

Herbert J. Storing, author and scholar, does not share the dominant opinion that the founding fathers deliberately excluded the slaves in the Constitution's protection of the "rights of man." He maintains that many delegates to the Constitutional Convention abhorred slavery and wished to see it ended. However, to appease delegates from slave-holding states, the drafters of the Constitution avoided a condemnation of slavery and made preserving the union the guiding principle of the document. Storing laments the fact that the rights of the slaves were sacrificed to a higher exigency: the white man's right to protect his self-interest. Storing does, though, exonerate the founding fathers from betraying any moral approval of slavery in the Constitution. At the time of writing, Herbert J. Storing was the Robert Kent Gooch Professor of Government at the University of Virginia. He also taught at the University of Chicago, Northern Illinois University, and Colgate University. Among his publications are *The Complete Anti-Federalist; Essays on the Scientific Study of Politics*; and *What Country Have I? Political Writings of Black Americans*.

The Founders did acknowledge slavery, they compromised with it. The effect was in the short run probably to strengthen it. Perhaps they could have done more to restrict it, though the words of a Missouri judge express what the Founders thought they were doing and, I think, probably the truth.

Herbert J. Storing, "Slavery and the Moral Foundations of the American Republic," *The Moral Foundations of the American Republic*, edited by Robert H. Horwitz. Charlottesville: University Press of Virginia, 1986. Copyright © 1986 by Kenyon Public Affairs Conference Center. Reproduced by permission of the publisher.

"When the States assumed the rights of self-government, they found their citizens claiming a right of property in a miserable portion of the human race. Sound national policy required that the evil should be restricted as much as possible. What they could, they did." "As those fathers marked it," [Abraham] Lincoln urged on the eve of the Civil War, "so let it be again marked, as an evil not to be extended, but to be tolerated and protected only because of and so far as its actual presence among us makes that toleration and protection a necessity." Slavery was an evil to be tolerated, allowed to enter the Constitution only by the back door, grudgingly, unacknowledged, on the presumption that the house would be truly fit to live in only when it was gone, and that it would ultimately be gone.

In their accommodation to slavery, the Founders limited and confined it and carefully withheld any indication of moral approval, while they built a Union that they thought was the greatest instrument of human liberty ever made, that they thought would lead and that did in fact lead to the extinction of Negro slavery. It is common today to make harsh reference to the irony of ringing declarations of human rights coming from the pens of men who owned slaves. . . . They saw better than their critics how difficult it was to extricate themselves from that [ironic] position in a reasonably equitable way. But they saw, too, a deeper irony: these masters knew that they were writing the texts in which their slaves would learn their rights.

A Problem in the Principles

Having, I hope, rescued the Founders from the common charge that they shamefully excluded Negroes from the principles of the Declaration of Independence, that they regarded their enslavement as just, and that in their Constitution they protected property in man like any other property, I must at least touch on a deeper question, where they do not come off so well. But at this deeper level the problem is not that they betrayed their principles, the common charge; the problem lies rather in the principles themselves. That very principle of individual liberty for which the Founders worked so brilliantly and successfully contains within itself an uncomfortably large opening toward slavery. The principle is the right of each individual to his life, his liberty, his pursuit of happiness as he sees fit. He is, to be sure, subject to constraints in the pursuit of his own interests because of the fact of other human beings with similar rights. But are these moral constraints or merely prudential ones? [English philosopher John] Locke says that under the law of nature each individual ought, as much as he can, "to preserve the rest of mankind" "when his own preservation comes not in competition." Each individual is of course the judge of what his own preservation does require, and it would be a foolish man, an unnatural man, who would not, under conditions of extreme uncertainty, give himself every generous benefit of the doubt. Does this not tend to mean in practice that each individual has a right to pursue his own interests, as he sees fit and as he can? And is there not a strong tendency for that "as he can" to become conclusive? In civil society, indeed, each of us gives up the claim of sovereign judgment for the sake of the milder, surer benefits of a supreme judge. Even in that case there is a question whether the first principle does not remain that one may do what one can do. The Founders often described the problem of civil society as resulting from that tendency. In any case, regarding persons outside civil society, there is a strong implication that any duty I have to respect their rights is whatever residue is left after I have amply secured my own.

Rights and Self-Preservation

Now, in the case of American slavery, especially in the South at the time of the writing of the Constitution, there clearly was a conflict between the rights of the slaves and the self-preservation of the masters. "[W]e have a wolf by the ears," Jefferson said, "and we can neither hold him, nor safely let him go. Justice is in one scale, and self preservation in the other." Only an invincible naiveté can deny that Jefferson spoke truly. But the deeper issue, as I think Jefferson knew, is the tendency, under the principles of the Declaration of Independence itself, for justice to be reduced to self-preservation, for self-preservation to be defined as self-interest, and for self-interest to be defined as what is convenient and achievable. Thus the slave owner may resolve that it is necessary to keep his slaves in bondage for the compelling reason that if they were free they would kill him; but he may also decide, on the same basic principle, that he must keep them enslaved in order to protect his plantation, his children's patrimony, his flexibility of action, on which his preservation ultimately depends; and from that he may conclude that he is entitled to keep his slaves in bondage if he finds it convenient to do so. All of this presumes of course that he *can* keep his slaves in

Benjamin Franklin's Last Cause

Benjamin Franklin figured in all the historic moments that spanned the revolutionary era. Self-taught, he excelled in all endeavors he engaged in—science, diplomacy, statemanship, politics, and literature. As historian Joseph J. Ellis reminds readers, Franklin embraced the abolition of slavery as the last cause of his life, believing slavery violated the principles on which the nation was founded.

His forceful presence at the defining moment of 1776 [the signing of the Declaration of Independence] had caused most observers to forget that, in truth, Franklin was a latecomer to the patriot cause, the man who had spent most of the 1760s in London attempting to obtain, of all things, a royal charter for Pennsylvania. He had actually lent his support to the Stamp Act in 1765 and lobbied for a position within the English government as late as 1771. But he had leapt back across the Atlantic and onto the American side of the imperial debate in the nick of time, a convert to the cause, who, by the dint of his international reputation, was quickly catapulted into the top echelon of the political leadership. Sent to France to negotiate a wartime alliance, he arrived in Paris just when the French ministry was ready to entertain such an idea. He remained in place long enough to lead the American delegation through the peace treaty with England, then relinquished his ministerial duties to Jefferson in 1784, just when all diplomatic initiatives on America's behalf in Europe bogged down and proved futile. (When bondage. Nor does it in any way deny the right of the slave to resist his enslavement and to act the part of the master if he can. This whole chain of reasoning is a chilling clarification of the essential war that seems always to exist, at bottom, between man and man.

American Negro slavery, in this ironic and terrible sense, can be seen as a radicalization of the principle of individual liberty on which the American polity was founded. Jefferson wrote in his *Notes on the State of Virginia* of the demoralization of the masters caused by slavery and its threat to the

---

asked if he was Franklin's replacement, Jefferson had allegedly replied that he was his successor, but that no one could replace him.) He arrived back in Philadelphia a conquering hero and in plenty of time to be selected as a delegate to the Constitutional Convention. . . .

At the Constitutional Convention he intended to introduce a proposal calling for the inclusion of a statement of principle, condemning both the slave trade and slavery, thereby making it unequivocally clear that the founding document of the new American nation committed the government to eventual emancipation. But several northern delegates, along with at least one officer in the Pennsylvania Abolition Society, persuaded him to withdraw his proposal on the grounds that it put the fragile Sectional Compromise, and therefore the Constitution itself, at risk. The petition submitted to the First Congress under his signature, then, was essentially the same proposal he had wanted to introduce at the Convention. With the Constitution now ratified and the new federal government safely in place, Franklin resumed his plea that slavery be declared incongruous with the revolutionary principles on which the nation was founded. The man with the impeccable timing was choosing to make the anomaly of slavery the last piece of advice he would offer his country.

Joseph J. Ellis, *Founding Brothers: The Revolutionary Generation.* New York: Alfred A. Knopf, 2000, pp. 109–111.

whole institution of free government. Masters become
tyrants and teach tyranny to their children (and, incidentally,
to their slaves). Even more important, slavery, through its
visible injustice, tends to destroy the moral foundation of
civil society. "And can the liberties of a nation be thought secure when we have removed their only firm basis, a conviction in the minds of the people that these liberties are of the
gift of God? That they are not to be violated but with His
wrath? Indeed I tremble for my country when I reflect that
God is just; that his justice cannot sleep forever; that . . . an
exchange of situation [between whites and blacks] is among
possible events; that it may become probably [*sic*] by super-
natural interference! The Almighty has no attribute which
can take side with us in such a contest." I do not think that
Jefferson was literally concerned with divine vengeance, but
he was concerned with the underlying tension—so ruthlessly
exposed in the institution of Negro slavery—between the
doctrine of individual rights and the necessary moral ground
of any government instituted to secure those rights.

Chapter 5

Critiques of the Constitution

Turning Points

IN WORLD HISTORY

The Constitution Is an Economic Document

Charles A. Beard

Scholar and history professor Charles A. Beard boldly asserts in the following article that the Constitution was designed by the framers mainly to regulate and protect property. The assertion, which is contained in his 1935 book *An Economic Interpretation of the Constitution of the United States*, met strong reaction from the academic community. Through the years, the book has remained an important work on the subject. To prove his point, Professor Beard dissects the contents of *The Federalist* papers—the brainchild of James Madison, Alexander Hamilton, and John Jay—which, he claims, contains the political thinking that underpins the Constitution. Beard, a distinguished historian, taught at Columbia University and Johns Hopkins University. He is the author and editor of dozens of books and hundreds of articles on government, history, politics, and economics. Among his major works are *The Industrial Revolution*, *Economic Origins of Jeffersonian Democracy*, *The Economic Basis of Politics*, and *American Government and Politics*. The last title, a definitive text for American government courses, has been published in ten editions.

The Federalist . . . presents in a relatively brief and systematic form an economic interpretation of the Constitution by the men best fitted, through an intimate knowledge of the ideals of the framers, to expound the political science of the new government. This wonderful piece of argumentation by Hamilton, Madison, and Jay is in fact the finest study in the economic interpretation of politics which exists in any language. . . .

Charles A. Beard, *An Economic Interpretation of the Constitution of the United States*. New York: The Macmillan Company, 1935. Copyright © 1935 by The Macmillan Company. All rights reserved. Reproduced by permission.

Before taking up the economic implications of the structure of the federal government, it is important to ascertain what, in the opinion of *The Federalist*, is the basis of all government. The most philosophical examination of the foundations of political science is made by Madison in the tenth number. Here he lays down, in no uncertain language, the principle that the first and elemental concern of every government is economic.

1. "The first object of government," he declares, is the protection of "the diversity in the faculties of men, from which the rights of property originate." The chief business of government, from which, perforce, its essential nature must be derived, consists in the control and adjustment of conflicting economic interests. After enumerating the various forms of propertied interests which spring up inevitably in modern society, he adds: "The regulation of these various and interfering interests forms the principal task of modern legislation, and involves the spirit of party and faction in the ordinary operations of the government."

2. What are the chief causes of these conflicting political forces with which the government must concern itself? Madison answers. Of course fanciful and frivolous distinctions have sometimes been the cause of violent conflicts; "but the most common and durable source of factions has been the various and unequal distribution of property. Those who hold and those who are without property have ever formed distinct interests in society. Those who are creditors, and those who are debtors, fall under a like discrimination. A landed interest, a manufacturing interest, a mercantile interest, a moneyed interest, with many lesser interests grow up of necessity in civilized nations, and divide them into different classes actuated by different sentiments and views."

3. The theories of government which men entertain are emotional reactions to their property interests. "From the protection of different and unequal faculties of acquiring property, the possession of different degrees and kinds of property immediately results; *and from the influence of these on the sentiments and views of the respective proprietors, ensues a di-*

vision of society into different interests and parties." Legislatures reflect these interests. "What," he asks, "are the different classes of legislators but advocates and parties to the causes which they determine?" There is no help for it. "The causes of faction cannot be removed," and "we well know that neither moral nor religious motives can be relied on as an adequate control."

·4. Unequal distribution of property is inevitable, and from it contending factions will rise in the state. The government will reflect them, for they will have their separate principles and "sentiments"; but the supreme danger will arise from the fusion of certain interests into an overbearing majority, which Madison, in another place, prophesied would be the landless proletariat,—an overbearing majority which will make its "rights" paramount, and sacrifice the "rights" of the minority. "To secure the public good," he declares, "and private rights against the danger of such a faction and at the same time preserve the spirit and the form of popular government is then the great object to which our inquiries are directed."

5. How is this to be done? Since the contending classes cannot be eliminated and their interests are bound to be reflected in politics, the only way out lies in making it difficult for enough contending interests to fuse into a majority, and in balancing one over against another. The machinery for doing this is created by the new Constitution and by the Union. (*a*) Public views are to be refined and enlarged "by passing them through the medium of a chosen body of citizens." (*b*) The very size of the Union will enable the inclusion of more interests so that the danger of an overbearing majority is not so great. "The smaller the society, the fewer probably will be the distinct parties and interests composing it; the fewer the distinct parties and interests, the more frequently will a majority be found of the same party. . . . Extend the sphere, and you take in a greater variety of parties and interests; you make it less probable that a majority of the whole will have a common motive to invade the rights of other citizens; or if such a common motive exists, it will be more difficult for all who feel it to discover their strength

and to act in unison with each other."

Q.E.D., "in the extent and proper structure of the Union, therefore, we behold a republican remedy for the diseases most incident to republican government."

The Balance of Powers

The fundamental theory of political economy thus stated by Madison was the basis of the original American conception of the balance of powers which is formulated at length in four numbers of *The Federalist* and consists of the following elements:

1. No mere parchment separation of departments of government will be effective. "The legislative department is everywhere extending the sphere of its activity, and drawing all power into its impetuous vortex. The founders of our republic . . . seem never for a moment to have turned their eyes from the danger to liberty from the overgrown and all-grasping prerogative of an hereditary magistrate, supported and fortified by an hereditary branch of the legislative authority. They seem never to have recollected the danger from legislative usurpations, which, by assembling all power in the same hands, must lead to the same tyranny as is threatened by executive usurpations."

2. Some sure mode of checking usurpations in the government must be provided, other than frequent appeals to the people. "There appear to be insuperable objections against the proposed recurrence to the people as a provision in all cases for keeping the several departments of power within their constitutional limits." In a contest between the legislature and the other branches of the government, the former would doubtless be victorious on account of the ability of the legislators to plead their cause with the people.

3. What then can be depended upon to keep the government in close rein? "The only answer that can be given is, that as all these exterior provisions are found to be inadequate, the defect must be supplied by so contriving the interior structure of the government as that its several constituent parts may, by their mutual relations, be the means of keeping each other in their proper places. . . . It is of great

importance in a republic not only to guard the society against the oppression of its rulers, but to guard one part of the society against the injustice of the other part. Different interests necessarily exist in different classes of citizens. If a majority be united by a common interest, the rights of the minority will be insecure." There are two ways of obviating this danger: one is by establishing a monarch independent of popular will, and the other is by reflecting these contending interests (so far as their representatives may be enfranchised) in the very structure of the government itself so that a majority cannot dominate the minority—which minority is of course composed of those who possess property that may be attacked. "Society itself will be broken into so many parts, interests, and classes of citizens, that the rights of individuals, or of the minority, will be in little danger from interested combinations of the majority."

4. The structure of the government as devised at Philadelphia reflects these several interests and makes improbable any danger to the minority from the majority. "The House of Representatives being to be elected immediately by the people, the Senate by the State legislatures, the President by electors chosen for that purpose by the people, there would be little probability of a common interest to cement these different branches in a predilection for any particular class of electors."

5. All of these diverse interests appear in the amending process but they are further reinforced against majorities. An amendment must receive a two-thirds vote in each of the two houses so constituted and the approval of three-fourths of the states.

6. The economic corollary of this system is as follows: Property interests may, through their superior weight in power and intelligence, secure advantageous legislation whenever necessary, and they may at the same time obtain immunity from control by parliamentary majorities.

Barriers to Majority Rule

If we examine carefully the delicate instrument by which the framers sought to check certain kinds of positive action that might be advocated to the detriment of established and acquired rights, we cannot help marvelling at their skill. Their leading idea was to break up the attacking forces at the starting point: the source of political authority for the several branches of the government. This disintegration of positive action at the source was further facilitated by the differentiation in the terms given to the respective departments of the government. And the crowning counterweight to "an interested and over-bearing majority," as Madison phrased it, was secured in the peculiar position assigned to the judiciary, and the use of the sanctity and mystery of the law as a foil to democratic attacks.

It will be seen on examination that no two of the leading branches of the government are derived from the same source. The House of Representatives springs from the mass of the people whom the states may see fit to enfranchise. The Senate is elected by the legislatures of the states, which were, in 1787, almost uniformly based on property qualifications, sometimes with a differentiation between the sources of the upper and lower houses. The President is to be chosen by electors selected as the legislatures of the states may determine—at all events by an authority one degree removed from the voters at large. The judiciary is to be chosen by the President and the Senate, both removed from direct popular control and holding for longer terms than the House.

A sharp differentiation is made in the terms of the several authorities, so that a complete renewal of the government at one stroke is impossible. The House of Representatives is chosen for two years; the Senators for six, but not at one election, for one-third go out every two years. The President is chosen for four years. The judges of the Supreme Court hold for life. Thus "popular distempers," as eighteenth century publicists called them, are not only restrained from working their havoc through direct elections, but they are further checked by the requirement that they must last six years in order to make their effects felt in the political department of the government, providing they can break through the barriers imposed by the indirect election of the Senate and the President. Finally, there is the check of judicial control that can be overcome only through the manipulation of the appointing power which requires time, or through the operation of a cumbersome amending system.

Judicial Control

The keystone of the whole structure is, in fact, the system provided for judicial control—the most unique contribution to the science of government which has been made by American political genius. It is claimed by some recent writers that it was not the intention of the framers of the Constitution to confer upon the Supreme Court the power of passing upon the constitutionality of statutes enacted by Congress; but in view of the evidence on the other side, it is incumbent upon those who make this assertion to bring forward positive evidence to the effect that judicial control was not a part of the Philadelphia programme. Certainly, the authors of *The Federalist* entertained no doubts on the point, and they conceived it to be such an excellent principle that they were careful to explain it to the electors to whom they addressed their arguments.

After elaborating fully the principle of judicial control over legislation under the Constitution, Hamilton enumerates the advantages to be derived from it. Speaking on the point of tenure during good behavior, he says: "In a monarchy it is an excellent barrier to the despotism of the prince; in a republic it is no less an excellent barrier to the encroachments and oppressions of the representative body. . . . If, then, the courts of justice are to be considered as the bulwarks of a limited Constitution against legislative encroachments, this consideration will afford a strong argument for the permanent tenure of judicial offices, since nothing will contribute so much as this to that independent spirit in the judges which must be essential to the faithful performance of so arduous a duty. . . . But it is not with a view to infractions of the Constitution only that the independence of the judges may be an essential safeguard against the effects of occasional ill humors in the society. These sometimes extend no farther than to the injury of private rights of particular classes of citizens, by unjust and partial laws. Here also the firmness of the judicial magistracy is of vast importance in mitigating the severity and confining the operation of such laws. It not only serves to moderate the immediate mischiefs of those which may have been passed, but it operates as a check upon the legislative body in passing them; who, perceiving that obstacles to the success of iniquitous intention are to be expected from the scruples of the courts, are in a manner compelled, by the very motives of injustice they meditate, to qualify their attempts. This is a circumstance calculated to have more influence upon the character of our governments than but few may be aware of."

No Reference to Property Qualifications

Nevertheless, it may be asked why, if the protection of property rights lay at the basis of the new system, there is in the Constitution no provision for property qualifications for voters or for elected officials and representatives. This is, indeed, peculiar when it is recalled that the constitutional history of England is in a large part a record of conflict over the weight in the government to be enjoyed by definite economic groups, and over the removal of the property qualifications early imposed on members of the House of Commons and on the voters at large. But the explanation of the absence of property qualifications from the Constitution is not difficult.

The members of the Convention were, in general, not opposed to property qualifications as such, either for officers or voters. "Several propositions," says Mr. S. H. Miller, "were made in the federal Convention in regard to property qualifications. A motion was carried instructing the committee to fix upon such qualifications for members of Congress. The committee could not agree upon the amount and reported in favor of leaving the matter to the legislature. Charles Pinckney objected to this plan as giving too much power to the first legislature. . . . [Oliver] Ellsworth objected to a property qualification on account of the difficulty of fixing the amount. If it was made high enough for the South, it would not be applicable to the Eastern States. [Benjamin] Franklin was the only speaker who opposed the proposition to require property on principle, saying that 'some of the greatest rogues he was ever acquainted with were the richest rogues.' A resolution was also carried to require a property qualification for the Presidency. Hence it was evident that the lack of all property requirements for office in the United States Constitution was not owing to any opposition of the convention to such qualifications per se."

Madison's Reasoning

Propositions to establish property restrictions were defeated, not because they were believed to be inherently opposed to the genius of American government, but for economic reasons—strange as it may seem. These economic reasons were clearly set forth by Madison in the debate over landed qualifications for legislators in July, when he showed, first, that slight property qualifications would not keep out the small farmers whose paper money schemes had been so disastrous to personalty [wealth generated by personal property, not land holdings]; and, secondly, that landed property qualifications would exclude from Congress the representatives of "those classes of citizens who were not landholders," *i.e.* the personalty interests. This was true, he thought, because the mercantile and manufacturing classes would hardly be willing to turn their personalty into sufficient quantities of landed property to make them eligible for a seat in Congress. . . .

Madison had no confidence in the effectiveness of the landed qualification and moved to strike it out, adding, "Landed possessions were no certain evidence of real wealth. Many enjoyed them to a great extent who were more in debt than they were worth. The unjust laws of the states had proceeded more from this class of men than any others. It had often happened that men who had acquired landed property on credit got into the Legislatures with a view of promoting an unjust protection against their Creditors. In the next place, if a small quantity of land should be made the standard, it would be no security; if a large one, it would exclude the proper representatives of those classes of Citizens who were not landholders." For these and other reasons he opposed the landed qualifications and suggested that property qualifications on the voters would be better.

The motion to strike out the "landed" qualification for legislators was carried by a vote of ten to one. . . .

No Fear of Change

Indeed, there was little risk to personalty in thus allowing the Constitution to go to the states for approval without any property qualifications on voters other than those which the state might see fit to impose. Only one branch of new government, the House of Representatives, was required to be elected by popular vote; and, in case popular choice of presidential electors might be established, a safeguard was secured by the indirect process. Two controlling bodies, the Senate and Supreme Court, were removed altogether from the possibility of popular election except by constitutional amendment. Finally, the conservative members of the Convention were doubly fortified in the fact that nearly all of the state constitutions then in force provided real or personal property qualifications for voters anyway, and radical democratic changes did not seem perilously near.

Women Had to Fight to Become Equal Citizens

Sharon Whitney

The unamended Constitution did not make provisions that would allow women to participate in making laws that affected them. Women did not have the right to vote. Furthermore, a single woman could engage in business, make contracts, and sue for payment of debt, but once she was married, her legal rights ended. She could not buy or sell anything without her husband's permission, she could not sign a contract, and she could not own a home. Author Sharon Whitney credits Lucretia Mott, Elizabeth Cady Stanton, and Susan B. Anthony for spearheading the movement to draw people's attention to the social, civil, and religious rights of women. Women would achieve initial victory with the ratification of the Nineteenth Amendment, which provided for women's suffrage. Whitney, a journalist, was based in Alaska at the time of writing, serving on the board of the Juneau Women's Resource Center. She has written and produced radio and television programs on public affairs, human rights, and ethnic studies.

In the years surrounding the birth of the American republic many women worked vigorously to overthrow British rule and to create a new democracy. One way to protest the British was to hit them in the pocketbook, and the Daughters of Liberty were among the first to organize boycotts on British products. . . .

In New England, women organized Anti-Tea Leagues to object to British taxes on their favorite drink. They boycotted tea and encouraged their families to drink herbal

Sharon Whitney, *The Equal Rights Amendment: The History of the Movement.* New York: Franklin Watts, 1984. Copyright © 1984 by Sharon Whitney. Reproduced by permission.

brews and even coffee. Female protests were the background for more famous events like the Boston Tea Party.

In a small town in North Carolina a group of women published the *Edenton Proclamation*. The women said it was both their right and a duty to stand up and resist the British. They did not want to be protected from the confrontation. And when the Revolution turned into actual armed rebellion, dozens of women in different colonies disguised themselves as men in order to pick up guns and join the fight. Thousands of others went to the battlefields as nurses, doctors, cooks, laundry workers, maids, and wagon tenders. . . .

The Prejudices of the Day

It was Abigail Adams, [John Adams's] wife, who made a case for women [taking part in the new government]. An accomplished money manager, farmer, and businesswoman, Abigail learned these jobs by being thrust into them. It was she who maintained home and property for ten years while John was away from home building a career as a revolutionary and statesman. In John's absence, Abigail wrote hundreds of letters to him. . . . In one, Abigail reminded John of the unfairness of an all-male power structure.

> By the way, in the new code of laws which I suppose it will be necessary for you to make, I desire you would *remember the ladies* and be more generous and favorable to them than your ancestors! Do not put such unlimited power in the hands of husbands. Remember all men would be tyrants if they could. If particular care and attention is not paid to the ladies, we are determined to foment a rebellion, and will not hold ourselves bound by any laws in which we have no voice or representation.

The American Revolution was a direct response to a people's being governed without their having a say in it: government without representation. Yet when Abigail Adams argued that women also deserve to decide their own affairs, John Adams treated Abigail's argument as a joke. In effect John said, In these days of revolution, everybody's getting uppity, and now it's women. But don't worry your little head about anything,

Abigail. Women really run the country, anyway. If we gave you legal rights, we men would be completely at your mercy. . . . When in 1789 the Constitution of the United States was adopted, Abigail Adams's urgent request to "remember the ladies" was forgotten. The document did not include women, or black men, or red men. When the Founding Fathers reasoned that government must have the consent of the governed, and talked about the natural equality of all human beings, they didn't mean to secure equal rights for all persons in the new federal government system. In this regard the great documents of American history—the Declaration of Independence, the Constitution, and the Bill of Rights—merely reflected the prejudices of the day. . . .

No Legal Identity

According to most American laws, all of a woman's possessions became the property of her husband in marriage. The moment the vows were spoken, a woman's land, clothing, jewelry, money—even any wages she might earn—became her husband's. A married woman could not buy or sell anything without her husband's permission. She could not sign a contract, sue, or be sued. If her husband died without leaving a will, a woman was entitled to no more than the *use* of one-third of his estate. The rest of the estate went to any male heirs, and when the woman died, so did her one-third share. It could be said that a married woman had no legal identity. She could not own her own home or control her own possessions. Legally, she did not even own her own clothes. No state granted a woman the right to vote or in any way to participate in the making of laws that affected her. In fact, she did not exist as a person in her own right. Her relationship to property made this clear. . . .

It was frustration and anger about the discrimination in property laws and other conditions affecting the lives of women that finally led to the organization of the first feminist protest in the United States. Historians date the beginning of the women's rights movement back to that convention in 1848 at Seneca Falls, New York. The women credited with drawing attention to "the social, civil, and religious condition and rights of woman" were Lucretia Mott of Philadelphia and Elizabeth Cady Stanton of Seneca Falls.

Working as volunteers in the antislavery movement, Mott and Stanton discovered how it was to work hard for a political cause and still be treated as inferior citizens. In 1840 the women went to the World Anti-Slavery Convention in London. There they had a large dose of what twentieth-century feminists would call "consciousness raising"—whereby women analyze the situation they are in and become aware of their real status in life. Mott was an official delegate, yet she was not allowed to speak at the convention. All the female delegates were silenced and even made to sit out of sight behind curtains in the balcony, rather than take part in the lively discussions on the floor of the convention. Sitting behind the curtain, feeling insulted and angry over being isolated from the action, Mott and Stanton talked about other kinds of sex discrimination they had seen. The list included no free choice for women in education or job opportunities. There was no economic independence possible under state and federal property laws. With women not having the right to vote, they had no representation at any level of government. It was their opinion that women as citizens had no more real political power than children.

Working for Women's Causes

From the antislavery convention, Mott and Stanton returned to the United States to work for women's causes. Mott tried to raise support for women's suffrage, believing that the vote was crucial for women's progress. In New York state, Stanton helped get the Married Woman's Property Rights Act passed by the state assembly, granting married women the right to own real estate. When the two old friends finally met in Seneca Falls to plan the historic convention, they were experienced organizers. With other local women they planned a convention program and wrote up a Declaration of Sentiments. It was in part modeled after the Declaration of Independence:

> We hold these truths to be self-evident: that all men *and women* are created equal; that they are endowed by their cre-

ator with certain inalienable rights, that among these are life, liberty, and the pursuit of happiness.

After the eloquent beginning, the Declaration parted from its model and went on to state clearly and without apology what grievances the women had against the American legal and social system.

He (man) has never permitted her (woman) to exercise her inalienable rights to the elective franchise.

He has compelled her to submit to laws in the formation of which she has no voice.

He has withheld from her the rights which are given to the most ignorant and degraded men. . . .

He has made her, if married, in the eye of the law civilly dead. . . .

He closes against her all the avenues to wealth and distinction, which he considers most honorable to himself. As a teacher of theology, medicine, or law, she is not known. . . .

The Declaration was hard-hitting, but it was approved by most of the three hundred women and men at the convention. . . .

Elizabeth Cady Stanton became a close friend of Susan B. Anthony, "the guiding mind" of the nineteenth-century women's movement. Stanton and Anthony organized more conferences to stir public opinion. They wrote speeches, drew up petitions, and worked into the dark hours of the night together, sometimes arguing furiously over differences in their approach to issues. Stanton's seven children thought it was a wonder that the two remained friends. "After an argument they never explained to each other, nor apologized, nor wept, nor went through a make-up period, as most people do." Their commitment to women's rights was much deeper than any differences in opinion.

In 1860, thanks to the "incessant prodding and petitioning of Susan B. Anthony and her women," the New York assembly amended the Married Woman's Property Rights Act.

The law now permitted a married woman to control both her own property and her wages; for the first time she became coguardian of her children; and if she were widowed she now received the same rights to her husband's property that, had she died first, he would have had to hers. This "liberating legislation" became the model for similar laws in several other states, although it had been a fight to get it passed in New York. . . .

Civil War Buries Women's Issues

But concern for women's causes was more or less buried in the 1860s as the Civil War divided the country over the issue of slavery. Feminists—many of whom had worked for the freeing of slaves as well as for women's rights—now circulated petitions supporting the Thirteenth Amendment, which would end slavery. Anthony worked for the American Anti-Slavery Society and organized the Women's National Loyal League to urge emancipation. At the end of the war the Thirteenth Amendment, freeing the slaves, was passed, but many women were painfully disappointed with the wording of a second reconstruction amendment, the Fourteenth. This introduced into the Constitution the word *male* for the first time, giving the vote to former slaves, but stating clearly that the vote was a male privilege only. This indifference to women was all that Stanton and Anthony needed to open up the National Woman's Suffrage Association to whoever would help women get the vote. They decided to accept the support of anyone—including radical trade unionists and persons like Victoria Woodhull, a free-love advocate who spent time in jail for her unpopular views. People who believed in women's rights but didn't want to be associated with characters like Woodhull, joined the more conservative American Woman's Suffrage Association, headed by Lucy Stone.

In the coming decades, feminists continued to put their case before the people, even when they risked social ridicule. Lucy Stone became a well-known orator in an age when it was thought disgraceful for a woman to be heard in public. When Stone talked about women's rights and the vote, she could expect to be called names and even hit with rotten vegetables. But Stone and others pushed past their fears and spoke up. The wave of feminism rolled on. Susan B. Anthony published a newspaper called *The Revolution*. Its motto was, "The true republic—men, their rights and nothing more; women, their rights and nothing less."

Birth of Equal Rights Amendment

It was in the 1870s that the name *Equal Rights Amendment* was first used. This was the name attached to the first bill introduced into Congress to give women the vote. In 1878 the bill was voted on and failed.

Reform movements grew in the last part of the nineteenth century and women worked hard on a variety of issues. The Women's Christian Temperance Union (WCTU) was organized to fight alcoholism and its devastating effects on dependent families. The WCTU was a strong force for decades. In other areas, college-educated women joined forces to press for female admissions to graduate schools and to the professions. They collected research that disproved popular myths that said that higher education ruins women's health and that working women lower the wages of working men. Some reformers lobbied for protective labor legislation for women and children, and to establish juvenile courts. Others ran settlement houses for poor immigrants. By 1900, in addition to all the volunteer labor freely given in such causes, one out of five women was also a wage earner outside the home. The first cries for equal pay and equal employment opportunity were beginning to be heard. But getting the vote was still the overriding concern.

While the federal Constitution, the highest law in the land, now insured the right to vote for most qualified men, the various states continued to create their own rules about whoever else was eligible. In the early part of the twentieth century, more than a dozen states yielded to pressure and gave women the vote. But a national movement was necessary to get women's suffrage in the country at large. To organize on a national level, strong leadership was needed. Two women, Carrie Chapman Catt and Alice Paul, came forward, each bringing different qualities and styles of leadership to the task.

Alice Paul, the founder of the National Women's Party, was a dynamic, radical feminist who had learned protest techniques from British suffragists. In 1913 Paul led eight thousand women—all dressed in white—in a march on the nation's capital to force Congress to pay attention to the need for women's suffrage. The suffrage march competed with

Remember the Ladies

Abigail Adams, one of the first women to bring up the concerns of women, writes to her revolutionary husband, John Adams, from Boston in 1776. John Adams, one of the leaders who took active part in fighting the British, was in Philadelphia to help in drafting the Declaration of Independence on the eve of the American Revolution. Anxious that John and his colleagues might exclude the women in their deliberations, Abigail writes with a warning.

I long to hear that you have declared an independency—and by the way, in the new Code of Laws which I suppose it will be necessary for you to make, I desire you would Remember the Ladies, and be more generous and favourable to them than your ancestors. Do not put such unlimited power into the hands of the Husbands. Remember, all Men would be tyrants if they could. If perticular care and attention is not paid to the Ladies, we are determined to foment a Rebelion, and will not hold ourselves bound by any Laws in which we have no voice, or Representation.

That your Sex are Naturally Tyrannical is Truth so thoroughly established as to admit no dispute, but such of you as wish to be happy willingly give up the harsh title of Master for the more tender and endearing one of Friend. Why, then, not put it out of the power of the vicious and the Lawless to use us with cruelty and indignity with impunity. Men of Sense in all Ages abhor those customs which treat us only as the vassals of your Sex. Regard us then as Beings placed by providence under your protection, and in immitation of the Supreem Being, make use of that power only for our happiness.

Andrew Carroll, ed., *Letters of a Nation*. New York: Broadway Books, 1997, pp. 58–60.

President Woodrow Wilson's inaugural parade, and while Washington police looked away, bystanders spat on the women and men slapped them and burned them with cigar butts until the march was broken up. Later, when President Wilson showed indifference to the women's cause, Paul organized strong political opposition to Wilson. In 1917 pickets began a six-month vigil at the White House. Suffragists carried signs calling Wilson a tyrant and pointing out that while he led the country into World War I to fight for democracy, there was still no democracy for women at home. . . .

Multi-Pronged Campaign

Carrie Chapman Catt used completely different strategies from Alice Paul. She organized extensive grass-roots support for suffrage, recognizing that changing the minds of enough people would make women's suffrage seem both possible and desirable. On the national level, she believed it was foolish to attack the men in power. She frequently visited the president and was able to persuade him to speak at a national suffrage convention. She convinced him he would be remembered in history for helping women get the vote. . . . President Wilson eventually agreed to use his influence in Congress to get a women's suffrage amendment passed. . . .

In the end it was a combination of events that tipped the scales for women's suffrage. In 1919 the Eighteenth Amendment was passed. Male voters, without the help of women, had approved Prohibition. When this happened, the liquor lobby and its stand against suffrage fell apart. At the same time, the public was recognizing the contributions made by women in World War I, and there was a broad base of support for women to get the vote. So the year after the war, Congress passed the Nineteenth Amendment—also called the "Susan B. Anthony Amendment"—by a narrow margin. (It was twice defeated in the Senate before President Wilson called a special session to pass it.) It was then ratified by the required number of states in time for women to vote in the 1920 elections.

Some feminists believed that getting the vote was the end of women's struggle for equality. But Alice Paul, who had studied law and the Constitution, believed that a battle for women's rights had been won but the war was not over. Getting the vote was only one step on the road to equal rights. There remained an overwhelming number of laws, ordinances, court decisions, and administrative rulings that discriminated against people on the basis of sex. Some universal law would have to be passed to correct all these lesser laws. Paul continued to lobby members of Congress to finish the reform that had been started with the Nineteenth Amendment. And through her efforts, the first Equal Rights Amendment aimed at correcting all the various federal, state, and local laws that discriminated on the basis of sex was introduced to Congress in 1923.

The 1923 ERA was worded this way: "Men and women shall have equal rights throughout the United States and every place to its jurisdiction." But the campaign for women's suffrage was over and there was no longer a mass movement to push for such legislation. Without being pressured, few members of Congress were concerned with another amendment related to the status of women.

In the same wording this ERA would be reintroduced in nineteen subsequent Congresses. Each time it would get just a little attention and each time it would fail to be approved and sent to the states for ratification.

A Strategy of Evasion and Silence on the Slavery Issue

Joseph J. Ellis

In the following essay, excerpted from the 2002 bestseller *Founding Brothers: The Revolutionary Generation*, author Joseph J. Ellis analyzes the viability of the positions of the southern and northern states on two petitions seeking the abolition of slavery, which were filed at the House of Representatives in 1790. Ellis observes that the petitions met resistance because the southern states argued that the fledging government could not afford the cost of freeing and relocating the slaves. The author questions these assumptions. He also examines the motives of many founding fathers who remained silent on the issue in order to ensure the ratification of the Constitution. Finally, Ellis asserts that the crushing of the petition by the House in 1790 closed any further opportunity to negotiate an end to slavery, leaving the nation susceptible to sectional tensions and civil war. Ellis is the Ford Foundation Professor of History at Mount Holyoke College. He is the author of several books, including *Passionate Sage: The Character and Legacy of John Adams* and *American Sphinx: The Character of Thomas Jefferson*, which won the 1997 National Book Award.

On February 11, 1790, two Quaker delegations, one from New York and the other from Philadelphia, presented petitions to the House calling for the federal government to put an immediate end to the African slave trade. This was considered an awkward interruption. . . . Representative James Jackson from Georgia was positively apoplectic that such a petition would even be considered by any serious delibera-

Joseph J. Ellis, *The Founding Brothers: The Revolutionary Generation*. New York: Alfred A. Knopf, 2000. Copyright © 2000 by Joseph J. Ellis. Reproduced by permission of Alfred A. Knopf, a division of Random House, Inc., and by permission of Faber & Faber Ltd.

tive body. The Quakers, he argued, were infamous innocents incessantly disposed to drip their precious purity like holy water over everyone else's sins. They were also highly questionable patriots, having sat out the recent war against British tyranny in deference to their cherished consciences. What standing could such dedicated pacifists enjoy among veterans of the Revolution. . . ?

On February 12 . . . another petition arrived in the House, this one from the Pennsylvania Abolition Society. . . . This new petition made two additional points calculated to exacerbate the fears of men like Jackson: First, it claimed that both slavery and the slave trade were incompatible with the values for which the American Revolution had been fought, and it even instructed the Congress on its political obligation to "devise means for removing this inconsistency from the Character of the American people." Second, it challenged the claim that the Constitution prohibited any legislation by the federal government against the slave trade for twenty years, suggesting instead that the "general welfare" clause of the Constitution empowered the Congress to take whatever action it deemed "necessary and proper" to eliminate the stigma of traffic in human beings and to "Countenance the Restoration of Liberty for all Negroes." Finally, to top it all off and heighten its dramatic appeal, the petition arrived under the signature of Benjamin Franklin, whose patriotic credentials and international reputation were beyond dispute. . . .

Waning Revolutionary Fervor

The passionate conviction that the Revolution was like a mighty wave fated to sweep slavery off the American landscape actually created false optimism and fostered a misguided sense of inevitability that rendered human action or agency superfluous. (Why bother with specific schemes when history would soon arrive with all the answers?) Moreover, one of the reasons the Revolution proved so successful as a movement for independence was that its immediate and short-run goals were primarily political: removing royal governors and rewriting state constitutions that, in fact, already embodied many of the republican features the Revolution now sanctioned. Removing slavery, however, was not like removing British officials or revising constitutions. In isolated pockets of New York and New Jersey, and more panoramically in the entire region south of the Potomac, slavery was woven into the fabric of American society in ways that defied appeals to logic or morality. It also enjoyed the protection of one of the Revolution's most potent legacies, the right to dispose of one's property without arbitrary interference from others, especially when the others resided far away or claimed the authority of some distant government. There were, to be sure, radical implications latent in the "principles of '76" capable of challenging privileged appeals to property rights, but the secret of their success lay in their latency—that is, the gradual and surreptitious ways they revealed their egalitarian implications over the course of the nineteenth century. If slavery's cancerous growth was to be arrested and the dangerous malignancy removed, it demanded immediate surgery. The radical implications of the revolutionary legacy were no help at all so long as they remained only implications. . . .

Two Sides Defend Positions

The most forceful expression of the northern position on the slave trade came, somewhat ironically, from Luther Martin of Maryland, who denounced it as "an odious bargain with sin" that was "inconsistent with the principles of the revolution and dishonorable to the American character." The fullest expression of the northern position on abolition itself came from Gouverneur Morris, a New Yorker, but serving as a delegate from Pennsylvania, who described slavery as "a curse" that actually retarded the economic development of the South and "the most prominent feature in the aristocratic countenance of the proposed Constitution." Morris even proposed a national tax to compensate the slave owners, claiming that he would much prefer "a tax for paying for all the Negroes in the United States than saddle posterity with such a Constitution." In the speeches of Martin and Morris one can discern the clearest articulation of the view, later embraced by the leadership of the abolitionist movement, that slavery was a nonnegotiable issue; that this was the appropriate and propitious moment to place it on the road to ultimate extinction; and that any compromise of that long-term goal was a "covenant with death."

The southern position might more accurately be described as "deep southern," since it did not include Virginia. Its major advocates were South Carolina and Georgia, and the chief burden for making the case in the Constitutional Convention fell almost entirely on the South Carolina delegation. The underlying assumption of this position was most openly acknowledged by Charles Cotesworth Pinckney of South Carolina—namely, that "South Carolina and Georgia cannot do without slaves." What those from the Deep South wanted was open-ended access to African imports to stock their plantations. They also wanted equivalently open access to western lands, meaning no federal restrictions on slavery in the territories. Finally, they wanted a specific provision in the Constitution that would prohibit any federal legislation restricting the property rights of slave owners—in effect, a constitutional assurance that slavery as it existed in the Deep South would be permitted to flourish. The clearest statement of their concerns came from Pierce Butler and John Rutledge of South Carolina. Butler explained that "the security the southern states want is that their Negroes may not be taken from them." Rutledge added that "the people of those States will never be such fools as to give up so important an interest." The implicit but unmistakably clear message underlying their position, which later became the trump card played by the next generation of South Carolinians in the Nullification Crisis in 1832, then more defiantly by the secessionists in 1861, was the threat to leave the union if the federal government ever attempted to implement a national emancipation policy.

The Constitution's Evasion of the Issue

Neither side got what it wanted at Philadelphia in 1787. The Constitution contained no provision that committed the newly created federal government to a policy of gradual emancipation, or in any clear sense placed slavery on the road to ultimate extinction. On the other hand, the Constitution contained no provisions that specifically sanctioned slavery as a permanent and protected institution south of the Potomac or anywhere else. The distinguishing feature of the document when it came to slavery was its evasiveness. It was neither a "contract with abolition" nor a "covenant with death," but rather a prudent exercise in ambiguity. The circumlocutions required to place a chronological limit on the slave trade or to count slaves as three-fifths of a person for purposes of representation in the House, all without ever using the forbidden word, capture the intentionally elusive ethos of the Constitution. The underlying reason for this calculated orchestration of noncommitment was obvious: Any clear resolution of the slavery question one way or the other rendered ratification of the Constitution virtually impossible. . . .

If one wished to generalize, then, about the situation that obtained in 1790 at the moment of the congressional debate over the Quaker petitions, the one thing that seemed clear concerning slavery was that nothing was clear at all. The initial debate in February had, in fact, accurately reflected the competing and incompatible presumptions about slavery's fate in the American republic, with one side emphasizing the promissory note to end it purportedly issued in 1776, the other side emphasizing the gentlemen's agreement to permit it reached in 1787, and a middle group, dominated by the Virginians, straddling both sides and counseling moderation lest the disagreement produce a sectional rupture. Both sides could plausibly claim a core strand of the revolutionary legacy as their own. And all parties to the debate seemed to believe that history, as well as the future, was on their side. . . .

The Unspoken

The ultimate legacy of the American Revolution on slavery was not an implicit compact that it be ended, or a gentlemen's agreement between the two sections that it be tolerated, but rather a calculated obviousness that it not be talked about at all. Slavery was the unmentionable family secret, or the proverbial elephant in the middle of the room. What was truly new in the proslavery argument was not really the ideas or attitudes expressed, but the expression itself.

There was yet another new ingredient about to enter the debate in 1790, though it too was more a matter of making visible and self-conscious what had previously hovered in some twilight zone of hazy and unspoken recognition. Perhaps the least controversial decision of the First Congress was passage of legislation that authorized the census of 1790, an essential item because accurate population figures were necessary to determine the size of state delegations in the House. . . .

At the most obvious level, these numbers confirmed with enhanced precision the self-evident reality that slavery was a sectional phenomenon that was dying out in the North and flourishing in the South. The exceptions were New York and New Jersey, which, not incidentally, remained the only northern states to resist the passage of gradual emancipation laws. In general, then, there was a direct and nearly perfect correlation between demography and ideology—that is, between the ratio of blacks to whites in the population and the reluctance to consider abolition. When the proslavery advocates of the Deep South unveiled their racial argument— What will happen between the races after emancipation?— the census of 1790 allowed one to predict the response with near precision. Wherever the black population reached a threshold level, slavery remained the preferred means of assuring the segregation of the races.

The only possible exception to this rule was the Upper South, to include the states of Maryland, Virginia, and North Carolina. There the slave populations were large, in Virginia very large indeed, but so were the populations of free blacks. From a strictly demographic perspective, Virginia was almost as vulnerable to the specter of postemancipation racial fears as South Carolina, but the growing size of the free-black population accurately reflected the presence of multiple schemes for gradual emancipation within the planter class and the willingness of at least a few slave owners to act in accord with the undeniable logic of the American Revolution. The sheer size of Virginia's total population, amplified by the daunting racial ratio, and then further amplified by the political prowess of its leadership at the national level, all combined to make it the key state. If any national plan for ending slavery was to succeed, Virginia needed to be in the vanguard.

Financially Unviable

Finally, the census of 1790 provided unmistakable evidence that those antislavery advocates who believed that the future was on their side were deluding themselves. For the total slave population was now approaching 700,000, up from about 500,000 in the year of the Declaration of Independence. Despite the temporary end of the slave trade during the war, and despite the steady march of abolition in the North, the slave population in the South was growing exponentially at the same exploding rate as the American population as a whole, which meant it was doubling every twenty to twenty-five years. Given the political realities that defined the parameters of any comprehensive program for emancipation—namely, compensation for owners, relocation of freed slaves, and implementation over a sufficient time span to permit economic and social adjustments—the larger the enslaved population grew, the more financially and politically impractical any emancipation scheme became. (One interpretation of the Deep South's argument of 1790 was that, at least from their perspective, the numbers already made such a decision impossible.) The census of 1790 revealed that the window of opportunity to end slavery was not opening, but closing. . . . In effect, the fading revolutionary ideology and the growing racial demography were converging to close off the political options. With all the advantage of hindsight, a persuasive case can be made that the Quaker petitioners were calling for decisive action against slavery at the last possible moment, if indeed there was such a moment, when gradual emancipation had any meaningful prospect for success.

The chief strength of the proslavery argument that emerged from the Deep South delegation in the congressional debate of March 16–17 was its relentless focus on the impractical dimensions of all plans for abolition. In effect, their arguments exposed the two major weaknesses of the antislavery side: First, those ardent ideologues who believed that slavery would die a natural death after the Revolution were naïve utopians proven wrong by the stubborn realities reflected in the census of 1790; second, the gradual emancipation plans implemented in the northern states were inoperative models for the nation as a whole, because the northern states contained only about 10 percent of the slave population; for all those states from Maryland south, the cost of compensation and the logistical difficulties attendant upon the relocation of the freed slaves were simply insurmountable; the numbers, quite simply, did not work. . . .

The Cost of Emancipation

All the plans for gradual emancipation assumed that slavery was a moral and economic problem that demanded a political solution. All also assumed that the solution needed to combine speed and slowness, meaning that the plan needed to be put into action quickly, before the burgeoning slave population rendered it irrelevant, but implemented gradually, so the costs could be absorbed more easily. Everyone advocating gradual emancipation also made two additional assumptions: First, that slave owners would be compensated, the funds coming from some combination of a national tax and from revenues generated by the sale of western lands; second, that the bulk of the freed slaves would be transported elsewhere, the Fairfax plan favoring an American colony in Africa on the British model of Sierra Leone, others proposing what might be called a "homelands" location in some unspecified region of the American West, and still others preferring a Caribbean destination. . . .

The projected cost of compensation was a potent argument against gradual emancipation, and the argument has been echoed in most scholarly treatments of the topic ever since. Estimates vary according to the anticipated price for each freed slave, which ranges between one hundred and two hundred dollars. The higher figure produces a total cost of about $140 million to emancipate the entire slave population in 1790. Since the federal budget that year was less than $7 million, the critics seem to be right when they conclude that the costs were not just daunting but also prohibitively expensive. The more one thought about such numbers, in effect, the more one realized that further thought was futile. There is some evidence that reasoning of just this sort was going on in Jefferson's mind at this time, changing him from an advocate of emancipation to a silent and fatalistic procrastinator.

The flaw in such reasoning, however, would have been obvious to any accountant or investment banker with a modicum of Hamiltonian wisdom. For the chief virtue of a gradual approach was to extend the cost of compensation over several decades so that the full bill never landed at one time or even on one generation. In the scheme that St. George Tucker proposed, for example, purchases and payments would continue for the next century, delaying the arrival of complete emancipation, to be sure, but significantly reducing the impact of the current costs by spreading them into the distant future. The salient question in 1790 was not the total cost but, with an amortized debt, the initial cost of capitalizing a national fund (often called a "sinking fund") for such purposes. The total debt inherited from the states and the federal government in 1790 was $77.1 million. A reasonable estimate of the additional costs for capitalizing a gradual emancipation program would have increased the national debt to about $125 million. While daunting, these numbers were not fiscally impossible. And they became more palatable when folded into a total debt package produced by a war for independence.

The Issue of Relocation

The other major impediment, equally daunting as the compensation problem at first glance, even more so upon reflection, was the relocation of the freed slaves. Historians have not studied the feasibility of this feature as much as the compensation issue, preferring instead to focus on the racial prejudices that required its inclusion, apparently fearing that their very analysis of the problem might be construed as an endorsement of the racist and segregationist attitudes prevalent at the time. Two unpalatable but undeniable historical facts must be faced: First, that no emancipation plan without this feature stood the slightest chance of success; and second, that no model of a genuinely biracial society existed anywhere in the world at that time, nor had any existed in recorded history.

The gradual emancipation schemes adopted in the northern states never needed to face this question squarely, because the black population there remained relatively small. South of the Potomac was a different matter altogether, since approximately 90 percent of the total black population resided there. Any national plan for gradual emancipation needed to transform this racial demography by relocating at least a significant portion of that population elsewhere. But where? The subsequent failure of the American Colonization Society and the combination of logistical and economic difficulties in the colony of Liberia exposed the impracticality of any mass migration back to Africa. The more viable option was transportation to the unsettled lands of the American West, along the lines of the Indian removal program adopted over forty years later. In 1790, however, despite the presumptive dreams of a continental empire, the Louisiana Purchase remained in the future and the vast trans-Mississippi region continued under Spanish ownership. While the creation of several black "homelands" or districts east of the Mississippi was not beyond contemplation—it was mentioned in private correspondence by a handful of antislavery advocates—it was just as difficult to envision then as it is difficult to digest now.

Fear of Federal Control

More than the question of compensation, then, the relocation problem was perilously close to insoluble. To top it all off, and add yet another layer of armament to the institution of slavery, any comprehensive plan for gradual emancipation could only be launched at the national level under the auspices of a federal government fully empowered to act on behalf of the long-term interests of the nation as a whole. Much like Hamilton's financial plan, any effective emancipation initiative conjured up fears of the much-dreaded "consolidation" that the Virginians, more than anyone else, found so threatening. (Indeed, for at least some of the Virginians, the deepest dread and greatest threat was that federal power would be used in precisely this way.) All the constitutional arguments against the excessive exercise of government power at the federal level then kicked in to make any effort to shape public policy more problematic.

Any attempt to take decisive action against slavery in 1790, given all these considerations, confronted great, perhaps impossible, odds. The prospects for success were remote at best. But then the prospects for victory against the most powerful army and navy in the world had been remote in 1776, as had the likelihood that thirteen separate and sovereign states would create a unified republican government in 1787. Great leadership had emerged in each previous instance to transform the improbable into the inevitable. Ending slavery was a challenge on the same gigantic scale as these earlier achievements. Whether even a heroic level of leadership stood any chance was uncertain because—and here was the cruelest irony—the effort to make the Revolution truly complete seemed diametrically opposed to remaining a united nation.

Benjamin Franklin Takes Up the Cause

One person stepped forward to answer the challenge, unquestionably the oldest, probably the wisest, member of the revolutionary generation. (In point of fact, he was actually a member of the preceding generation, the grandfather among the fathers.) Benjamin Franklin was very old and very ill in March of 1790. He had been a fixture on the American scene for so long and had outlived so many contemporaries . . . that reports of his imminent departure lacked credibility; his last act seemed destined to go on forever; he was an American immortal. . . .

In addition to seeming eternal, ubiquitous, protean, and endlessly quotable, Franklin had the most sophisticated sense of timing among all the prominent statesmen of the revolutionary era. . . .

This gift of exquisite timing continued until the very end.

In April of 1787, Franklin agreed to serve as the new president of the revitalized Pennsylvania Abolition Society and to make the antislavery cause the final project of his life. Almost sixty years earlier, in 1729, as a young printer in Philadelphia, he had begun publishing Quaker tracts against slavery and the slave trade. Throughout the middle years of the century and into the revolutionary era, he had lent his support to Anthony Benezet and other Quaker abolitionists, and he had spoken out on occasion against the claim that blacks were innately inferior or that racial categories were immutable. Nevertheless, while his antislavery credentials were clear, at one point Franklin had owned a few household slaves himself, and he had never made slavery a priority target or thrown the full weight of his enormous prestige against it.

Starting in 1787, that changed. At the Constitutional Convention he intended to introduce a proposal calling for the inclusion of a statement of principle, condemning both the slave trade and slavery, thereby making it unequivocally clear that the founding document of the new American nation committed the government to eventual emancipation. But several northern delegates, along with at least one officer in the Pennsylvania Abolition Society, persuaded him to withdraw his proposal on the grounds that it put the fragile Sectional Compromise, and therefore the Constitution itself, at risk. The petition submitted to the First Congress under his signature, then, was essentially the same proposal he had wanted to introduce at the Convention. With the Constitution now ratified and the new federal government safely in place, Franklin resumed his plea that slavery be declared incongruous with the revolutionary principles on which the nation was founded. The man with the impeccable timing was choosing to make the anomaly of slavery the last piece of advice he would offer his country. . . .

Franklin Becomes a Catalyst

The great weight of Franklin's unequivocal endorsement made itself felt in the congressional debate and emboldened several northern representatives to answer the proslavery arguments of the Deep South with newfound courage. Franklin's reputation served as the catalyst in an exchange, as Smith of South Carolina attempted to discredit his views by observing that "even great men have their senile moments." This prompted rebuttals from the Pennsylvania delegation: "Instead of proving him superannuated," Franklin's anti-slavery views showed that "the qualities of his soul, as well as those of his mind, are yet in their vigour"; only Franklin still seemed able "to speak the language of America, and to call us back to our first principles"; critics of Franklin, it was suggested, only exposed the absurdity of the proslavery position, revealing clearly that "an advocate for slavery, in its fullest latitude, at this stage of the world, and on the floor of the American Congress too, is *a phenomenon in politics.* . . . They defy, yea, mock all belief." William Scott of Pennsylvania, his blood also up in defense of Franklin, launched a frontal assault on the constitutional position of the Deep South: "I think it unsatisfactory to be told that there was an understanding between the northern and southern members, in the national convention"; the Constitution was a written document, not a series of unwritten understandings; where did it say anything at all about slavery? Who were these South Carolinians to instruct us on what Congress could and could not do? "I believe," concluded Scott, "if Congress should at any time be of the opinion that a state of slavery was a quality inadmissible in America, they would not be barred . . . of prohibiting this baneful quality." He went on for nearly an hour. It turned out to be the high-water mark of the antislavery effort in the House.

In retrospect, Franklin's final gesture at leadership served to solidify his historic reputation as a man who possessed in his bones a feeling for the future. But in the crucible of the moment, another quite plausible definition of leadership was circulating in the upper reaches of the government. . . . And the man who stepped forward to implement this version of leadership was James Madison.

Madison's "Enlightened Obfuscation"

If Franklin's great gift was an uncanny knack for levitating above political camps, operating at an altitude that permitted him to view the essential patterns and then comment with great irony and wit on the behavior of those groveling about on the ground, Madison's specialty was just the opposite. He lived in the details and worked his magic in the context of the moment, mobilizing those forces on the ground more adroitly and with a more deft tactical proficiency than anyone else. Taken together, he and Franklin would have made a nearly unbeatable team. But in 1790, they were on different sides.

Madison's position on slavery captured the essence of what might be called "the Virginia straddle." On the one hand, he found the blatantly proslavery arguments "shamefully indecent" and described his colleagues from South Carolina and Georgia as "intemperate beyond all example and even all decorum." Like most of his fellow Virginians, he wanted it known that he preferred an early end to the slave trade and regarded the institution of slavery "a deep-rooted abuse." He claimed to be genuinely embarrassed at the stridently proslavery rhetoric of the delegates from the Deep South and much more comfortable on the high moral ground of his northern friends.

But a fault line ran through the center of his thinking, a kind of mysterious region where ideas entered going in one direction but then emerged headed the opposite way. . . .

Any effort to locate the core of Madison's position on slavery, therefore, misses the point, which is that there was no core, except perhaps the conviction that the whole subject was taboo. Like Jefferson and the other members of the Virginia dynasty, he regarded any explicit defense of slavery in the mode of South Carolina and Georgia as a moral embarrassment. On the other hand, he regarded any effort to end slavery as premature, politically impractical, and counterproductive. As a result, he developed a way of talking and writing about the problem that might be described as "enlightened obfuscation.". . .

In the midst of this willful confusion, one Madisonian conviction shone through with his more characteristic clarity—namely, that slavery was an explosive topic that must be removed from the political agenda of the new nation. It was taboo because it exposed the inherent contradictions of the Virginia position, which was much closer to the position of the Deep South than Madison wished to acknowledge, even to himself. And it was taboo because, more than any other controversy, it possessed the political potential to destroy the union. Franklin wanted to put slavery onto the national agenda before it was too late to take decisive action in accord with the principles of the Revolution. Madison wanted to take slavery off the national agenda because he believed that decisive action would result in the destruction of either the Virginia planter class or the nation itself. . . .

The Madisonian influence revealed itself in the House debate of March 23 when the committee report came up for a vote.

Something had changed. Several northern members, who had previously sided with the Quaker petitioners, now expressed their regret that the matter had gotten out of hand. . . .

Ending the Debate

The goal of the Deep South, now with support from Massachusetts and Virginia, was to have the committee report tabled, again threatening that further debate would risk disunion, which William Loughton Smith likened to "heaving out an anchor to windward." Madison, however, wanted more than just an end to the debate. He wished to establish a precedent that clarified the constitutional ambiguities concerning the power of Congress over slavery. Therefore he welcomed the positive vote (29 to 25) to accept the committee report (details of which forthcoming), because he had resolved to use the occasion to establish a constitutional precedent. In the twentieth century, what Madison aimed to achieve would have required a decision by the Supreme Court. But in 1790 the Supreme Court was a woefully weak third branch of the federal government and the principle of judicial review had yet to be established. Madison wanted to use the vote on the committee report to create the equivalent of a landmark decision prohibiting any national scheme for emancipation.

It happened just as he desired. The committee report

consisted of seven resolutions that addressed this salient question: What are "the powers vested in Congress, under the present constitution, relating to the abolition of slavery"? The first resolution was designed to appease the Deep South by confirming that the Constitution prohibited any federal legislation limiting or ending the slave trade until 1808. The fourth was a gesture toward the northern interests, authorizing Congress to levy a tax on slave imports designed to discourage the practice without prohibiting it. The seventh was a nod toward the Quaker petitioners, declaring that "in all cases, to which the authority of Congress extends, they will exercise it for the humane objects of the memorialists, so far as they can be promoted on the principles of justice, humanity and good policy." But what did this deliberately vague promise mean? Specifically, how far did the authority of Congress extend? The implicit answer was in the second resolution. It read: "That Congress, by a fair construction of the Constitution, are equally restrained from interfering in the emancipation of slaves, who already are, or who may, within the period mentioned, be imported into, or born within any of the said States."

This was the key provision. In keeping with the compromise character of the committee report, it gave the Deep South the protection it had demanded by denying congressional authority to pass any gradual emancipation legislation. But it also set a chronological limit to this moratorium. The prohibition would only last "within the period mentioned"— that is, until 1808. In effect, the committee report extended the deadline for the consideration of emancipation to bring it into line with the deadline for the end of the slave trade. The Deep South would get its way, but only for a limited time. After 1808, Congress possessed the authority to do what it wished; then all constitutional restraints would lapse.

The Case Is Closed

At this decisive moment, the Madisonian magic worked its will. The House went into committee of the whole to revise the language of the report. In parliamentary maneuverings of this sort, Madison had no peer. The Virginia delegation had already received its marching orders to mobilize behind an amended version of the report. And several northern delegations, chiefly those of Massachusetts and New York, had clearly been lobbied to support the amendments, though no one will ever know what promises were made. In the end, the seven resolutions were reduced to three. The tax on the slave trade was dropped altogether, as was the seventh resolution, with its vague declaration of solidarity with the benevolent goals of the Quaker petitioners. The latter gesture had become irrelevant because of the new language of the second resolution. It now read: "The Congress have no authority to interfere in the emancipation of slaves, or in the treatment of them within any of the States; it remaining with the several States alone to provide any regulation therein, which humanity and true policy may require." During the debate over this language, Madison provided the clearest gloss on its fresh meaning by explaining that, instead of imposing an eighteen-year moratorium on congressional action against slavery, the amendment made it unconstitutional "to attempt to manumit them at any time." The final report passed by the House in effect placed any and all debate over slavery as it existed in the South out of bounds forever. What had begun as an initiative to put slavery on the road to extinction had been transformed into a decision to extinguish all federal plans for emancipation. By a vote of 29 to 25 the House agreed to transcribe this verdict in the permanent record. A relieved George Washington wrote home to a Virginia friend that "the slave business has at last [been] put to rest and will scarce awake."

As usual, Washington was right. Congress had moved gradual emancipation off its political agenda; its decision in the spring of 1790 became a precedent with the force of common law. In November of 1792, for example, when another Quaker petition came forward under the sponsorship of Fisher Ames, William Loughton Smith referred his colleague to the earlier debate of 1790. The House had then decided never again to allow itself to become inflamed by the "mere rant and rhapsody of a meddling fanatic" and had argued "that the subject would never be stirred again." The petition was withdrawn. Over forty years later, in 1833, Daniel Webster cited the same precedent: "My opinion of the powers of Congress on the subject of slaves and slavery is that Congress has no authority to interfere in the emancipation of slaves. This was so resolved by the House in 1790 . . . and I do not know of a different opinion since."

Whatever window of opportunity had existed to complete the one glaring piece of unfinished business in the revolutionary era was now closed. . . . Perhaps the window, if in fact there ever was a window, had already closed by 1790, so the debate and decision in the House merely sealed shut what the formidable combination of racial demography, Anglo-Saxon presumptions, and entrenched economic interests had already foreclosed.

List of Delegates

There were seventy-seven designated delegates by the states, but only fifty-five attended the sessions. Most of them were property owners; educated in the best schools; in possession of economic status, social class, and pedigree; and experienced in government. Words such as venerable, demigods, and elite of the elite, have been used to describe them. Some historians have questioned their motives, with a few claiming that as property owners, the men went to Philadelphia with only one goal—to protect their self-interest. Unperturbed by this minority view, most Americans agree that the framers were engaged in the honorable task of forging a strong and durable nation in fulfillment of the Revolution.

NEW HAMPSHIRE
John Langdon (signer of final document); John Pickering (did not attend); Nicholas Gilman (signer); Benjamin West (did not attend)

MASSACHUSETTS
Francis Dana (did not attend); Elbridge Gerry; Nathaniel Gorham (signer); Rufus King (signer); Caleb Strong

RHODE ISLAND
No appointment

CONNECTICUT
William Samuel Johnson (signer); Roger Sherman (signer); Oliver Ellsworth; Erastus Wolcott (elected but declined to serve)

NEW YORK
Robert Yates; Alexander Hamilton (signer); John Lansing, Junior

NEW JERSEY
David Brearley (signer); William Churchill Houston; William Paterson (signer); John Neilson (did not attend); William Liv-

ingston (signer); Abraham Clark (did not attend); Jonathan Dayton (signer)

PENNSYLVANIA
Thomas Mifflin (signer); Robert Morris (signer); George Clymer (signer); Jared Ingersoll (signer); Thomas Fitzsimons (signer); James Wilson (signer); Gouverneur Morris (signer); Benjamin Franklin (signer)

DELAWARE
George Read (signer); Gunning Bedford, Junior (signer); John Dickinson (signer); Richard Bassett (signer); Jacob Broom (signer)

MARYLAND
James McHenry (signer); Daniel of St. Thomas Jenifer (signer); Daniel Carroll (signer); John Francis Mercer; Luther Martin; Charles Carroll of Carrollton, Gabriel Duvall, Robert Hanson Harrison, Thomas Sim Lee, and Thomas Stone (elected but declined to serve)

VIRGINIA
George Washington (signer); Edmund Randolph; John Blair (signer); James Madison, Junior (signer); George Mason; George Wythe; James McClurg; Patrick Henry, Richard Henry Lee, and Thomas Nelson (elected but declined to serve)

NORTH CAROLINA
Alexander Martin; William Richardson Davie; Richard Dobbs Spaight (signer); William Blount (signer); Hugh Williamson (signer); Richard Caswell and Willie Jones (elected but declined to serve)

SOUTH CAROLINA
John Rutledge (signer); Charles Pinckney (signer); Charles Cotesworth Pinckney (signer); Pierce Butler (signer); Henry Laurens (did not attend)

GEORGIA
William Few (signer); Abraham Baldwin (signer); William Pierce; George Walton (did not attend); William Houstoun; Nathaniel Pendleton (did not attend)

The Constitution of the United States

The text of the 1787 draft-Constitution was submitted to the various states for ratification in September 1787. The first state to ratify was Delaware, followed by Pennsylvania and New Jersey, all in the month of December. In early 1788, Georgia ratified the Constitution, followed by Connecticut and Massachusetts. Maryland followed suit in April, South Carolina in May, New Hampshire and Virginia in June, and New York in July. By August 1788, eleven states had ratified the Constitution. North Carolina rejected the Constitution, while Rhode Island refused to even call a convention. Because of their refusal to support the Constitution, the two states were for some time called the "wayward sisters." North Carolina finally came around approving the Constitution in November 1789 in a second convention, with a list of recommended amendments. Rhode Island relented in May 1790, also with a list of recommended amendments.

We the People of the United States, in Order to form a more perfect Union, establish Justice, insure domestic Tranquility, provide for the common defence, promote the general Welfare, and secure the Blessings of Liberty to ourselves and our Posterity, do ordain and establish this Constitution for the United States of America.

Article I

Section 1. All legislative Powers herein granted shall be vested in a Congress of the United States, which shall consist of a Senate and House of Representatives.

Section 2. The House of Representatives shall be composed of Members chosen every second Year by the People of the several States, and the Electors in each State shall have the Qualifications requisite for Electors of the most numerous Branch of the State Legislature.

No Person shall be a Representative who shall not have attained to the age of twenty five Years, and been seven Years a Citizen of the United States, and who shall not, when elected, be an Inhabitant of that State in which he shall be chosen.

Representatives and direct Taxes shall be apportioned among the several States which may be included within this Union, according to their respective Numbers, which shall be determined by adding to the whole Number of free Persons, including those bound to Service for a Term of Years, and excluding Indians not taxed, three fifths of all other Persons. The actual Enumeration shall be made within three Years after the first Meeting of the Congress of the United States, and within every subsequent Term of ten Years, in such Manner as they shall by Law direct. The Number of Representatives shall not exceed one for every thirty Thousand, but each State shall have at Least one Representative; and until such enumeration shall be made, the State of New Hampshire shall be entitled to chuse three, Massachusetts eight, Rhode-Island and Providence Plantations one, Connecticut five, New-York six, New Jersey four, Pennsylvania eight, Delaware one, Maryland six, Virginia ten, North Carolina five, South Carolina five, and Georgia three.

When vacancies happen in the Representation from any State, the Executive Authority thereof shall issue Writs of Election to fill such Vacancies.

The House of Representatives shall chuse their Speaker and other Officers; and shall have the sole Power of Impeachment.

Section 3. The Senate of the United States shall be composed of two Senators from each State, chosen by the Legislature thereof, for six Years; and each Senator shall have one Vote.

Immediately after they shall be assembled in Consequence of the first Election, they shall be divided as equally as may be into three Classes. The Seats of the Senators of the first Class shall be vacated at the Expiration of the second Year, of the second Class at the Expiration of the fourth Year, and the third Class at the Expiration of the sixth Year, so that one third may be chosen every second Year; and if Vacancies happen by Resignation, or otherwise, during the

Recess of the Legislature of any State, the Executive thereof may make temporary Appointments until the next Meeting of the Legislature, which shall then fill such Vacancies.

No Person shall be a Senator who shall not have attained to the Age of thirty Years, and been nine Years a Citizen of the United States and who shall not, when elected, be an Inhabitant of that State for which he shall be chosen.

The Vice President of the United States shall be President of the Senate, but shall have no Vote, unless they be equally divided.

The Senate shall chuse their other Officers, and also a President pro tempore, in the Absence of the Vice President, or when he shall exercise the Office of President of the United States.

The Senate shall have the sole Power to try all Impeachments. When sitting for that Purpose, they shall be on Oath or Affirmation. When the President of the United States is tried, the Chief Justice shall preside: And no Person shall be convicted without the Concurrence of two thirds of the Members present.

Judgment in Cases of Impeachment shall not extend further than to removal from Office, and disqualification to hold and enjoy any Office of Honor, Trust or Profit under the United States: but the Party convicted shall nevertheless be liable and subject to Indictment, Trial, Judgment and Punishment, according to Law.

Section 4. The Times, Places and Manner of holding Elections for Senators and Representatives, shall be prescribed in each State by the Legislature thereof; but the Congress may at any time by Law make or alter such Regulations, except as to the Places of chusing Senators.

The Congress shall assemble at least once in every Year, and such Meeting shall be on the first Monday in December, unless they shall by Law appoint a different Day.

Section 5. Each House shall be the Judge of the Elections, Returns and Qualifications of its own Members, and a Majority of each shall constitute a Quorum to do Business; but a smaller Number may adjourn from day to day, and may be authorized to compel the Attendance of absent Members, in such Manner, and under such Penalties as each House may provide.

Each House may determine the Rules of its Proceedings, punish its Members for disorderly Behaviour, and, with the Concurrence of two thirds, expel a Member.

Each House, shall keep a Journal of its Proceedings, and from time to time publish the same, excepting such Parts as may in their Judgment require Secrecy; and the Yeas and Nays of the Members of either House on any question shall, at the Desire of one fifth of those Present, be entered on the Journal.

Neither House, during the Session of Congress, shall, without the Consent of the other, adjourn for more than three days, nor to any other Place than that in which the two Houses shall be sitting.

Section 6. The Senators and Representatives shall receive a Compensation for their Services, to be ascertained by Law, and paid out of the Treasury of the United States. They shall in all Cases, except Treason, Felony and Breach of the Peace, be privileged from Arrest during their Attendance at the Session of their respective Houses, and in going to and returning from the same; and for any Speech or Debate in either House, they shall not be questioned in any other Place.

No Senator or Representative shall, during the Time for which he was elected, be appointed to any civil Office under the Authority of the United States, which shall have been created, or the Emoluments whereof shall have been encreased during such time: and no Person holding any Office under the United States, shall be a Member of either House during his Continuance in Office.

Section 7. All Bills for raising Revenue shall originate in the House of Representatives: but the Senate may propose or concur with Amendments as on other Bills.

Every Bill which shall have passed the House of Representatives and the Senate, shall, before it become a Law, be presented to the President of the United States; if he approve he shall sign it, but if not he shall return it, with his Objections to that House in which it shall have originated, who shall enter the Objections at large on their Journal, and proceed to reconsider it. If after such Reconsideration two thirds of that House shall agree to pass the Bill, it shall be sent, together with the Objections, to the other House, by which it shall likewise be reconsidered, and if approved by two thirds of that House, it shall become a Law. But in all such Cases the Votes of both Houses shall be determined by Yeas and Nays, and the Names of the Persons voting for and against the Bill shall be entered on the Journal of each House respectively. If any Bill shall not be returned by the President within ten Days (Sundays excepted) after it shall have been presented to him, the Same shall be a Law, in like Manner as if he had signed it, unless the Congress by their Adjournment prevent its Return, in which Case it shall not be a Law.

Every Order, Resolution, or Vote to which the Concurrence of the Senate and House of Representatives may be necessary (except on a question of Adjournment) shall be presented to the President of the United States: and before the Same shall take effect, shall be approved by him, or being disapproved by him, shall be repassed by two thirds of the Senate and House of Representatives, according to the Rules and Limitations prescribed in the Case of a Bill.

Section 8. The Congress shall have Power to lay and collect Taxes, Duties, Imposts and Excises, to pay the Debts and provide for the common Defence and general Welfare of the United States; but all Duties, Imposts and Excises shall be uniform throughout the United States;

To borrow Money on the credit of the United States;

To regulate Commerce with foreign Nations, and among the several States, and with the Indian Tribes;

To establish an uniform Rule of Naturalization, and uniform Laws on the subject of Bankruptcies throughout the United States;

To coin Money, regulate the Value thereof, and of foreign Coin, and fix the Standard of Weights and Measures;

To provide for the Punishment of counterfeiting the Securities and current Coin of the United States;

To establish Post Offices and post Roads;

To promote the Progress of Science and useful Arts, by securing for limited Times to Authors and Inventors the exclusive Right to their respective Writings and Discoveries;

To constitute Tribunals inferior to the supreme Court;

To define and punish Piracies and Felonies committed on the high Seas, and Offences against the Law of Nations;

To declare War, grant Letters of Marque and Reprisal, and make Rules concerning Captures on Land and Water;

To raise and support Armies, but no Appropriation of Money to that Use shall be for a longer Term than two Years;

To provide and maintain a Navy;

To make Rules for the Government and Regulation of the land and naval Forces;

To provide for calling forth the Militia to execute the Laws of the Union, suppress Insurrections and repel Invasions;

To provide for organizing, arming, and disciplining, the Militia, and for governing such Part of them as may be employed in the Service of the United States, reserving to the States respectively, the Appointment of the Officers, and the Authority of training the Militia according to the discipline prescribed by Congress;

To exercise exclusive Legislation in all Cases whatsoever, over such District (not exceeding ten Miles square) as may, by Cession of particular States, and the Acceptance of Congress, become the Seat of the Government of the United States, and to exercise like Authority over all Places purchased by the Consent of the Legislature of the State in which the Same shall be, for the Erection of Forts, Magazines, Arsenals, dock-Yards, and other needful Buildings;—And

To make all Laws which shall be necessary and proper for carrying into Execution the foregoing Powers, and all other Powers vested by this Constitution in the Government of the United States, or in any Department or Officer thereof.

Section 9. The Migration or Importation of such Persons as any of the States now existing shall think proper to admit, shall not be prohibited by the Congress prior to the Year one thousand eight hundred and eight, but a Tax or duty may be imposed on such Importation, not exceeding ten dollars for each Person.

The Privilege of the Writ of Habeas Corpus shall not be suspended, unless when in Cases of Rebellion or Invasion the public Safety may require it.

No Bill of Attainder or ex post facto Law shall be passed.

No Capitation, or other direct, Tax shall be laid, unless in Proportion to the Census or Enumeration herein before directed to be taken.

No Tax or Duty shall be laid on Articles exported from any State.

No Preference shall be given by any Regulation of Commerce or Revenue to the Ports of one State over those of another: nor shall Vessels bound to, or from, one State, be obliged to enter, clear or pay Duties in another.

No Money shall be drawn from the Treasury, but in Consequence of Appropriations made by Law; and a regular Statement and Account of Receipts and Expenditures of all public Money shall be published from time to time.

No Title of Nobility shall be granted by the United States: And no Person holding any Office of Profit or Trust under them, shall, without the Consent of the Congress, accept of any present, Emolument, Office, or Title, of any kind whatever, from any King, Prince, or foreign State.

Section 10. No State shall enter into any Treaty, Alliance, or Confederation; grant Letters of Marque and Reprisal; coin Money; emit Bills of Credit; make any Thing but gold and silver Coin a Tender in Payment of Debts; pass any Bill of Attainder, ex post facto Law, or Law impairing the Obligation of Contracts, or grant any Title of Nobility.

No State shall, without the Consent of the Congress, lay any Imposts or Duties on Imports or Exports, except what may be absolutely necessary for executing its inspection Laws: and the net Produce of all Duties and Imposts, laid by any State on Imports or Exports, shall be for the Use of the Treasury of the United States; and all such Laws shall be subject to the Revision and Controul of the Congress.

No State shall, without the Consent of Congress, lay any Duty of Tonnage, keep Troops, or Ships of War in time of Peace, enter into any Agreement or Compact with another State, or with a foreign Power, or engage in War, unless actually invaded, or in such imminent Danger as will not admit of delay.

Article II

Section 1. The executive Power shall be vested in a President of the United States of America. He shall hold his Office during the Term of four Years, and, together with the Vice President, chosen for the same Term, be elected, as follows:

Each State shall appoint, in such Manner as the Legislature thereof may direct, a Number of Electors, equal to the whole Number of Senators and Representatives to which the State may be entitled in the Congress: but no Senator or Representative, or Person holding an Office of Trust or Profit under the United States, shall be appointed an Elector.

The Electors shall meet in their respective States, and vote by Ballot for two Persons, of whom one at least shall not be an Inhabitant of the same State with themselves. And they shall make a List of all the Persons voted for, and of the Number of Votes for each; which List they shall sign and certify, and transmit sealed to the Seat of the Government of the United States, directed to the President of the Senate. The President of the Senate shall, in the Presence of the Senate and House of Representatives, open all the Certificates, and the Votes shall then be counted. The Person having the greatest Number of Votes shall be the President, if such Number be a Majority of the whole Number of Electors appointed; and if there be more than one who have such Majority, and have an equal Number of Votes, then the House of Representatives shall immediately chuse by Ballot one of them for President; and if no Person have a Majority, then from the five highest on the List the said House shall in like Manner chuse the President. But in chusing the President, the Votes shall be taken by States, the Representation from each State having one Vote; A quorum for this Purpose shall consist of a Member or Members from two thirds of the States, and a Majority of all the States shall be necessary to a Choice. In every Case, after the Choice of the President, the Person having the greatest Number of Votes of the Electors shall be the Vice President. But if there should remain two or more who have equal Votes, the Senate shall chuse from them by Ballot the Vice President.

The Congress may determine the Time of chusing the

Electors, and the Day on which they shall give their Votes; which Day shall be the same throughout the United States.

No Person except a natural born Citizen, or a Citizen of the United States, at the time of the Adoption of this Constitution, shall be eligible to the Office of President; neither shall any Person be eligible to that Office who shall not have attained to the Age of thirty five Years, and been fourteen Years a Resident within the United States.

In Case of the Removal of the President from Office, or of his Death, Resignation, or Inability to discharge the Powers and Duties of the said Office, the Same shall devolve on the Vice President, and the Congress may by Law provide for the Case of Removal, Death, Resignation or Inability, both of the President and Vice President, declaring what Officer shall then act as President, and such Officer shall act accordingly, until the Disability be removed, or a President shall be elected.

The President shall, at stated Times, receive for his Services, a Compensation, which shall neither be encreased nor diminished during the Period for which he shall have been elected, and he shall not receive within that Period any other Emolument from the United States, or any of them.

Before he enter on the Execution of his Office, he shall take the following Oath or Affirmation:—"I do solemnly swear (or affirm) that I will faithfully execute the Office of President of the United States, and will to the best of my Ability, preserve, protect and defend the Constitution of the United States."

Section 2. The President shall be Commander in Chief of the Army and Navy of the United States, and of the Militia of the several States, when called into the actual Service of the United States; he may require the Opinion, in writing, of the principal Officer in each of the executive Departments, upon any Subject relating to the Duties of their respective Offices, and he shall have Power to grant Reprieves and Pardons for Offences against the United States, except in Cases of Impeachment.

He shall have Power, by and with the Advice and Consent of the Senate, to make Treaties, provided two thirds of the

Senators present concur; and he shall nominate, and by and with the Advice and Consent of the Senate, shall appoint Ambassadors, other public Ministers and Consuls, Judges of the supreme Court, and all other Officers of the United States, whose Appointments are not herein otherwise provided for, and which shall be established by Law: but the Congress may by Law vest the Appointment of such inferior Officers, as they think proper, in the President alone, in the Courts of Law, or in the Heads of Departments.

The President shall have Power to fill up all Vacancies that may happen during the Recess of the Senate, by granting Commissions which shall expire at the End of their next Session.

Section 3. He shall from time to time give to the Congress Information of the State of the Union, and recommend to their Consideration such Measures as he shall judge necessary and expedient; he may, on extraordinary Occasions, convene both Houses, or either of them, and in Case of Disagreement between them, with Respect to the Time of Adjournment, he may adjourn them to such Time as he shall think proper; he shall receive Ambassadors and other public Ministers; he shall take Care that the Laws be faithfully executed, and shall Commission all the Officers of the United States.

Section 4. The President, Vice President and all civil Officers of the United States, shall be removed from Office on Impeachment for, and Conviction of, Treason, Bribery, or other high Crimes and Misdemeanors.

Article III

Section 1. The judicial Power of the United States, shall be vested in one supreme Court, and in such inferior Courts as the Congress may from time to time ordain and establish. The Judges, both of the supreme and inferior Courts, shall hold their Offices during good Behaviour, and shall, at stated Times, receive for their Services, a Compensation, which shall not be diminished during their Continuance in Office.

Section 2. The judicial Power shall extend to all Cases, in Law and Equity, arising under this Constitution, the Laws of the United States, and Treaties made, or which shall be made, under their Authority;—to all Cases affecting Ambassadors, other public Ministers and Consuls;—to all Cases of admiralty and maritime Jurisdiction;—to Controversies to which the United States shall be a Party;—to Controversies between two or more States;—between a State and Citizens of another State;—between Citizens of different States;—between Citizens of the same State claiming Lands under Grants of different States, and between a State, or the Citizens thereof, and foreign States, Citizens or Subjects.

In all Cases affecting Ambassadors, other public Ministers and Consuls, and those in which a State shall be Party, the supreme Court shall have original Jurisdiction. In all the other Cases before mentioned, the supreme Court shall have appellate Jurisdiction, both as to Law and Fact, with such Exceptions, and under such Regulations as the Congress shall make.

The Trial of all Crimes, except in Cases of Impeachment, shall be by Jury; and such Trial shall be held in the State where the said Crimes shall have been committed; but when not committed within any State, the Trial shall be at such Place or Places the Congress may by Law have directed.

Section 3. Treason against the United States, shall consist only in levying War against them, or in adhering to their Enemies, giving them Aid and Comfort. No Person shall be convicted of Treason unless on the Testimony of two Witnesses to the same overt Act, or on Confession in open Court.

The Congress shall have Power to declare the Punishment of Treason, but no Attainder of Treason shall work Corruption of Blood, or Forfeiture except during the Life of the Person attainted.

Article IV

Section 1. Full Faith and Credit shall be given in each State to the public Acts, Records, and judicial Proceedings of every other State. And the Congress may by general Laws prescribe the Manner in which such Acts, Records, and Proceedings shall be proved, and the Effect thereof.

Section 2. The Citizens of each State shall be entitled to all Privileges and Immunities of Citizens in the several States.

A Person charged in any State with Treason, Felony, or other Crime, who shall flee from Justice, and be found in another State, shall on Demand of the executive Authority of the State from which he fled, be delivered up, to be removed to the State having Jurisdiction of the Crime.

No Person held to Service or Labour in one State, under the Laws thereof escaping into another, shall, in Consequence of any Law or Regulation therein, be discharged from such Service or Labour, but shall be delivered up on Claim of the Party to whom such Service or Labour may be due.

Section 3. New States may be admitted by the Congress into this Union; but no new States shall be formed or erected within the Jurisdiction of any other State; nor any State be formed by the Junction of two or more States, or Parts of States, without the Consent of the Legislatures of the States concerned as well as of the Congress.

The Congress shall have Power to dispose of and make all needful Rules and Regulations respecting the Territory or other Property belonging to the United States; and nothing in this Constitution shall be so construed as to Prejudice any Claims of the United States, or of any particular State.

Section 4. The United States shall guarantee to every State in this Union a Republican Form of Government, and shall protect each of them against Invasion; and on Application of the Legislature, or of the Executive (when the Legislature cannot be convened) against domestic Violence.

Article V

The Congress, whenever two thirds of both Houses shall deem it necessary, shall propose Amendments to this Constitution, or, on the Application of the Legislatures of two thirds of the several States, shall call a Convention for proposing Amendments, which, in either Case, shall be valid to all Intents and Purposes, as Part of this Constitution, when ratified by the Legislatures of three fourths of the several States, or by Conventions in three fourths thereof, as the one or the other Mode of Ratification may be proposed by the Congress; Provided that no Amendment which may be made prior to the Year One thousand eight hundred and eight shall in any Manner affect the first and fourth Clauses in the Ninth Section of the first Article; and that no State, without its Consent, shall be deprived of its equal Suffrage in the Senate.

Article VI

All Debts contracted and Engagements entered into, before the Adoption of this Constitution, shall be as valid against the United States under this Constitution, as under the Confederation.

This Constitution, and the Laws of the United States which shall be made in Pursuance thereof; and all Treaties made, or which shall be made, under the Authority of the United States, shall be the supreme Law of the Land; and the Judges in every State shall be bound thereby, any Thing in the Constitution or Laws of any State to the Contrary notwithstanding.

The Senators and Representatives before mentioned, and the Members of the several State Legislatures, and all executive and judicial Officers, both of the United States and of the several States, shall be bound by Oath or Affirmation, to support this Constitution; but no religious Test shall ever be required as a Qualification to any Office or public Trust under the United States.

Article VII

The Ratification of the Conventions of nine States, shall be sufficient for the Establishment of this Constitution between the States so ratifying the Same.

Done in Convention by the Unanimous Consent of the States present the Seventeenth Day of September in the Year of our Lord one thousand seven hundred and Eighty seven and of the Independence of the United States of America the Twelfth.

Note: This is the 1787 unamended Constitution of the United States. Between 1791 and 1992, twenty-seven amendments were added to the Constitution.

Appendix of Documents

Document 1: Articles of Confederation

In September 1774, delegates from the colonies gathered in Philadelphia during the First Continental Congress to adopt a series of petitions to pressure the British Crown to act on the colonies' grievances. After these efforts failed, the colonies convened the Second Continental Congress in 1775 that created an army and sought help from European nations. Before the First Congress and Second Congress, the colonies had no collective body to act on their behalf. Each had its own domestic form of government and its line of connection to the British Crown. During the Second Congress in 1775, the colonies organized a committee that would draft a set of rules for a central government. In March 1781, the states ratified the Articles of Confederation which defined the powers of such a government. This government, which ruled the thirteen states as a confederation, lasted until 1789.

Whereas the Delegates of the United States of America in Congress assembled did on the fifteenth day of November in the Year of our Lord One Thousand Seven Hundred and Seventyseven, and in the Second Year of the Independence of America agree to certain articles of Confederation and perpetual Union between the States of Newhampshire, Massachusetts-bay, Rhodeisland, and Providence Plantations, Connecticut, New York, New Jersey, Pennsylvania, Delaware, Maryland, Virginia, North-Carolina, South-Carolina and Georgia in the Words following. . . .

ARTICLE I. The stile of this confederacy shall be "The United States of America."

ARTICLE II. Each State retains its sovereignty, freedom and independence, and every power, jurisdiction and right, which is not by this confederation expressly delegated to the United States, in Congress assembled.

ARTICLE III. The said States hereby severally enter into a firm league of friendship with each other, against all force offered to, of attacks made upon them, or any of them, on account of religion, sovereignty, trade, or any other pretence whatever.

ARTICLE IV. The better to secure and perpetuate mutual friendship and intercourse among people of the different States in this Union, the free inhabitants of each of these States, paupers, vagabonds and fugitives from justice excepted, shall be entitled to all privileges and immunities of free citizens in the several States; and the people of each State shall have free ingress and regress to and from any other State, and shall enjoy therein all the privileges of trade and commerce, subject to the same duties, impositions and restrictions as the inhabitants thereof respectively, provided that such restrictions shall not extend so far as to prevent the removal of property imported into any State, to any other State of which the owner is an inhabitant; provided also that no imposition, duties or restriction shall be laid by any State, on the property of the United States, or either of them. . . .

ARTICLE V. For the more convenient management of the general interests of the United States, delegates shall be annually appointed in such manner as the legislature of each State shall direct, to meet in Congress on the first Monday in November, in every year, with a power reserved to each State, to recall its delegates, or any of them, at any time within the year, and to send others in their stead, for the remainder of the year.

No State shall be represented in Congress by less than two, not by more than seven members; and no person shall be capable of being a delegate for more than three years in any term of six years; nor shall any person, being a delegate, be capable of holding any office under the United States, for which he, or another for his benefit receives any salary, fees or emolument of any kind. . . .

In determining questions in the United States, in Congress assembled, each State shall have one vote.

Freedom of speech and debate in Congress shall not be impeached or questioned in any court, or place out of Congress, and the members of Congress shall be protected in their persons from arrests and imprisonments, during the time of their going to and from, any attendance on Congress, except for treason, felony, or breach of the peace.

ARTICLE VI. No State without the consent of the United States in Congress assembled, shall send any embassy to, or receive any embassy from, or enter into any conference, agreement, alliance or treaty with any king prince or state. . . .

No two or more States shall enter into any treaty, confederation or alliance whatever between them, without the consent of the United States in Congress assembled, specifying accurately the purposes for which the same is to be entered into, and how long it shall continue.

No State shall lay any imposts or duties, which may interfere with any stipulations in treaties, entered into by the United States in Congress assembled, with any king, prince or state, in pursuance of any treaties already proposed by Congress, to the courts of France and Spain.

No vessels of war shall be kept up in time of peace by any State, except such number only, as shall be deemed necessary by the United States in Congress assembled, for the defence of such State, or its trade: nor shall any body of forces be kept up by any State, in time of peace, except such number only, as in the judgment of the United States, in Congress assembled, shall be deemed requisite to garrison the forts necessary for the defence of such State; but every State shall always keep up a well regulated and disciplined militia, sufficiently armed and accoutered, and shall provide and constantly have ready for use, in public stores, a due number of field pieces and tents, and a proper quantity of arms, ammunition and camp equipage. . . .

ARTICLE VIII. All charges of war, and all other expenses that shall be incurred for the common defence or general welfare, and allowed by the United States in Congress assembled, shall be defrayed out of a common treasury, which shall be supplied by the several States, in proportion to the value of all land within each State, granted to or surveyed for any person, as such land and the buildings and improvements thereon shall be estimated according to such mode as the United States in Congress assembled, shall from time to time direct and appoint.

The taxes for paying that proportion shall be laid and levied by the authority and direction of the Legislature of the several States within the time agreed upon by the United States in Congress assembled.

ARTICLE IX. The United States in Congress assembled, shall have the sole and exclusive right and power of determining on peace and war, . . . of sending and receiving ambassador, [or] entering into treaties and alliances. . . .

The United States in Congress assembled shall also be the last resort on appeal in all disputes and differences now subsisting or that hereafter may arise between two or more States concerning boundary, jurisdiction or any other cause whatever: which authority shall always be exercised in the manner following. Whenever the legislative or executive authority or lawful agent of any State in controversy with another shall present a petition to Congress, stating the matter in question and praying for a hearing, notice thereof shall be given by order of Congress to the legislative or executive authority of the other State in controversy, and a day assigned for the appearance of the parties by their lawful agents, who shall then be directed to appoint by joint consent, commissioners or judges to constitute a court for hearing and determining the matter in question. . . . And the judgment and sentence of the court to be appointed, in the manner before prescribed, shall be final and conclusive; and if any of the parties shall refuse to submit to the authority of such court, or to appear or defend their claim or cause, the court shall nevertheless proceed to pronounce sentence, or judgment, which shall in like manner be final and decisive, the judgment or sentence and other proceedings being in either case transmitted to Congress, and lodged among the acts of Congress for the security of the parties concerned: provided that every commissioner, before he sits in judgment, shall take an oath to be administered by one of the judges of the supreme or superior court of the State where the cause shall be tried, "well and truly to hear and determine the matter in question, according to the best of his judgment, without favour, affection or hope of reward:" provided also that no State shall be deprived of territory for the benefit of the United States. . . .

The United States in Congress assembled shall also have the sole and exclusive right and power of regulating the alloy and value of coin struck by their own authority, or by that of the respective States—fixing the standard of weights and measure throughout the United States—regulating the trade and managing all affairs with the Indians, not members of any of the States, provided that the legislative right of any State within its own limits be not infringed or violated—establishing and regulating post-offices from one State to another, throughout all the United States, and exacting such postage on the papers passing thro' the same as may be requisite to defray the expenses of the said office—appointing all officers of the land forces, in the service of the United States, excepting regimental officers—appointing all the officers of the naval forces, and commissioning all officers whatever in the service of the United States—making rules for the government and regulation of the said land and naval forces, and directing their operations.

The United States in Congress assembled shall have authority to appoint a committee, to sit in the recess of Congress, to be denominated "a Committee of the States," and to consist of one delegate from each State; and to appoint such other committees and civil officers as may be necessary for managing the general affairs of the United States under their direction—to appoint one of their number to preside, provided that no person be allowed to serve in the office of president more than one year in any term of three years; to ascertain the necessary sums of money to be raised for the service of the United States, and to appropriate and apply the same for defraying the public expenses—to borrow money, or emit bills on the credit of the United States, transmitting every half year to the respective States an account of the sums of money so borrowed or emitted,—to build and equip a navy—to agree upon the number of land forces, and to make requisitions from each State for its quota, in proportion to the number of white inhabitants in such State; which requisition shall be binding, and thereupon the Legislature of each State shall appoint the regimental officers, raise the men and cloath, arm and equip them in a soldier like manner, at the expense of the United States; and the officers and men so cloathed, armed and equipped shall march to the place appointed, and within the time agreed on by the United States in Congress assembled. . . .

The United States in Congress assembled shall never engage in a war, nor grant letters of marque and reprisal in time of peace, nor enter into any treaties or alliances, nor coin money, nor regulate the value thereof, nor ascertain the sums and expenses necessary for the defence and welfare of the United States, or any of them, nor emit bills, nor borrow money on the credit of the United States, nor appropriate money, nor agree upon the number of vessels of war, to be built or purchased, or the number of land or sea forces to be raised, nor appoint a commander in chief of the army or navy, unless nine States assent to the same: nor shall a question on any other point, except for adjourning from day to day be determined, unless by the votes of a majority of the United States in Congress assembled.

The Congress of the United States shall have power to adjourn to any time within the year, and to any place within the United States, so that no period of adjournment be for a longer duration than the space of six months, and shall publish the journal of the proceedings monthly. . . .

ARTICLE X. The committee of the States, or any nine of them, shall be authorized to execute, in the recess of Congress, such of the powers of Congress as the United States in Congress assembled, by the consent of nine States, shall from time to time think expedient to vest them with; provided that no power be delegated to the said committee, for the exercise of which, by the articles of confederation, the voice of nine States in the Congress of the United States assembled is requisite.

ARTICLE XI. Canada acceding to this confederation, and joining in the measures of the United States, shall be admitted into, and entitled to all the advantages of this Union: but no other colony shall be admitted into the same, unless such admission be agreed to by nine States.

ARTICLE XII. All bills of credit emitted, monies borrowed and debts contracted by, or under the authority of Congress, before the assembling of the United States, in pursuance of the present confederation, shall be deemed and considered as a charge against the United States, for payment and satisfaction whereof the said United States, and the public faith are hereby solemnly pledged.

ARTICLE XIII. Every State shall abide by the determinations of the United States in Congress assembled, on all questions which by this confederation are submitted to them. And the articles of this confederation shall be inviolably observed by every State, and the Union shall be perpetual; nor shall any alteration at any time hereafter be made in any of them; unless such alteration be agreed to in a Congress of the United States, and be afterwards confirmed by the Legislatures of every State.

And whereas it has pleased the Great Governor of the world to incline the hearts of the Legislatures we respectively represent in Congress, to approve of, and to authorize us to ratify the said articles of confederation and perpetual union.

In witness whereof we [the signers] have hereunto set our hands in Congress. Done at Philadelphia in the State of Pennsylvania the ninth day of July in the year of our Lord one thousand seven hundred and seventy-eight, and in the third year of the Independence of America.

The Articles of Confederation, 1781.

Document 2: The Declaration of Independence

The Declaration of Independence, written by Thomas Jefferson, was adopted by Congress on July 2, 1776, when the Americans realized their efforts at conciliation with Britain had failed. Earlier in June, Congress instructed the individual colonies to form independent governments. The declaration is the American manifesto which aimed to justify the American Revolution. It starts by enumerating a chronicle of abuses that the British had committed, violating the rights of the American colonies. It moves on to elucidate its fundamental philosophy of the sovereignty of the people. At its heart is the idea of man having inalienable rights—those of life, liberty, and the pursuit of happiness—which a government should protect and secure.

When, in the course of human events, it becomes necessary for one people to dissolve the political bonds which have connected them with another, and to assume among the powers of the earth, the separate and equal station to which the laws of nature and of nature's God entitle them, a decent respect to the opinions of mankind requires that they should declare the causes which impel them to the separation.

We hold these truths to be self-evident, that all men are created equal, that they are endowed by their Creator with certain unalienable rights, that among these are life, liberty and the pursuit of happiness. That to secure these rights, governments are instituted among men, deriving their just powers from the consent of the governed. That whenever any form of government becomes destructive to these ends, it is the right of the people to alter or to abolish it, and to institute new government, laying its foundation on such principles and organizing its powers in such form, as to them shall seem most likely to effect their safety and happiness. Prudence, indeed, will dictate that governments long established should not be changed for light and transient causes; and accordingly all experience hath shown that mankind are more disposed to suffer, while evils are sufferable, than to right themselves by abolishing the forms to which they are accustomed. But when a long train of abuses and usurpations, pursuing invariably the same object evinces a design to reduce them under absolute despotism, it is their right, it is their duty, to throw off such government, and to provide new guards for their future security.—Such has been the patient sufferance of these colonies; and such is now the necessity which constrains them to alter their former systems of government. The history of the present King of Great Britain is a history of repeated injuries and usurpations, all having in direct object the establishment of an absolute tyranny over these states. To prove this, let facts be submitted to a candid world.

He has refused his assent to laws, the most wholesome and necessary for the public good.

He has forbidden his governors to pass laws of immediate and pressing importance, unless suspended in their operation till his assent should be obtained; and when so suspended, he has utterly neglected to attend to them.

He has refused to pass other laws for the accommodation of large districts of people, unless those people would relinquish the right of representation in the legislature, a right inestimable to them and formidable to tyrants only.

He has called together legislative bodies at places unusual, uncomfortable, and distant from the depository of their public records, for the sole purpose of fatiguing them into compliance with his measures.

He has dissolved representative houses repeatedly, for opposing with manly firmness his invasions on the rights of the people.

He has refused for a long time, after such dissolutions, to cause others to be elected; whereby the legislative powers, incapable of annihilation, have returned to the people at large for their exercise; the state remaining in the meantime exposed to all the dangers of invasion from without, and convulsions within.

He has endeavored to prevent the population of these states; for that purpose obstructing the laws for naturalization of foreigners; refusing to pass others to encourage their migration hither, and raising the conditions of new appropriations of lands.

He has obstructed the administration of justice, by refusing his assent to laws for establishing judiciary powers.

He has made judges dependent on his will alone, for the tenure of their offices, and the amount and payment of their salaries.

He has erected a multitude of new offices, and sent hither swarms of officers to harass our people, and eat out their substance.

He has kept among us, in times of peace, standing armies without the consent of our legislature.

He has affected to render the military independent of and superior to civil power.

He has combined with others to subject us to a jurisdiction foreign to our constitution, and unacknowledged by our laws; giving his assent to their acts of pretended legislation:

For quartering large bodies of armed troops among us:

For protecting them, by mock trial, from punishment for any murders which they should commit on the inhabitants of these states:

For cutting off our trade with all parts of the world:

For imposing taxes on us without our consent:

For depriving us in many cases, of the benefits of trial by jury:

For transporting us beyond seas to be tried for pretended offenses:

For abolishing the free system of English laws in a neighboring province, establishing therein an arbitrary government, and enlarging its boundaries so as to render it at once an example and fit instrument for introducing the same absolute rule in these colonies:

For taking away our charters, abolishing our most valuable laws, and altering fundamentally the forms of our governments:

For suspending our own legislatures, and declaring themselves invested with power to legislate for us in all cases whatsoever.

He has abdicated government here, by declaring us out of his protection and waging war against us.

He has plundered our seas, ravaged our coasts, burned our towns, and destroyed the lives of our people.

He is at this time transporting large armies of foreign mercenaries to complete the works of death, desolation and tyranny, already begun with circumstances of cruelty and perfidy scarcely paralleled in the most barbarous ages, and totally unworthy the head of a civilized nation.

He has constrained our fellow citizens taken captive on the high seas to bear arms against their country, to become the executioners of their friends and brethren, or to fall themselves by their hands.

He has excited domestic insurrections amongst us, and has endeavored to bring on the inhabitants of our frontiers, the merciless Indian savages, whose known rule of warfare, is undistinguished destruction of all ages, sexes and conditions.

In every stage of these oppressions we have petitioned for redress in the most humble terms: our repeated petitions have been answered only by repeated injury. A prince, whose character is thus marked by every act which may define a tyrant, is unfit to be the ruler of a free people.

Nor have we been wanting in attention to our British brethren. We have warned them from time to time of attempts by their legislature to extend an unwarrantable jurisdiction over us. We have reminded them of the circumstances of our emigration and settlement here. We have appealed to their native justice and magnanimity, and we have conjured them by the ties of our common kindred to disavow these usurpations, which, would inevitably interrupt our connections and correspondence. We must, therefore, acquiesce in the necessity, which denounces our separation, and hold them, as we hold the rest of mankind, enemies in war, in peace friends.

We, therefore, the representatives of the United States of America, in General Congress, assembled, appealing to the Supreme Judge of the world for the rectitude of our intentions, do, in the name, and by the authority of the good people of these colonies, solemnly publish and declare, that these united colonies are, and of right ought to be free and independent states; that they are absolved from all allegiance to the British Crown, and that all political connection between them and the state of Great Britain, is and ought to be totally dissolved; and that as free and independent states, they have full power to levy war, conclude peace, contract alliances, establish commerce, and to do all other acts and things which independent states may of right do. And for the support of this declaration, with a firm reliance on the protection of Divine Providence, we mutually pledge to each other our lives, our fortunes and our sacred honor.

The Declaration of Independence, 1776.

Document 3: Resolution to Hold a Constitutional Convention

In February 1787, Congress convened and passed a resolution that called for the holding of a constitutional convention that would revise the Articles of Confederation. The resolution sets May 1787 for the convention and asks the states to designate their delegates.

1787, February 21.

Whereas there is provision in the Articles of Confederation & perpetual Union for making alterations therein by the Assent of a Congress of the United States and of the legislatures of the several States; And whereas experience hath evinced that there are defects in the present Confederation, as a mean to remedy which several of the States and particularly the State of New York by express instructions to their delegates in Congress have suggested a convention for the purposes expressed in the following resolution and such Convention appearing to be the most probable mean of establishing in these states a firm national government

Resolved that in the opinion of Congress it is expedient that on the second Monday in May next a Convention of delegates who shall have been appointed by the several states be held at Philadelphia for the sole and express purpose of revising the Articles of Confederation and reporting to Congress and the several legislatures such alterations and provisions therein as shall when agreed to in Congress and confirmed by the states render the federal constitution adequate to the exigencies of Government & the preservation of the Union

Max Farrand, ed., *The Records of the Federal Convention of 1787*, Vol. III, Revised Edition. New Haven, CT: Yale University Press, 1937, pp. 13–14.

Document 4: Letter of Alexander Hamilton to George Washington on the Need for a Strong Government

During the deliberations of the Constitutional Convention in 1787, Alexander Hamilton and other nationalists argued for a strong central government that would address the expanding collective concerns of the

states. Their opponents, advocates of state rights, argued for the retention of the states' sovereignty and a smaller, less centralized federal government. In the following letter, dated July 3, 1787, Hamilton writes to George Washington, whose opinion he trusted and expected to influence decision makers at the time.

Dr. Sir,

In my passage through the Jerseys and since my arrival here I have taken particular pains to discover the public sentiment and I am more and more convinced that this is the critical opportunity for establishing the prosperity of this country on a solid foundation. I have conversed with men of information not only of this City but from different parts of the state; and they agree that there has been an astonishing revolution for the better in the minds of the people. The prevailing apprehension among thinking men is that the Convention, from a fear of shocking the popular opinion, will not go far enough. They seem to be convinced that a strong, well mounted government will better suit the popular palate than one of a different complexion. Men in office are indeed taking all possible pains to give an unfavourable impression of the Convention; but the current seems to be running strongly the other way.

A plain but sensible man, in a conversation I had with him yesterday, expressed himself nearly in this manner. The people begin to be convinced that their "excellent form of government" as they have been used to call it, will not answer their purpose: and that they must substitute something not very remote from that which they have lately quitted.

These appearances though they will not warrant a conclusion that the people are yet ripe for such a plan as I advocate, yet serve to prove that there is no reason to despair of their adopting one equally energetic, if the Convention should think proper to propose it. They serve to prove that we ought not to allow too much weight to objections drawn from supposed repugnancy of the people to an efficient constitution. I confess I am more and more inclined to believe that former habits of thinking are regaining their influence with more rapidity than is generally imagined.

Not having compared ideas with you, Sir, I cannot judge how far our sentiments agree; but as I persuade myself the genuiness of my representations will receive credit with you, my anxiety for the event of the deliberations of the Convention induces me to make this communication of what appears to be the tendency of the public mind. I own to you Sir that I am seriously and deeply distressed at the aspect of the Councils which prevailed when I left Philadelphia. I fear that we shall let slip the golden opportunity of rescuing the American empire from disunion anarchy and misery. No motley or feeble measure can answer the end or will finally receive the public support. Decision is true wisdom and will be not less reputable to the Convention than salutary to the community.

I shall of necessity remain here ten or twelve days; if I have reason to believe that my attendance at Philadelphia will not be mere waste of time, I shall after that period rejoin the Convention.

I shall remain with sincere esteem Dr Sir Yr. Obed ser A Hamilton

Andrew Carroll, ed., *Letters of a Nation.* New York: Broadway Books, 1997, pp. 73–74.

Document 5: The Virginia Plan

The Virginia Plan, proposed by the Virginia delegates, contains many of the principles and provisions eventually adopted by the Constitutional Convention. It entirely scraps the Articles of Confederation and introduces a new instrument of government for the United States. It authorizes the new government to operate directly on the American people rather than through the mediation of the state governments. The plan, which favors a strong central government, introduces the principle of separation of powers and divides the functions of government into the legislative, executive, and judiciary. It also provides for a national legislature with two branches.

1. RESOLVED, That the articles of Confederation ought to be so corrected and enlarged as to accomplish the objects proposed by their institution; namely, common defence, security of liberty and general welfare.

2. Resolved, therefore, That the rights of suffrage, in the National Legislature ought to be proportioned to the Quotas of contribution, or to the number of free inhabitants, as the one or the other rule may seem best in different cases.

3. Resolved, That the National Legislature ought to consist of two branches.

4. Resolved, That the members of the first branch of the National Legislature ought to be elected by the people of the several States every   for the term of   ; to be of the age of   years at least; to receive liberal stipends by which they may be compensated for the devotion of their time to public service; to be ineligible to any office established by a particular State, or under the authority of the United States, except those peculiarly belonging to

the functions of the first branch, during the term of service, and for the space of   after its expiration; to be incapable of re-election for the space of   after the expiration of their term of service; and to be subject to recall.

5. Resolved, That the members of the second branch of the National Legislature ought to be elected by those of the first, out of a proper number of persons nominated by the individual Legislatures; to be of the age of   years, at least; to hold their offices for a term sufficient to ensure their independency; to receive liberal stipends, by which they may be compensated for the devotion of their time to public service; and to be ineligible to any office established by a particular State, or under the authority of the United States, except those peculiarly belonging to the functions of the second branch, during the term of service, and for the space of   after the expiration thereof.

6. Resolved, That each branch ought to possess the right of originating Acts; that the National Legislature ought to be impowered to enjoy the Legislative Rights vested in Congress by the Confederation, and moreover to legislate in all cases to which the separate States are incompetent, or in which the harmony of the United States may be interrupted by the exercise of individual Legislation; to negative all laws passed by the several States, contravening in the opinion of the National Legislature the articles of Union; and to call forth the force of the Union against any member of the Union failing to fulfil its duty under the articles thereof.

7. Resolved, That a national executive be instituted; to be chosen by the National Legislature for the term of   years; to receive punctually at stated times, a fixed compensation for the services rendered, in which no increase or diminution shall be made so as to affect the Magistracy existing at the time of increase or diminution; and to be ineligible a second time; and that besides a general authority to execute the National laws, it ought to enjoy the Executive rights vested in Congress by the Confederation.

8. Resolved, That the executive and a convenient number of the National Judiciary, ought to compose a council of revision with authority to examine every act of the National Legislature before it shall operate, and every act of a particular Legislature before a Negative thereon shall be final; and that the dissent of the said Council shall amount to a rejection, unless the act of the National Legislature be again passed, or that of a particular Legislature be again negatived by   of the members of each branch.

9. Resolved, That a national judiciary be established to consist

of one or more supreme tribunals, and of inferior tribunals to be chosen by the National Legislature, to hold their offices during good behaviour; and to receive punctually at stated times fixed compensations for their services, in which no increase or diminution shall be made so as to affect the person actually in office at the time of such increase or diminution. That the jurisdiction of the inferior tribunals shall be to hear and determine in the first instance, and of the supreme tribunal to hear and determine, in the dernier resort, all piracies and felonies on the high seas; captures from an enemy; cases in which foreigners or citizens of other States applying to such jurisdictions may be interested, or which respect the collection of the National revenue; impeachments of any National officer; and questions which involve the national peace or harmony.

10. Resolved, That provision ought to be made for the admission of States lawfully arising within the limits of the United States, whether from a voluntary junction of Government and Territory, or otherwise, with the consent of a number of voices in the National Legislature less than the whole.

11. Resolved, That a Republican Government and the territory of each State, except in the instance of a voluntary junction of Government and territory, ought to be guaranteed by the United States to each State.

12. Resolved, That provision ought to be made for the continuance of Congress and their authorities and privileges, until a given day after the reform of the articles of Union shall be adopted, and for the completion of all their engagements.

13. Resolved, That provision ought to be made for the amendment of the articles of Union whensoever it shall seem necessary; and that the assent of the National Legislature ought not to be required thereto.

14. Resolved, That the legislative, executive, and judiciary powers within the several States, ought to be hound by oath to support the articles of union.

15. Resolved, That the amendments which shall be offered to the Confederation, by the Convention ought at a proper time, or times, after the approbation of Congress, to be submitted to an assembly or assemblies of Representatives, recommended by the several Legislatures to be expressly chosen by the people, to consider and decide thereon.

Clinton Rossiter, *1787: The Grand Convention*. New York: MacMillan, 1966, pp. 361–63.

Document 6: The New Jersey Plan

The New Jersey Plan was hatched by small-state delegates as a foil to the strong national government bent of the Virginia Plan. The Plan preserves the one-house legislature of the Articles of Confederation with each state having one vote. The contention of the small states was that if representation in the legislature was based on population, they would be outvoted by the big states. After three days of debate, the plan lost to the Virginia Plan.

1. RESOLVED, That the articles of Confederation ought to be so revised, corrected and enlarged, as to render the federal Constitution adequate to the exigencies of Government, and the preservation of the Union.

2. Resolved, That in addition to the powers vested in the United States in Congress, by the present existing articles of Confederation, they be authorized to pass acts for raising a revenue, by levying a duty or duties on all goods and merchandizes of foreign growth or manufacture, imported into any part of the United States, by Stamps on paper, vellum, or parchment, and by a postage on all letters and packages passing through the general post-office, to be applied to such federal purposes as they shall deem proper and expedient; to make rules and regulations for the collection thereof; and the same from time to time, to alter and amend in such manner as they shall think proper; to pass Acts for the regulation of trade and commerce, as well with foreign nations as with each other: provided that all punishments, fines, forfeitures, and penalties to be incurred for contravening such rules and regulations shall be adjudged by the Common law Judiciarys of the State in which any offence contrary to the true intent and meaning of such Acts, rules and regulations shall have been committed or perpetrated, with liberty of commencing in the first instance all suits or prosecutions for that purpose, in the superior Common law Judiciary of such State; subject nevertheless, for the correction of all errors, both in law and fact in rendering judgment, to an appeal to the Judiciary of the United States.

3. Resolved, That whenever requisitions shall be necessary, instead of the rule for making requisitions mentioned in the articles of Confederation the United States in Congress be authorized to make such requisitions in proportion to the whole number of white and other free citizens and inhabitants of every age, sex, and condition, including those bound to servitude for a term of years, and three fifths of all other persons not comprehended in the fore-

going description, except Indians not paying taxes; that if such requisitions be not complied with, in the time specified therein, to direct the collection thereof in the non-complying States, and for that purpose to devise and pass acts directing and authorizing the same; provided that none of the powers hereby vested in the United States in Congress shall be exercised without the consent of at least   States; and in that proportion, if the number of confederated States should hereafter be increased or diminished.

4. Resolved, That the United States in Congress be authorized to elect a federal Executive to consist of   persons, to continue in office for the term of   years; to receive punctually at stated times a fixed compensation for their services in which no increase or diminution shall be made so as to affect the persons composing the Executive at the time of such increase or diminution, to be paid out of the federal treasury; to be incapable of holding any other office or appointment during their term of service, and for   years thereafter; to be ineligible a second time, and removable by Congress on application by a majority of the Executives of the several States. That the executive, besides their general authority to execute the federal acts ought to appoint all federal officers not otherwise provided for, and to direct all military operations; provided, that none of the persons composing the federal executive shall on any occasion take command of any troops, so as personally to conduct any military enterprise as General, or in any other capacity.

5. Resolved, That a federal Judiciary be established, to consist of a supreme Tribunal the Judges of which to be appointed by the Executive, and to hold their offices during good behaviour; to receive punctually at stated times a fixed compensation for their services, in which no increase or diminution shall be made, so as to affect the persons actually in office at the time of such increase or diminution. That the Judiciary so established shall have authority to hear and determine in the first instance on all impeachments of federal officers, and by way of appeal in the dernier resort in all cases touching the rights and privileges of Ambassadors; in all cases of captures from an enemy; in all cases of piracies and felonies on the high seas; in all cases in which foreigners may be interested, in the construction of any treaty or treaties, or which may arise on any of the acts for regulation of trade, or the collection of the federal Revenue. That none of the Judiciary shall during the time they remain in Office be capable of receiving or holding any other office or appointment during their term of service, or for   thereafter.

6. Resolved, That all acts of the United States in Congress, made by virtue and in pursuance of the powers hereby and by the articles of confederation vested in them, and all treaties made and ratified under the authority of the United States, shall be the supreme law of the respective States as far forth as those Acts or Treaties shall relate to the said States or their Citizens; and that the judiciary of the several States shall be bound thereby in their decisions, any thing in the respective laws of the Individual States to the contrary notwithstanding; and if any State, or any body of men in any State, shall oppose or prevent the carrying into execution such acts or treaties, the federal Executive shall be authorized to call forth the powers of the Confederated States, or so much thereof as may be necessary, to enforce and compel an obedience to such Acts, or an Observance of such Treaties.

7. Resolved, That provision be made for the admission of new States into the Union.

8. Resolved, That the rule for naturalization ought to be the same in every State.

9. Resolved, That a citizen of one State committing an offence in another State of the Union shall be deemed guilty of the same offence as if it had been committed by a citizen of the State in which the offence was committed.

Clinton Rossiter, *1787: The Grand Convention*. New York: MacMillan, 1966, pp. 367–69.

Document 7: Federalist No. 10: Preventing Factions in a Republic

During the debate on the draft-Constitution, delegates were divided into two camps, those who favored the approval of the Constitution, or the Federalists, and those who opposed its ratification, or the Anti-Federalists. The Federalists were called such because the main theme of their argument was that the draft-Constitution had the essence and devices of a republican government. It assured people of representation, which was the main contention against British rule. The Federalists presented their case and arguments to the general public in a series of anonymous newspaper articles that were published extensively prior to the ratification dates. These writings, subsequently called the Federalist Papers, *were later known to have been written by James Madison, Alexander Hamilton, and John Jay.*

Federalist No. 10, written by James Madison, is a seminal work on the soundness of a republican form of government in controlling "factions," which, Madison claimed to be inherent in human nature and the source of all instability and injustice in society. He argued that a large country like the United States was suited for a republican government since the many opposing parties would check each other, preventing any one faction from dominating the others.

To the People of the State of New York:

Among the numerous advantages promised by a well-constructed Union, none deserves to be more accurately developed than its tendency to break and control the violence of faction. The friend of popular governments never finds himself so much alarmed for their character and fate as when he contemplates their propensity to this dangerous vice. He will not fail, therefore, to set a due value on any plan which, without violating the principles to which he is attached, provides a proper cure for it. The instability, injustice, and confusion introduced into the public councils, have, in truth, been the mortal diseases under which popular governments have everywhere perished; as they continue to be the favourite and fruitful topics from which the adversaries to liberty derive their most specious declamations. . . . Complaints are everywhere heard from our most considerate and virtuous citizens, equally the friends of public and private faith, and of public and personal liberty, that our governments are too unstable, that the public good is disregarded in the conflicts of rival parties, and that measures are too often decided, not according to the rules of justice and the rights of the minor party, but by the superior force of an interested and overbearing majority. However anxiously we may wish that these complaints had no foundation, the evidence of known facts will not permit us to deny that they are in some degree true. It will be found, indeed, on a candid review of our situation, that some of the distresses under which we labour have been erroneously charged on the operation of our governments; but it will be found, at the same time, that other causes will not alone account for many of our heaviest misfortunes; and, particularly, for that prevailing and increasing distrust of public engagements, and alarm for private rights, which are echoed from one end of the continent to the other. These must be chiefly, if not wholly, effects of the unsteadiness and injustice with which a factious spirit has tainted our public administrations.

By a faction, I understand a number of citizens, whether amounting to a majority or minority of the whole, who are united and actuated by some common impulse of passion, or of interest, adverse to the rights of other citizens, or to the permanent and aggregate interests of the community.

There are two methods of curing the mischiefs of faction: the one, by removing its causes; the other, by controlling its effects.

There are again two methods of removing the causes of faction: the one, by destroying the liberty which is essential to its existence; the other, by giving to every citizen the same opinions, the same passions, and the same interests.

It could never be more truly said than of the first remedy, that it was worse than the disease. Liberty is to faction what air is to fire, an aliment without which it instantly expires. But it could not be less folly to abolish liberty, which is essential to political life, because it nourishes faction, than it would be to wish the annihilation of air, which is essential to animal life, because it imparts to fire its destructive agency.

The second expedient is as impracticable as the first would be unwise. As long as the reason of man continues fallible, and he is at liberty to exercise it, different opinions will be formed. . . . From the protection of different and unequal faculties of acquiring property, the possession of different degrees and kinds of property immediately results; and from the influence of these on the sentiments and views of the respective proprietors, ensues a division of the society into different interests and parties.

The latent causes of faction are thus sown in the nature of man; and we see them everywhere brought into different degrees of activity, according to the different circumstances of civil society. . . . But the most common and durable source of factions has been the various and unequal distribution of property. Those who hold and those who are without property have ever formed distinct interests in society. Those who are creditors, and those who are debtors, fall under a like discrimination. A landed interest, a manufacturing interest, a mercantile interest, a moneyed interest, with many lesser interests, grow up of necessity in civilised nations, and divide them into different classes, actuated by different sentiments and views. The regulation of these various and interfering interests forms the principal task of modern legislation, and involves the spirit of party and faction in the necessary and ordinary operations of the government. . . .

It is in vain to say that enlightened statesmen will be able to adjust these clashing interests, and render them all subservient to the public good. Enlightened statesmen will not always be at the helm. Nor, in many cases, can such an adjustment be made at all without taking into view indirect and remote considerations, which will rarely prevail over the immediate interest which one party may find in disregarding the rights of another or the good of the whole.

The inference to which we are brought is, that the *causes* of faction cannot be removed, and that relief is only to be sought in the means of controlling its *effects*.

If a faction consists of less than a majority, relief is supplied by the republican principle, which enables the majority to defeat its sinister views by regular vote. It may clog the administration, it may convulse the society; but it will be unable to execute and mask its violence under the forms of the Constitution. When a majority is included in a faction, the form of popular government, on the other hand, enables it to sacrifice to its ruling passion or interest both the public good and the rights of other citizens. To secure the public good and private rights against the danger of such a faction, and at the same time to preserve the spirit and the form of popular government, is then the great object to which our inquiries are directed. . . .

By what means is this object obtainable? Evidently by one of two only. Either the existence of the same passion or interest in a majority at the same time must be prevented, or the majority, having such co-existent passion or interest, must be rendered, by their number and local situation, unable to concert and carry into effect schemes of oppression. If the impulse and the opportunity be suffered to coincide, we well know that neither moral nor religious motives can be relied on as an adequate control. They are not found to be such on the injustice and violence of individuals, and lose their efficacy in proportion to the number combined together, that is, in proportion as their efficacy becomes needful.

From this view of the subject it may be concluded that a pure democracy, by which I mean a society consisting of a small number of citizens, who assemble and administer the government in person, can admit of no cure for the mischiefs of faction. . . .

A republic, by which I mean a government in which the scheme of representation takes place, opens a different prospect, and promises the cure for which we are seeking. Let us examine the points in which it varies from pure democracy, and we shall comprehend both the nature of the cure and the efficacy which it must derive from the Union.

The two great points of difference between a democracy and a republic are: first, the delegation of the government, in the latter, to a small number of citizens elected by the rest; secondly, the greater number of citizens, and greater sphere of country, over which the latter may be extended.

The effect of the first difference is, on the one hand, to refine and enlarge the public views, by passing them through the medium of a chosen body of citizens, whose wisdom may best discern the true interest of their country, and whose patriotism and love of justice will be least likely to sacrifice it to temporary or partial considerations. Under such a regulation, it may well happen that the public voice, pronounced by the representatives of the people, will be more consonant to the public good than if pronounced by the people themselves, convened for the purpose. On the other hand, the effect may be inverted. Men of factious tempers, of local prejudices, or of sinister designs, may, by intrigue, by corruption, or by other means, first obtain the suffrages, and then betray the interests, of the people. The question resulting is, whether small or extensive republics are more favourable to the election of proper guardians of the public weal; and it is clearly decided in favour of the latter by two obvious considerations:

In the first place, it is to be remarked that, however small the republic may be, the representatives must be raised to a certain number, in order to guard against the cabals of a few; and that, however large it may be, they must be limited to a certain number, in order to guard against the confusion of a multitude. Hence the number of representatives in the two cases not being in proportion to that of the two constituents, and being proportionally greater in the small republic, it follows that, if the proportion of fit characters be not less in the large than in the small republic, the former will present a greater option, and consequently a greater probability of a fit choice.

In the next place, as each representative will be chosen by a greater number of citizens in the large than in the small republic, it will be more difficult for unworthy candidates to practise with success the vicious arts by which elections are too often carried; and the suffrages of the people being more free, will be more likely to centre in men who possess the most attractive merit and the most diffusive and established character.

It must be confessed that in this, as in most other cases, there is a mean, on both sides of which inconveniences will be found to lie. By enlarging too much the number of electors, you render the representative too little acquainted with all their local circumstances and lesser interests; as by reducing it too much, you render him unduly attached to these, and too little fit to comprehend and pursue great and national objects. The federal Constitution forms a happy combination in this respect; the great and aggregate interests being referred to the national, the local and particular to the State legislatures.

The other point of difference is, the greater number of citizens and extent of territory which may be brought within the compass of republican than of democratic government; and it is this circumstance principally which renders factious combinations less to be dreaded in the former than in the latter. The smaller the society, the fewer probably will be the distinct parties and interests composing it; the fewer the distinct parties and interests, the more frequently will a majority be found of the same party; and the smaller the number of individuals composing a majority, and the smaller the compass within which they are placed, the more easily will they concert and execute their plans of oppression. Extend the sphere, and you take in a greater variety of parties and interests; you make it less probable that a majority of the whole will have a common motive to invade the rights of other citizens; or if such a common motive exists, it will be more difficult for all who feel it to discover their own strength, and to act in unison with each other. Besides other impediments, it may be remarked that, where there is a consciousness of unjust or dishonourable purposes, communication is always checked by distrust in proportion to the number whose concurrence is necessary. . . .

The influence of factious leaders may kindle a flame within their particular States, but will be unable to spread a general conflagration through the other States. A religious sect may degenerate into a political faction in a part of the Confederacy; but the variety of sects dispersed over the entire face of it must secure the national councils against any danger from that source. A rage for paper money, for an abolition of debts, for an equal division of property, or for any other improper or wicked project, will be less apt to pervade the whole body of the Union than a particular member of it; in the same proportion as such a malady is more likely to taint a particular county or district, than an entire State.

In the extent and proper structure of the Union, therefore, we behold a republican remedy for the diseases most incident to republican government. And according to the degree of pleasure and pride we feel in being republicans, ought to be our zeal in cherishing the spirit and supporting the character of Federalists.

Alexander Hamilton, James Madison, and John Jay, *The Federalist*. With an introduction by W.R. Brock. New York: E.P. Dutton, 1961, pp. 41–48.

Document 8: Federalist No. 3: On Safety

In Federalist No. 3, John Jay puts forward the issue of safety as the single most important matter the Americans should consider in determining the merits of the draft-Constitution. He notes that instability does not come only from external sources like foreign countries, but from domestic sources as well. He persuades the American public that a strong and efficient national government can provide the security that America needs at that time.

To the People of the State of New York:

It is not a new observation that the people of any country (if, like the Americans, intelligent and well-informed) seldom adopt and steadily persevere for many years in an erroneous opinion respecting their interests. That consideration naturally tends to create great respect for the high opinion which the people of America have so long and uniformly entertained of the importance of their continuing firmly united under one federal government, vested with sufficient powers for all general and national purposes.

The more attentively I consider and investigate the reasons which appear to have given birth to this opinion, the more I become convinced that they are cogent and conclusive.

Among the many objects to which a wise and free people find it necessary to direct their attention, that of providing for their *safety* seems to be the first. The *safety* of the people doubtless has relation to a great variety of circumstances and considerations, and consequently affords great latitude to those who wish to define it precisely and comprehensively.

At present I mean only to consider it as it respects security for the preservation of peace and tranquillity, as well as against dangers from *foreign arms and influence*, as from dangers of the *like kind* arising from domestic causes. As the former of these comes first in order, it is proper it should be the first discussed. Let us therefore proceed to examine whether the people are not right in their opinion that a cordial Union, under an efficient national government, affords them the best security that can be devised against *hostilities* from abroad.

The number of wars which have happened or will happen in the world will always be found to be in proportion to the number and weight of the causes, whether *real* or *pretended*, which *provoke* or *invite* them. If this remark be just, it becomes useful to inquire whether so many *just* causes of war are likely to be given by *United America* as by *disunited* America; for if it should turn out that

United America will probably give the fewest, then it will follow that in this respect the Union tends most to preserve the people in a state of peace with other nations.

The *just* causes of war, for the most part, arise either from violations of treaties or from direct violence. America has already formed treaties with no less than six foreign nations, and all of them, except Prussia, are maritime, and therefore able to annoy and injure us. She has also extensive commerce with Portugal, Spain, and Britain, and, with respect to the two latter, has, in addition, the circumstance of neighbourhood to attend to.

It is of high importance to the peace of America that she observe the laws of nations towards all these powers, and to me it appears evident that this will be more perfectly and punctually done by one national government than it could be either by thirteen separate States or by three or four distinct confederacies.

Because when once an efficient national government is established, the best men in the country will not only consent to serve, but also will generally be appointed to manage it; for, although town or country, or other contracted influence, may place men in State assemblies, or senates, or courts of justice, or executive departments, yet more general and extensive reputation for talents and other qualifications will be necessary to recommend men to offices under the national government—especially as it will have the widest field for choice, and never experience that want of proper persons which is not uncommon in some of the States. Hence, it will result that the administration, the political counsels, and the judicial decisions of the national government will be more wise, systematical, and judicious than those of individual States, and consequently more satisfactory with respect to other nations, as well as more *safe* with respect to us.

Because, under the national government, treaties and articles of treaties, as well as the laws of nations, will always be expounded in one sense and executed in the same manner—whereas adjudications on the same points and questions, in thirteen States, or in three or four confederacies, will not always accord or be consistent; and that, as well from the variety of independent courts and judges appointed by different and independent governments, as from the different local laws and interests which may affect and influence them. The wisdom of the convention, in committing such questions to the jurisdiction and judgment of courts appointed by and responsible only to one national government, cannot be too much commended.

Because the prospect of present loss or advantage may often tempt the governing party in one or two States to swerve from good faith and justice; but those temptations, not reaching the other States, and consequently having little or no influence on the national government, the temptation will be fruitless, and good faith and justice be preserved. The case of the treaty of peace with Britain adds great weight to this reasoning.

Because, even if the governing party in a State should be disposed to resist such temptations, yet, as such temptations may, and commonly do, result from circumstances peculiar to the State, and may affect a great number of the inhabitants, the governing party may not always be able, if willing, to prevent the injustice meditated, or to punish the aggressors. But the national government, not being affected by those local circumstances, will neither be induced to commit the wrong themselves, nor want power or inclination to prevent or punish its commission by others.

So far, therefore, as either designed or accidental violations of treaties and the laws of nations afford *just* causes of war, they are less to be apprehended under one general government than under several lesser ones, and in that respect the former most favours the *safety* of the people.

As to those just causes of war which proceed from direct and unlawful violence, it appears equally clear to me that one good national government affords vastly more security against dangers of that sort than can be derived from any other quarter.

Because such violences are more frequently caused by the passions and interests of a part than of the whole; of one or two States than of the Union. Not a single Indian war has yet been occasioned by aggressions of the present federal government, feeble as it is; but there are several instances of Indian hostilities having been provoked by the improper conduct of individual States, who, either unable or unwilling to restrain or punish offences, have given occasion to the slaughter of many innocent inhabitants.

The neighbourhood of Spanish and British territories, bordering on some States and not on others, naturally confines the causes of quarrel more immediately to the borderers. The bordering States, if any, will be those who, under the impulse of sudden irritation, and a quick sense of apparent interest or injury, will be most likely, by direct violence, to excite war with these nations; and nothing can so effectually obviate that danger as a national government, whose wisdom and prudence will not be diminished by the passions which actuate the parties immediately interested.

But not only fewer just causes of war will be given by the national government, but it will also be more in their power to accommodate and settle them amicably. They will be more temperate and cool, and in that respect, as well as in others, will be more in capacity to act advisedly than the offending State. The pride of states, as well as of men, naturally disposes them to justify all their actions, and opposes their acknowledging, correcting, or repairing their errors and offences. The national government, in such cases, will not be affected by this pride, but will proceed with moderation and candour to consider and decide on the means most proper to extricate them from the difficulties which threaten them.

Besides, it is well known that acknowledgements, explanations, and compensations are often accepted as satisfactory from a strong united nation, which would be rejected as unsatisfactory if offered by a State or confederacy of little consideration or power.

In the year 1685, the state of Genoa having offended Louis XIV., endeavoured to appease him. He demanded that they should send their *Doge*, or chief magistrate, accompanied by four of their senators, to *France*, to ask his pardon and receive his terms. They were obliged to submit to it for the sake of peace. Would he on any occasion either have demanded or have received the like humiliation from Spain, or Britain, or any other *powerful* nation?

Alexander Hamilton, James Madison, and John Jay, *The Federalist*. With an introduction by W.R. Brock. New York: E.P. Dutton, 1961, pp. 9–12.

Document 9: Anti-Federalist No. 17: Federal Power Will Subvert State Authority

Signed by a political figure that identified himself only as "Brutus," Anti-Federalist No. 17 is considered the most brilliant elucidation of the opposing arguments against the federal principles and tools stated in the Constitution. The essay strongly reacts to the extensive powers vested in the national government. It maintains that the broad powers given to the executive, legislative, and judicial branches of the government will undermine state authority and abolish eventually the state legislatures.

This [new] government is to possess absolute and uncontrollable powers, legislative, executive and judicial, with respect to every object to which it extends, for by the last clause of section eighth, article first, it is declared, that the Congress shall have power "to make all laws which shall be necessary and proper for carrying into execution the foregoing powers, and all other powers vested by this Constitution in the government of the United States, or in any department or office thereof." And by the sixth article, it is declared, "that this Constitution, and the laws of the United States, which shall be made in pursuance thereof, and the treaties made, or which shall be made, under the authority of the United States, shall be the supreme law of the land; and the judges in every State shall be bound thereby, any thing in the Constitution or law of any State to the contrary notwithstanding." It appears from these articles, that there is no need of any intervention of the State governments, between the Congress and the people, to execute any one power vested in the general government, and that the Constitution and laws of every State are nullified and declared void, so far as they are or shall be inconsistent with this Constitution, or the laws made in pursuance of it, or with treaties made under the authority of the United States. The government, then, so far as it extends, is a complete one, and not a confederation. . . . It has the authority to make laws which will affect the lives, the liberty, and property of every man in the United States; nor can the Constitution or laws of any State, in any way prevent or impede the full and complete execution of every power given. The legislative power is competent to lay taxes, duties, imposts, and excises;—there is no limitation to this power, unless it be said that the clause which directs the use to which those taxes and duties shall be applied, may be said to be a limitation. But this is no restriction of the power at all, for by this clause they are to be applied to pay the debts and provide for the common defence and general welfare of the United States; but the legislature have authority to contract debts at their discretion; they are the sole judges of what is necessary to provide for the common defence, and they only are to determine what is for the general welfare. This power, therefore, is neither more nor less than a power to lay and collect taxes, imposts, and excises, at their pleasure; not only the power to lay taxes unlimited, as to the amount they may require, but it is perfect and absolute to raise them in any mode they please. No State legislature, or any power in the State governments, have any more to do in carrying this into effect than the authority of one State has to do with that of another. In the business, therefore, of laying and collecting taxes, the idea of confederation is totally lost, and that of one entire republic is embraced. It is proper here to remark, that the authority to lay and collect taxes is the most important of any power that can be granted; it connects with it almost all other powers, or at least will in process of time draw all others after it; it is the great mean of protection, security, and defence, in a good government, and the great engine of oppression and tyranny in a bad one. . . . The only means, therefore, left for any State to support its government and discharge its debts, is by direct taxation; and the United States have also power to lay and collect taxes, in any way they please. Everyone who has thought on the subject, must be convinced that but small sums of money can be collected in any country, by direct tax; when the federal government begins to exercise the right of taxation in all its parts, the legislatures of the several states will find it impossible to raise monies to support their governments. Without money they cannot be supported, and they must dwindle away, and, as before observed, their powers be absorbed in that of the general government.

It might be here shown, that the power in the federal legislature, to raise and support armies at pleasure, as well in peace as in war, and their control over the militia, tend not only to a consolidation of the government, but the destruction of liberty. I shall not, however, dwell upon these, as a few observations upon the judicial power of this government, in addition to the preceding, will fully evince the truth of the position.

The judicial power of the United States is to be vested in a supreme court, and in such inferior courts as Congress may, from time to time, ordain and establish. The powers of these courts are very extensive. . . . These courts will be, in themselves, totally independent of the States, deriving their authority from the United States, and receiving from them fixed salaries; and in the course of human events it is to be expected that they will swallow up all the powers of the courts in the respective States.

How far the clause in the eighth section of the first article may operate to do away with all idea of confederated States, and to effect an entire consolidation of the whole into one general government, it is impossible to say. The powers given by this article are very general and comprehensive, and it may receive a construction to justify the passing almost any law. A power to make all laws, which shall be *necessary and proper*, for carrying into execution all powers vested by the Constitution in the government of the United States, or any department or officer thereof, is a power very comprehensive and definite, and may, for aught I know, be exercised in such manner as entirely to abolish the State legislature. . . . By such a law, the government of a particular State might be overturned at one stroke, and thereby be deprived of every means of its support.

It is not meant, by stating this case, to insinuate that the Constitution would warrant a law of this kind! Or unnecessarily to alarm the fears of the people, by suggesting that the Federal legislature would be more likely to pass the limits assigned them by the Constitution, than that of an individual State, further than they are less responsible to the people. But what is meant is, that the legislature of the United States are vested with the great and uncontrollable powers of laying and collecting taxes, duties, imposts, and excises; of regulating trade, raising and supporting armies, organizing, arming, and disciplining the militia, instituting courts, and other general powers; and are by this clause invested with the power of making all laws, proper and necessary, for carrying all these into execution; and they may so exercise this power as entirely to annihilate all the State governments, and reduce this country to one single government. And if they may do it, it is pretty certain they will; for it will be found that the power retained by individual States, small as it is, will be a clog upon the wheels of the government of the United States; the latter, therefore, will be naturally inclined to remove it out of the way. . . . It must be very evident, then, that what this Constitution wants of being a complete consolidation of the several parts of the union into one complete government, possessed of perfect legislative, judicial, and executive powers, to all intents and purposes, it will necessarily acquire in its exercise in operation.

The Antifederalist Papers, with an introduction by Morton Borden. East Lansing, Michigan: Michigan State University Press, 1965, pp. 42–45.

Document 10: Anti-Federalist No. 26: The Use of Coercion by the New Government

Anti-Federalist No. 26, signed by another anonymous commentator who identifies himself as "A Farmer and a Planter," re-echoes a major theme of the Anti-Federalists—that of the federal government emasculating the state governments and legislatures. Grounding its strength on its emotional appeal, the commentary warns the American people that the government being proposed in the Constitution is an aristocracy, the rule of rich men who will be bent on securing power for themselves. The piece was published in the Maryland Journal *and* Baltimore Advertiser *on April 1, 1788.*

The time is nearly at hand, when you are called upon to render up that glorious liberty you obtained, by resisting the tyranny and oppression of George the Third, King of England, and his ministers. The first Monday in April is the day appointed by our assembly, for you to meet and choose delegates in each county, to take into consideration the new Federal Government, and either adopt or refuse it. Let me entreat you, my fellows, to consider well what you are about. Read the said constitution, and consider it well before you act. I have done so, and can find that we are to receive but little good, and a great deal of evil. Aristocracy, or government in the hands of a very few nobles, or RICH MEN, is therein concealed in the most artful wrote plan that ever was formed to entrap a free people. The contrivers of it have so completely entrapped you, and laid their plans so sure and secretly, that they have only left you to do one of two things—that is either to receive or refuse it. And in order to bring you into their snare, you may daily read new pieces published in the newspapers, in favor of this new government; and should a writer dare to publish any piece against it, he is immediately abused and vilified.

Look round you and observe well the RICH MEN, who are to be your only rulers, lords and masters in future! Are they not all for it? Yes! Ought not this to put you on your guard? Does not riches beget power, and power, oppression and tyranny? . . . The new form of government gives Congress liberty at any time, by their laws, to alter the state laws, and the time, places and manner of holding elections for representatives. By this clause they may command, by their laws, the people of Maryland to go to Georgia, and the people of Georgia to go to Boston, to choose their representatives. Congress, or our future lords and masters, are to have power to lay and collect taxes, duties, imposts, and excises. Excise is a new thing in America, and few country farmers and planters know the meaning of it. But it is not so in Old England, where I have seen the effects of it, and felt the smart. It is there a duty, or tax, laid upon almost every necessary of life and convenience, and a great number of other articles. The excise on salt in the year 1762, to the best of my recollection, in England, was 4s. sterling per bushel, for all that was made use of in families; and the price of salt per bushel about 6s. sterling, and the excise 4s.–6d. on every gallon of rum made use of. If a private family make their own soap, candles, beer, cider, etc., they pay an excise duty on them. And if they neglect calling in an excise officer at the time of making these things, they are liable to grievous fines and forfeitures, besides a long train of evils and inconveniences attending this detestable excise—to enumerate particularly would fill a volume. The excise officers have power to enter your houses at all times, by night or day, and if you refuse them entrance, they can, under pretense of searching for exciseable goods, that the duty has not been paid on, break open your doors, chests, trunks, desks, boxes, and rummage your houses from bottom to top. Nay, they often search the clothes, petticoats and pockets of ladies or gentlemen (particularly when they are coming from on board an East-India ship), and if they find any the least article that you cannot prove the duty to be paid on, seize it and carry it away with them: . . . Do you expect the Congress excise-officers will be any better—if God, in his anger, should think it proper to punish us for our ignorance, and sins of ingratitude to him, after carrying us through the late war, and giving us liberty, and now so tamely to give it up by adopting this aristocratical government?

Representatives and direct taxes shall be apportioned among the several states which may be included within this union according to their respective numbers. This seems to imply, that we shall be taxed by the poll again, which is contrary to our Bill of Rights. But it is possible that the rich men, who are the great land holders, will tax us in this manner, which will exempt them from paying assessments on their great bodies of land in the old and new parts of the United States; many of them having but few taxable by the poll. Our great Lords and Masters are to lay taxes, raise and support armies, provide a navy, and may appropriate money for two years, call forth the militia to execute their laws, suppress insurrections, and the President is to have the command of the militia. Now, my countrymen, I would ask you, why are all these things directed and put into their power? . . . You labored under many hardships while the British tyrannized over you! You fought, conquered and gained your liberty—then keep it, I pray you, as a precious jewel. Trust it not out of your own hands; be assured, if you do, you will never more regain it. The train is laid, the match is on fire, and they only wait for yourselves to put it to the train, to blow up all your liberty and commonwealth governments, and introduce aristocracy and monarchy, and despotism will follow of course in a few years. Four-years President will be in time a King for life; and after him, his son, or he that has the greatest power among them, will be King also. View your danger, and find out good men to represent you in convention—men of your own profession and station in life; men who will not adopt this destructive and diabolical form of a federal government. There are many among you that will not be led by the nose by rich men, and would scorn a bribe. Rich men can live easy under any government, be it ever so tyrannical. They come in for a great share of the tyranny, because they are the ministers of tyrants, and always engross the places of honor and profit, while the greater part of the common people are led by the nose, and played about by these very men, for the destruction of themselves and their class. Be wise, be virtuous, and catch the precious moment as it passes, to refuse this new-fangled federal government, and extricate yourselves and posterity from tyranny, oppression, aristocratical or monarchical government.

The Antifederalist Papers, with an introduction by Morton Borden. East Lansing, Michigan: Michigan State University Press, 1965, pp. 70–72.

Document 11: Anti-Federalist No. 84: On the Omission of a Bill of Rights

The essay, signed by "Brutus," opposes the Constitution on the grounds that it does not provide for a bill of rights. The writer argues that man is born with inherent rights which no one has the authority to take away. He argues that a declaration of rights is necessary in the face of a national government that has been vested with extensive authority and one that might abuse its power. He asserts that the protection of these rights, expressly stated in the state constitutions, should be expressly stated in the national constitution.

When a building is to be erected which is intended to stand for ages, the foundation should be firmly laid. The Constitution proposed to your acceptance is designed, not for yourselves alone, but for generations yet unborn. The principles, therefore, upon which the social compact is founded, ought to have been clearly and precisely stated, and the most express and full declaration of rights to have been made. But on this subject there is almost an entire silence.

If we may collect the sentiments of the people of America, from their own most solemn declarations, they hold this truth as self-evident, that all men are by nature free. No one man, therefore, or any class of men, have a right, by the law of nature, or of God, to assume or exercise authority over their fellows. The origin of society, then, is to be sought, not in any natural right which one man has to exercise authority over another but in the united consent of those who associate. . . . How great a proportion of natural freedom is necessary to be yielded by individuals, when they submit to government, I shall not inquire. So much, however, must be given, as will be sufficient to enable those to whom the administration of the government is committed, to establish laws for the promoting the happiness of the community, and to carry those laws into effect. But it is not necessary, for this purpose, that individuals should relinquish all their natural rights. Some are of such a nature that they cannot be surrendered. Of this kind are the rights of conscience, the right of enjoying and defending life, etc. Others are not necessary to be resigned in order to attain the end for which government is instituted; these therefore ought not to be given up. To surrender them, would counteract the very end of government, to wit, the common good. From these observations it appears, that in forming a government on its true principles, the foundation should be laid in the manner I before stated, by expressly reserving to the people such of their essential rights as are not necessary to be parted with. The same reasons which at first induced mankind to associate and institute government, will operate to influence them to observe this precaution. If they had been disposed to conform themselves to the rule of immutable righteousness, government would not have been requisite. It was because one part exercised fraud, oppression and violence on the other, that men came together, and agreed that certain rules should be formed to regulate the conduct of all, and the power of the whole community lodged in the hands of rulers to enforce an obedience to them. But rulers have the same propensities as other men; they are as likely to use the power with which they are vested, for private purposes, and to the injury and oppression of those over whom they are placed, as individuals in a state of nature are to injure and oppress one another. It is therefore as proper that bounds should be set to their authority, as that government should have at first been instituted to restrain private injuries.

This principle, which seems so evidently founded in the reason and nature of things, is confirmed by universal experience. Those who have governed, have been found in all ages ever active to enlarge their powers and abridge the public liberty. This has induced the people in all countries, where any sense of freedom remained, to fix barriers against the encroachments of their rulers. The country from which we have derived our origin, is an eminent example of this. Their magna charta and bill of rights have long been the boast, as well as the security of that nation. I need say no more, I presume, to an American, than that this principle is a fundamental one. . . . To set this matter in a clear light, permit me to instance some of the articles of the bills of rights of the individual States, and apply them to the case in question.

For the security of life, in criminal prosecutions, the bills of rights of most of the States have declared, that no man shall be held to answer for a crime until he is made fully acquainted with the charge brought against him; he shall not be compelled to accuse, or furnish evidence against himself—the witnesses against him shall be brought face to face, and he shall be fully heard by himself or counsel. That it is essential to the security of life and liberty, that trial of facts be in the vicinity where they happen. Are not provisions of this kind as necessary in the general government, as in that of a particular State? The powers vested in the new Congress extend in many cases to life; they are authorized to provide for the punishment of a variety of capital crimes, and no restraint is laid upon them in its exercise, save only, that "the trial of all crimes, except in cases of impeachment, shall be by jury; and such trial shall be in the State where the said crimes shall have been committed." No man is secure of a trial in the county where he is charged to have committed a crime; he may he brought from Niagara to New York, or carried from Kentucky to Richmond for trial for an offence supposed to be committed. What security is there, that a man shall be furnished with a full and plain description of the charges against him? That he shall be allowed to produce all proof he can in his favor? That he shall see the witnesses against him face to face, or that he shall be fully heard in his own defense by himself or counsel?

For the security of liberty it has been declared, "that excessive bail should not be required, nor excessive fines imposed, nor cruel or unusual punishments inflicted. That all warrants, without oath or affirmation, to search suspected places, or seize any person, his papers or property, are grievous and oppressive."

These provisions are as necessary under the general government as under that of the individual States; for the power of the former is as complete to the purpose of requiring bail, imposing fines, inflicting punishments, granting search warrants, and seizing persons, papers, or property, in certain cases, as the other.

For the purpose of securing the property of the citizens, it is declared by all the States, "that in all controversies at law, respecting property, the ancient mode of trial by jury is one of the best securities of the rights of the people, and ought to remain sacred and inviolable."

Does not the same necessity exist of reserving this right under their national compact, as in that of the States? Yet nothing is said respecting it. In the bills of rights of the States it is declared, that a well regulated militia is the proper and natural defense of a free government; that as standing armies in time of peace are dangerous, they are not to be kept up, and that the military should be kept under strict subordination to, and controlled by, the civil power.

The same security is as necessary in this Constitution, and much more so; for the general government will have the sole power to raise and to pay armies, and are under no control in the exercise of it; yet nothing of this is to be found in this new system. . . .

Of what avail will the Constitutions of the respective States be to preserve the rights of its citizens? Should they be pled, the answer would be, the Constitution of the United States, and the laws made in pursuance thereof, is the supreme law, and all legislatures and judicial officers, whether of the General or State governments, are bound by oath to support it. No privilege, reserved by the bills of rights, or secured by the State governments, can limit the power granted by this, or restrain any laws made in pursuance of it. It stands, therefore, on its own bottom, and must receive a construction by itself, without any reference to any other. And hence it was of the highest importance, that the most precise and express declarations and reservations of rights should have been made.

This will appear the more necessary, when it is considered, that not only the Constitution and laws made in pursuance thereof, but all treaties made, under the authority of the United States, are the supreme law of the land, and supersede the Constitutions of all the States. The power to make treaties, is vested in the president, by and with the advice and consent of two-thirds of the senate. I do not find any limitation or restriction to the exercise of this power. The most important article in any Constitution may therefore be repealed, even without a legislative act. Ought not a government, vested with such extensive and indefinite authority, to have been restricted by a declaration of rights? It certainly ought.

So clear a point is this, that I cannot help suspecting that persons who attempt to persuade people that such reservations were less necessary under this Constitution than under those of the States, are wilfully endeavoring to deceive, and to lead you into an absolute state of vassalage.

The Antifederalist Papers, with an introduction by Morton Borden. East Lansing Michigan: Michigan State University Press, 1965, pp. 242–46.

Document 12: The Bill of Rights

During the deliberations of the Constitutional Convention, James Madison and company did not envision including a bill of rights in the Constitution. They argued that the "We, the People" clause was sufficient to embody the document's adherence to rights. Their assumption was proven wrong during the ratification contest. The single greatest objection to the Constitution was the omission of a bill of rights. To convince the people of their commitment to the public good, the Federalists made a campaign pledge to introduce a bill of rights after ratification. It was Madison himself who drafted the document that came to be called the Bill of Rights, the first amendment to the Constitution, which was ratified by nine states in July 1790. On March 1, 1792, Thomas Jefferson, then secretary of state, announced the Bill of Rights was now part of the Constitution.

Article I

After the first enumeration required by the first article of the Constitution, there shall be one representative for every thirty thousand, until the number shall amount to one hundred, after which the proportion shall be so regulated by Congress, that there shall be not less than one hundred representatives, nor less than one representative for every forty thousand persons, until the number of representatives shall amount to two hundred; after which the proportion shall be so regulated by Congress, that there shall be not less than two hundred representatives, nor more than one representative for every fifty thousand persons.

Article II

No law varying the compensation for the services of the Senators and Representatives, shall take effect, until an election of Representatives shall have intervened.

Article III

Congress shall make no law respecting an establishment of religion, or prohibiting the free exercise thereof; or abridging the freedom of speech, or of the press; or the right of the people peaceably to assemble, and to petition the Government for a redress of grievances.

Article IV

A well regulated Militia, being necessary to the security of a free State, the right of the people to keep and bear Arms, shall not be infringed.

Article V

No Soldier shall, in time of peace be quartered in any house, without the consent of the Owner, nor in time of war, but in a manner to be prescribed by law.

Article VI

The right of the people to be secure in their persons, houses, papers, and effects, against unreasonable searches and seizures, shall not be violated, and no Warrants shall issue, but upon probable cause, supported by Oath or affirmation, and particularly describing the place to be searched, and the persons or things to be seized.

Article VII

No person shall be held to answer for a capital, or otherwise infamous crime, unless on a presentment or indictment of a Grand Jury, except in cases arising in the land or naval forces, or in the Militia, when in actual service in time of War or public danger; nor shall any person be subject for the same offence to be twice put in jeopardy of life or limb; nor shall be compelled in any criminal case to be a witness against himself, nor be deprived of life, liberty, or property, without due process of law; nor shall private property be taken for public use, without just compensation.

Article VIII

In all criminal prosecutions, the accused shall enjoy the right to a speedy and public trial, by an impartial jury of the State and district wherein the crime shall have been committed, which district shall have been previously ascertained by law, and to be informed of the nature and cause of the accusation; to be confronted with the witnesses against him; to have compulsory process for obtaining witnesses in his favor, and to have the Assistance of Counsel for his defence.

Article IX

In Suits at common law, where the value in controversy shall exceed twenty dollars, the right of trial by jury shall be preserved, and no fact tried by a jury, shall be otherwise re-examined in any Court of the United States, than according to the rules of the common law.

Article X

Excessive bail shall not be required, nor excessive fines imposed, nor cruel and unusual punishments inflicted.

Article XI

The enumeration in the Constitution, of certain rights, shall not be construed to deny or disparage others retained by the people.

Article XII

The powers not delegated to the United States by the Constitution, nor prohibited by it to the States, are reserved to the States respectively, or to the people.

The Bill of Rights, 1792.

Chronology

1763

With the end of the French and Indian War, American settlements fall under the rule of England as prescribed by the Treaty of Paris.

1765

England imposes the Stamp Act, requiring the American colonies to pay a tax on some imported goods as well as some paper items (such as legal documents) within the colonies. Colonial representatives meet in New York and decide to resist the law.

1766

The Stamp Act is repealed after a year of protests and disobedience. Parliament, however, reasserts its authority to make laws or levy taxes in the American colonies.

1767

England issues the Townshend Acts, imposing a new set of levies on the colonies. Colonist John Dickinson publishes his first "Letter from a Pennsylvania Farmer" denouncing British policy.

1770

British troops fire upon a crowd of taunting colonists in Boston. Colonist firebrands use this, "The Boston Massacre," to rally support for resisting English tyranny.

1773

In protest over taxes a crowd of eight thousand Bostonians take part in dumping a shipload of British tea into the harbor. England considers the Boston Tea Party an act of rebellion.

1774

In response to the unrest in Boston, England passes the Coercive Acts (Americans call them the Intolerable Acts), closing Boston Harbor and limiting Massachusetts's self-governance. Colonial representatives gather in Philadelphia at the First Continental Congress. The discussions focus on how best to redress the growing rift with England. Most delegates favor reconciliation.

1775

British troops and colonists clash at Lexington and Concord in Massachusetts. With reconciliation no longer an option, the Second Continental Congress convenes. It acts as a national government for the colonies and organizes the armed forces.

1776
On July 4, Congress passes America's Declaration of Independence. A committee produces the Articles of Confederation, the colonies' first charter for a central government. Eight states adopt new state constitutions—New Hampshire, South Carolina, Virginia, New Jersey, Delaware, Pennsylvania, Maryland, and North Carolina. Rhode Island and Connecticut revise their charters, removing all references to Great Britain and the king.

1777
Georgia and New York adopt their state constitutions, while Vermont adopts its constitution, declaring itself an independent republic.

1778
America looks to France for support. The two sign treaties of alliance, amity, and commerce in Paris.

1781
Major fighting in the war for independence ends. The states ratify the Articles of Confederation.

1783
The colonies and England sign the Treaty of Paris. America becomes an independent nation.

1784
The colonies contend with a faltering union, economic difficulties, social and political tensions, interstate rivalries, and an empty treasury.

1785
The colonies hold the Mount Vernon Conference where delegates from Maryland and Virginia discuss problems of interstate commerce under the Articles of Confederation.

1786
Delegates from five states meet in Annapolis, Maryland, and decide to call a constitutional convention in Philadelphia to revise the Articles of Confederation.

1787
May—The states and Congress approve a constitutional conven-

tion, slated to begin in May in Philadelphia. A total of seventy-four delegates are appointed, but only fifty-five attend the convention.

June—The delegates to the convention adopt rules and create committees. They also discuss specific proposals on the role and strength of the central government under the Virginia Plan and the New Jersey Plan.

July—Discussion focuses on representation in the House of Representatives and Senate. Delegates adopt a compromise on representation in Congress and taxation.

August—Delegates strike another compromise: continuation of the slave trade and simple majority vote on some commerce laws. The first draft of the Constitution is presented to the delegates.

September—George Mason proposes the inclusion of a bill of rights as part of the Constitution. The majority of delegates rejects this proposal. The convention concludes. Only thirty-nine delegates sign the final draft of the Constitution. This version is sent to the states for ratification.

December—Three states ratify the Constitution—Delaware, Pennsylvania, and New Jersey.

1788
Six more states—Georgia, Connecticut, Massachusetts, Maryland, South Carolina, and New Hampshire—ratify the Constitution. Nine states are required for the Constitution to become effective. Virginia, New York, and North Carolina ratify later in the year.

1789
First Congress convenes. The first amendment to the Constitution, the Bill of Rights, is proposed by James Madison. In April, George Washington becomes the first president of the United States of America. Rhode Island ratifies the Constitution in May.

1791
The Bill of Rights is sent to the states for ratification. In December it is ratified, becoming the first ten amendments to the Constitution.

1798–1992
The rest of the amendments—eleven through twenty-seven—are passed by Congress and ratified by the states.

For Further Research

Primary Documents

Morton Borden, ed., *The Antifederalist Papers*. East Lansing: Michigan State University Press, 1965.

Andrew Carroll, ed., *Letters of a Nation*. New York: Broadway Books, 1997.

Max Farrand, *The Records of the Federal Convention*. Vols. 1–3. New Haven, CT: Yale University Press, 1937.

Alexander Hamilton, James Madison, and John Jay, *The Federalist Papers*. New York: Bantam, 1982.

Michael Kammen, ed., *The Origins of the American Constitution: A Documentary History*. New York: Penguin Books, 1986.

Joseph A. Melusky, *The Constitution: Our Written Legacy*. Malabar, FL: Krieger, 1991.

John H. Rhodehamel, *Letters of Liberty*. Los Angeles: Constitutional Rights Foundation, 1988.

General History of the Era

Herbert Aptheker, *The American Revolution: 1763–1783*. New York: International Publishers, 1960.

Richard B. Bernstein and Kym S. Rice, *Are We to Be a Nation? The Making of the Constitution*. Cambridge, MA: Harvard University Press, 1987.

Catherine Drinker Bowen, *Miracle at Philadelphia*. Boston: Little, Brown, 1966.

J.A.C. Chandler, ed., *Genesis and Birth of the Federal Constitution*. New York: Macmillan, 1924.

William Dudley, ed., *The Creation of the Constitution: Opposing Viewpoints*. San Diego, CA: Greenhaven Press, 1995.

Max Farrand, *The Framing of the Constitution of the United States*. New Haven, CT: Yale University Press, 1913.

Homer Carey Hockett, *The Constitutional History of the United States*. New York: Macmillan, 1939.

Andrew McLaughlin, *A Constitutional History of the United States.* New York: D. Appleton-Century, 1935.

John C. Miller, *Origins of the American Revolution.* Stanford, CA: Stanford University Press, 1959.

John H. Rhodehamel, Stephen F. Rohde, and Paul Von Blum, *Foundations of Freedom.* Los Angeles: Constitutional Rights Foundation, 1991.

Clinton Rossiter, *1787: The Grand Convention.* New York: Macmillan, 1966.

Carl Brent Swisher, *American Constitutional Development.* Boston: Houghton Mifflin, 1943.

Charles Warren, *The Making of the Constitution.* Boston: Little, Brown, 1929.

Michael P. Zuckert, *Natural Rights and the New Republicanism.* Princeton, NJ: Princeton University Press, 1994.

Social, Cultural, Political, and Moral Aspects of the Constitution

Charles M. Andrews, *The Colonial Background of the American Revolution.* New Haven, CT: Yale University Press, 1931.

Bernard Bailyn, *The Ideological Origins of the American Revolution.* Cambridge, MA: Harvard University Press, 1967.

———, *The Origins of American Politics.* New York: Alfred A. Knopf, 1968.

Charles A. Beard, *An Economic Interpretation of the Constitution of the United States.* New York: Macmillan, 1935.

Christopher Collier and James Lincoln Collier, *Decision in Philadelphia: The Constitutional Convention of 1787.* New York: Random House, 1986.

Robert H. Horwitz, ed., *The Moral Foundations of the American Republic.* Charlottesville: University Press of Virginia, 1986.

Merrill Jensen, *The Making of the American Constitution.* New York: Van Nostrand Reinhold, 1964.

Calvin C. Jillson, *Constitution Making: Conflict and Consensus in the Federal Convention of 1787.* New York: Agathon Press, 1988.

Jack N. Rakove, *Original Meanings: Politics and Ideas in the Making of the Constitution.* New York: Vintage Books, 1996.

Gordon S. Wood, *The Creation of the American Republic*. Chapel Hill: University of North Carolina Press, 1969.

Alfred F. Young, ed., *The American Revolution: Explorations in the History of American Radicalism*. DeKalb: Northern Illinois University Press, 1976.

Personalities Who Shaped the Constitution

Joseph J. Ellis, *Founding Brothers: The Revolutionary Generation*. New York: Alfred A. Knopf, 2000.

Charles Mee Jr., *The Genius of the People*. New York: Harper & Row, 1987.

David C. Whitney, *Founders of Freedom in America*. Chicago: J.G. Ferguson, 1965.

Women During the Revolution and After

Linda Grant De Pauw, *Founding Mothers: Women of America in the Revolutionary Era*. Boston: Houghton Mifflin, 1975.

Sharon Whitney, *The Equal Rights Amendment: The History of the Movement*. New York: Franklin Watts, 1984.

Specific Aspects of the Constitution

Merrill Jensen, *The Articles of Confederation*. Madison: University of Wisconsin Press, 1970.

Earl Latham, ed., *The Declaration of Independence and the Constitution*. Lexington, MA: D.C. Heath, 1956.

Staughton Lynd, *Class Conflict, Slavery, and the United States Constitution*. New York: Bobbs-Merrill, 1967.

J.R. Pole, ed., *The American Constitution: For and Against*. New York: Hill and Wang, 1987.

Impact and Legacy of the Constitution

Charles A. Beard, *The Supreme Court and the Constitution*. Englewood Cliffs, NJ: Prentice Hall, 1962.

Walter Berns, *The First Amendment and the Future of American Democracy*: Lake Bluff, IL: Regnery Gateway, 1985.

Richard B. Bernstein with Jerome Agel, *Amending America*. New York: Times Books, 1993.

Allan Bloom, ed., with the assistance of Steven J. Kautz, *Confronting the Constitution*. Washington, DC: American Enterprise Institute, 1990.

Edward S. Corwin, rev. Harold W. Chase and Craig R. Ducat, *The Constitution and What It Means Today*. Princeton, NJ: Princeton University Press, 1973.

George J. Graham Jr. and Scarlett G. Graham, eds., *Founding Principles of American Government: Two Hundred Years of Democracy on Trial*. Bloomington: Indiana University Press, 1977.

Periodicals

E.L. Doctorow, "A Citizen Reads the Constitution," *Nation*, vol. 244. February 21, 1987, pp. 208+.

John Greenwald, "A Gift to All Nations," *Time*, vol. 130, July 6, 1987, pp. 92–95.

Nation's Business, "200 and Going Strong," vol. 75, July 1987, p. 49.

Bertell Ollman, "Toward a Marxist Interpretation of the U.S. Constitution," *Monthly Review*, vol. 39, no. 7, December 1987, pp. 18+.

Websites

Archiving Early America, www.earlyamerica.com. Contains historical accounts taken from newspapers, magazines, maps, and other writings that comprised the media in early America.

The History Place, www.historyplace.com. Contains historical accounts on the American Revolution.

The Holt House, www.innercity.org. Contains a chronology on the history of slavery and racism in the United States.

NARA: National Archives and Records Administration, www.archives.gov. Contains important documents related to various periods of American history.

Native Web, www.nativeweb.org. Contains historical accounts on Native Americans during the European incursions into the Americas and after.

Index